A LIFE
IN MOVIES

A LIFE
IN MOVIES

STORIES FROM
50 YEARS IN HOLLYWOOD

IRWIN WINKLER

Abrams Press, New York

Library of Congress Control Number: 2018936294

ISBN: 978-1-4197-3452-6
eISBN: 978-1-68335-528-1

Printed and bound in the United States
10 9 8 7 6 5 4 3 2 1

ABRAMS The Art of Books
195 Broadway, New York, NY 10007
abramsbooks.com

TO MARGO

There was a star danced, and under that was *she* born.

CONTENTS

PART I

WHEN I WALKED ONTO the MGM lot in Culver City in January 1966, it was not the MGM I had imagined. When I was growing up, the MGM lion roared, promising the greatest movie stars, tuneful musicals, inspirational family dramas, and an occasional comedy or period film. It was America in all its small-town wholesomeness—no accident that the families in *Meet Me in St. Louis* or the Andy Hardy series featured happy, secure, middle-class, white fathers and mothers who never seemed to have a job other than taking care of the household and children (however, you never did see a pregnant woman or a gay man or woman). The MGM musicals were glamorous, inventive, and brought the great composers (Irving Berlin, Aaron Copeland, George and Ira Gershwin, Cole Porter) to a mass audience. They also brought unbelievably talented dancers (Gene Kelly, Fred Astaire, Cyd Charisse), vocalists (Judy Garland, Frank Sinatra, Debbie Reynolds), even Olympic swimmers (Esther Williams), and the movie stars Clark Gable, Greta Garbo, Mickey Rooney, Joan Crawford, Katharine Hepburn, Spencer Tracy, Greer Garson, Walter Pidgeon, Van Johnson, Lana Turner—all working for Mr. Mayer and company. For every nook and corner of America there was a film a week, fifty-two a year. MGM boasted hundreds of actors under multi-year exclusive contracts, schools for the child actors (Elizabeth Taylor, Mickey Rooney), dance classes, elocution lessons, doctors, dentists, barbers, bankers, chiropractors, and a team of masseuses to soothe the bodies of the executives and stars. The back lot, a couple of miles south of the main studio, had an authentic-looking French town with a lake and a moat (why travel all the way to Europe?), a New York City street (why go east?), a small-town Andy Hardy village, a railroad station, and an MGM-owned-and-operated generator plant (so MGM didn't have to depend on the city for its power). Storage facilities housed the valuable antiques that were used on sets, costumes from janitor overalls to glamorous gowns, even jewels for actors to flash. A large group of ex-Los Angeles police officers made up the security force to protect the actors and executives, who might themselves get into trouble on or more probably off the lot.

By 1966, most of that was gone. The man whose name was over the lion, Louis B. Mayer, was also gone, and an auction was soon to sell off the costumes, the props, and the real estate. A few television shows were renting out the soundstages where Gene Kelly had danced with Leslie Caron to George Gershwin's "An American in Paris." The once-bustling "dream factory" was sad and sparse.

Movies thrived before and after World War II, but in 1947 the United States government broke up the ownership of the theaters and the studios. No longer could the moviemakers control where the films played, and no longer could the movie theaters control the films that were produced. Television soon came along, and by the time I showed up at MGM, more than 90 percent of the homes in America had TV sets. As television audiences grew, movie attendance shrank. In the 1940s, almost 60 percent of America went to the movies once a week; by 1965 only 10 percent went that often. Not only MGM but all of the once-powerful studios had experienced a radical upheaval. In 1958 the talent agency MCA took over Universal Studios, primarily to produce television shows through the subsidiary Revue Productions. Twentieth Century Fox had lost its leader, Darryl Zanuck, and, to keep the movie studio running, sold most of its back lot, now known as Century City. In October 1966, Paramount was sold to Gulf and Western, a conglomerate run by a very shady Charles Bluhdorn. Warner Bros. Studio, despite winning an Academy Award for Best Picture with *My Fair Lady* in 1965, ended up in the hands of the New York parking lot owner Steve Ross after Jack Warner sold it to a small company, Seven Arts. Columbia Pictures lost its leader, the autocratic, much-hated Harry Cohn, in 1958 (at his funeral the actor Red Skelton, upon seeing the massive turnout, remarked, "Give the public what they want, and they'll come out for it"). Columbia Pictures was on the verge of bankruptcy until the mid-1960s, when a young producer, Bert Schneider, made a bunch of successful low-budget movies starting with *Easy Rider.* The Walt Disney Company we know now as one of the (if not the) most successful entertainment companies in the world was a mere shell of what it had been in the glory days of Mickey Mouse and the Seven Dwarfs, as Walt Disney himself died on December 15, 1966.

When I stepped out of my dilapidated car and looked up at the MGM sign, I was in awe, but when I walked around the lot trying to find my office, I ended up in the barber shop, where Slick the shoeshine man (who, I was told, had been shining shoes at MGM since the 1930s) pointed me to the Thalberg Building, named after the creative head of MGM's glory days, Irving Thalberg, who died in 1936. That seemed to be all that was left of an era when the studio's motto was "More stars than there are in heaven."

The MGM sign (without the lion) now sits atop a small office building on Beverly Drive in the commercial district of Beverly Hills, just one block east of the much more famous and glamorous Rodeo Drive. No lot, no soundstages.

As I wrote this memoir, we finished shooting *Creed II*, a spin-off of the Rocky series, with Michael B. Jordan and Sylvester Stallone, and *The Irishman*, the story of mob hit man Frank Sheeran, with Marty Scorsese directing Bob De Niro, Al Pacino, and Joe Pesci. Both *Creed II* and *The Irishman* prove that, although the dream factories may be gone, the dreams live on.

CHAPTER ONE

From Coney Island to William Morris to Hollywood

MY INTRODUCTION TO SHOW business came via a circuitous route (don't many important things in life?). Growing up in Coney Island, I played and worked on the famous boardwalk, selling hot dogs and cotton candy and taking tickets for kiddie rides. Whenever I had free time, I would end up in one of the two local movie theaters. The one that showed mostly MGM films was the favorite for dates—those were the romances and the musicals in blazing color. The other movie houses showed the much tougher Warner Bros.' James Cagney, Humphrey Bogart gangster films. For those films, no dates. I graduated from high school early and was seventeen and a half when I entered New York University.

It was 1949, and NYU was crowded with mature students who were attending college under the GI Bill. I was lost, had few friends, didn't like school, and after a couple of years I enlisted in the United States Army, figuring if I couldn't study with soldiers, I'd fight alongside them. The infantry unit I was assigned to in Camp Polk, Louisiana, was training for duty in Korea, where the North Koreans had invaded South Korea. (A useless war in which fifty-two thousand Americans died, and we seem to be at it again!)

When our sergeant asked if anyone could type, I raised my hand, figuring it would be a lot better than schlepping a forty-pound mortar on my back. They discovered I wasn't the greatest typist in the army, but before they might have sent me to the ice-cold front lines, I luckily became indispensable when I located some misplaced service records of Korean-assigned infantry men. After my discharge I returned to NYU a lot more grown up than when I'd left. One of the classes I signed up for was contemporary American literature. The instructor was a Professor Leahey, who introduced me to John Steinbeck, Ernest

Hemingway, John Dos Passos, William Faulkner, and F. Scott Fitzgerald. I was engrossed in the creativity of these writers, and, instead of an indifferent student who joined the army to get away from studying, I became a constant presence in the library as I consumed book after book until I graduated.

When I was a student at New York University, I had a lengthy subway ride from Coney Island in Brooklyn, where I lived, to Manhattan. To take a break from studying the great American writers, I picked up a pulp-fiction novel, *The Carpetbaggers* by Harold Robbins, about the early pioneers in the film industry, from the nickelodeon to the modern day (at the time: 1958). I was intrigued, read the book twice, and remembered I had grown up with a fellow who always looked great in a black suit, white shirt, and tie, who was with MCA, then a renowned talent agency. Upon graduating from NYU a short time later, I had to get a job. Remembering *The Carpetbaggers* and not knowing any better, I called and somehow got an interview for a job in the MCA mail room. Going from the reception area to my interview, I passed a couple of the black-suited agents who were on the phone in animated conversations, and I caught snippets of one talking to "Burt," who I realized was Burt Lancaster, another to "Tony," who was Tony Curtis, and I thought, *Wow, this is a lot better than my father's cotton goods business.* The interview, however, wasn't "wow." Far from it. I was asked a dozen questions, none of which I answered with any knowledge. I was quickly shown the door and told why didn't I try that other agency, William Morris.

At William Morris a very sweet receptionist handed me an application form, and after a short wait the head of the mail room, sure enough, asked me pretty much the same questions as the MCA fellow. But now I knew what not to say. I was hired for eight weeks at $40 per week to fill in for summer-vacationing messenger "boys" (no women), with the understanding that I would be let go when the vacations were over. Fair enough. I was more curious than ambitious.

After six or seven weeks of sorting mail, I was given a pack of savings bank books in the name of Abe Lastfogel, the head man at

William Morris. I was instructed to take each one of the twenty to thirty savings bank books to different banks all over Manhattan and Brooklyn and have the interest on the savings accounts entered. It seemed Mr. Lastfogel didn't trust any one bank with all his money and was also protecting himself from multiple bank failures, so he deposited the maximum amount protected by law, $5,000, in each bank. This was the man who was running a giant talent agency, advising clients from Frank Sinatra to Marilyn Monroe to Danny Kaye about their careers. I thought about my degree from NYU and that this procedure certainly wasn't what I'd been taught about economics and financial planning, but Lastfogel was the boss, and I was the mail boy.

As Labor Day approached, I was told I would be let go, as all the vacationers were returning. I was starting to enjoy the simplicity of the mail room and the camaraderie of my colleagues, who included future producers Bernie Brillstein, Jerry Weintraub, and George Shapiro. I was also enjoying the Broadway theater, as a couple of times a week clients would cancel at the last minute, and I got to see (and fall in love with) the musicals *My Fair Lady, Bells Are Ringing, The Most Happy Fella, Auntie Mame,* and legit shows like *Long Day's Journey into Night* and *Separate Tables.* Although that $40 a week didn't give me much to live on, I found myself really liking my little corner of showbiz.

As my departure date loomed, I was given an envelope and $4 in cab fare to take a contract to the singer Billy Eckstine for a performance that night. I was told to get it signed and brought right back. I walked from the Morris office on 55th Street to the subway on 59th Street, the express train took me to Eckstine's apartment on 125th Street, he signed the contract, and the express took me back to the office in just about twenty minutes! The office manager accused me of not only pocketing the $4 cab fare but also forging Eckstine's signature, since it was impossible for me to get back and forth so quickly. I protested and asked him to call Eckstine, who would verify his signature and my credibility. My boss was so embarrassed when Eckstine told him the kid had been there that he kept me on in the mail room.

Twenty-five years later an old friend, Jerry Perenchio, had a birthday party and had Eckstine perform, after which the singer coincidentally sat next to me for dinner. I told him the story of my long-ago trip to his apartment, and he looked at me blankly. The defining moment in my career was a completely insignificant moment in his. I guess it depends on which side of the aisle you're sitting on.

Now settled into the mail room, I had corresponded with a fellow clerk in the Los Angeles William Morris office mail room. He "introduced" me to Margo Melson, a beautiful young woman who had recently moved to New York from California. We met at the lounge of the Park Sheraton Hotel right next to the Morris office, had dinner that night, the next night, and, except for a couple of early days, we haven't separated in sixty years. Margo and I had come together in spite of her mother warning her to "Never marry an agent or a Jew." Margo was brought up in a non-practicing Jewish home by parents who were formerly vaudeville performers.

In the early part of the twentieth century, before television, radio, and widespread moviegoing, vaudeville was the primary source of entertainment in much of the United States. Performances featured an act, be it a juggler, acrobat, singer, comedian, dancer, you name it. The act traveled from city to city, town to town, the performers very often staying in rooming houses that bore signs No DOGS OR JEWS ALLOWED. Margo's mother, Irma, went by the name Irmanette, and her act was playing Beethoven violin concertos while on her toes and doing a backbend (she also seriously played at Carnegie Hall). Charlie Melson, Margo's father, was a bandleader who did "sand dance," a soft-shoe routine on sand spread on the stage. When Margo was growing up, however, these talents were no longer of use, nor was vaudeville.

Margo and I married eight months after we met. Margo's show business genes played well when she had a small part in the The Strawberry Statement, one of my earliest movies, right up through Marty Scorsese's After Hours, The King of Comedy, and Goodfellas, as well as Night and the City, The Net, and Guilty by Suspicion.

To supplement my meager income from the Morris office trainee program, I was able to "laugh" on two live television shows. Both *The Walter Winchell Show* and *The Buddy Hackett Show* had me laugh and applaud when the audience didn't. (It was pretty often.)

When a job opened up for a projectionist at William Morris, I applied and found myself running a 16mm projection machine, rather ineptly, and booking auditions in the conference room (including one for Elvis Presley, whom I got to know under very different circumstances, but that's for later) until I was promoted to secretary to an agent in the syndication department. The glamour of showbiz proved very unglamorous when my job consisted of selling foreign rights to half-hour television shows, like *Make Room for Daddy* starring Danny Thomas and *The Dick Van Dyke Show*, that the Morris office represented. Toward the fifth boring year I was introduced to the brilliant magazine editor (and lifelong friend) Clay Felker. Although I had little background in talent management, I had learned a lot by osmosis, hanging around with the talent agents, reading the odd script, and the like. Because of my Morris office pedigree, Clay asked if I would handle his young and gorgeous wife, the actress Pamela Tiffin. In short order Clay introduced me to the group of extremely talented writers who represented the "new" form of journalism: Tom Wolfe, Gloria Steinem, Nick Pileggi, Jimmy Breslin, Gail Sheehy, and Nora Ephron. Clay had assembled that group of writers when he was editor of the *New York Herald Tribune* and founder of *New York* magazine (I was a minor investor). Clay would introduce me to a whole new world far from the tedium of selling syndication rights, and through Pamela I was introduced to the world of the movies.

Examining my years as a mediocre (and that's an overstatement) agent, I decided to go into the personal management business with Bob Chartoff, a recent graduate of Columbia Law School who had no desire to be a lawyer. Bob and I met one night when one of his clients, the comic Jackie Mason, was on *The Ed Sullivan Show* and I was covering it for another William Morris agent who was sick. Bob then wanted me to see a singer he was interested in, who was appearing in a club downtown. I didn't think much of the singer, but I thought Bob was interesting, ambitious, and very smart. Bob soon after asked if I would handle Mason at William Morris. We booked Mason into some high-profile clubs and multiple appearances on live variety shows. Bob then suggested I leave William Morris and join him in the management business. I brought in to our partnership a few of my clients whom the Morris office had no interest in. One, an Englishman, Nat Cohen, was the producer of *Carry On Nurse*, one of a series of lowbrow comedies, and some minor television dramas. Bob, of course, had his list of singers and comics. Margo never blinked when I told her I was thinking of leaving my secure job at William Morris for the unknown world of personal management. We had no money and two young boys, Charles and David (Adam was yet to come), but Margo, rather than urging caution, was encouraging when I was unsure. It's been the same ever since.

Out of character, Nat Cohen had financed a small feature film called *Billy Liar* starring Tom Courtenay and the young British actress Julie Christie, directed by John Schlesinger (who later went on to direct *Midnight Cowboy*). When Cohen signed Christie for *Billy Liar*, he also got options on her acting services for six more films with the right to lend her out to other films (at a profit, of course). He asked us to represent those loans or, as he put it, "get her a big movie." We found *Billy Liar* playing at a small art house on Long Island. Watching the movie, Bob and I kept waiting for Julie Christie to show up on-screen. After thirty minutes or so she came bopping down the street, her hair flowing, beautiful face and figure, the epitome of English "hip" in the mid-1960s. One look at Christie and I poked my partner and said, "Bob, we're gonna be in the movie business!" Shortly thereafter Cohen told us he was financing another film directed by Schlesinger starring Christie called *Darling*, and would we help Schlesinger in the casting of *Darling* when he came to New York? In the meantime, we started looking for a movie for Christie after *Darling*. We checked all the upcoming films, and I heard about David Lean casting *Doctor Zhivago*, based on Boris Pasternak's novel about the Russian Revolution. We called Lean and Lee Steiner, who was producer Carlo Ponti's lawyer in New

York. Steiner told us to send him a letter on behalf of Julie Christie and that he would pass it on to Ponti. The suggestion of "sending a letter" seemed pretty much like a brush-off. It wasn't. At least not after Steiner called and we arranged for Christie to test for the starring role of Lara. Christie's test was successful, she got the part (beating out Jane Fonda), and Cohen asked us to come to London to see the half-completed *Darling* so that we could advise him on selling the film in the States.

The only problem we had at that point was finding the money to get to London. With my two small children and Bob's three, and not all of our clients paying commission, we were living hand to mouth. Bob found out about a gambling junket flying from New York to London with a planeload of high rollers, and they must have been short two players, because we were off to London in short order. We were put up at a fancy West End hotel and ferried to the Victoria Sporting Club, where

Irwin Winkler at MGM Studios

we were given dinner and expected to gamble. Bob and I bought $500 in chips and during the rest of our stay kept cashing in our supposed winnings, buying more chips for the sum of $500, then cashing them in again, looking very active but really risking nothing. In the meantime, we saw a rough cut of *Darling* and realized it was not only a very fine film but cutting-edge cinema that would make Julie Christie a star.

Back in New York we figured that MGM, the financiers behind *Doctor Zhivago*, would be a natural to buy and distribute *Darling* in the United States. MGM's CEO, Bob O'Brien, whom we were introduced to by Lee Steiner, thought so too and said he planned to go to London to see Stanley Kubrick's *2001: A Space Odyssey* and that we should meet him there and screen *Darling* for him. Luckily there was another junket, and back to London we went. O'Brien liked what he saw and agreed to buy the U.S. rights for $1.1 million. Cohen was thrilled, Julie Christie was thrilled, and I guess the Victoria Sporting Club was less so, as we were never able to get on another junket.

A couple of weeks after we returned from London the second time, Bob O'Brien asked us to his office and bluntly told us he was not going to go ahead on the *Darling* deal. It seems he was up for a papal knighthood, and he was sure that when the Catholic Legion of Decency saw the nudity and sexuality in the film, they would condemn it and him. There was no way of convincing him otherwise, and we dejectedly returned to our office. But in the time we had walked the mere five or six blocks, the word was out, and a small independent distributor, Joe Levine, who had made his reputation (and fortune) by distributing Italian epics like *Hercules Unchained* and some other minor foreign films, had called. Levine had been tipped off that O'Brien was pulling out of *Darling*, and he offered to buy it sight unseen for $800,000 or, if he flew to London and liked it, $1.1 million. When I informed Nat Cohen, he told me to "grab the eight hundred," as he was sure that Levine would pass on it if he saw the film. To this day I don't think Joe Levine ever saw *Darling*, but the film received great critical (and audience) acclaim. It was nominated for five Oscars (including Best Picture), and Julie Christie won for Best Actress.

Julie Christie went right from the set of *Darling* to the Madrid set of *Doctor Zhivago* for an unheard of 104-week schedule (at a salary of $1,000 per week). Taking into account that Christie had to do postproduction work on *Darling* in London, we negotiated for her to leave the *Zhivago* location and return to London after eight weeks. Seven weeks after Christie started *Zhivago*, I called the head of MGM Business Affairs, Peter Shaw, to give him notice that Christie would be leaving the set that Saturday as per her contract. Strangely, nothing happened; no response came from Shaw. Days passed and still no word, so this time I called Ben Melniker, the head of MGM Business Affairs in New York, and reminded him of Christie's leaving. No response. On that Friday afternoon Melniker called, hysterical, and asked us to come to O'Brien's office immediately. When we got there, O'Brien, who sweat a lot normally, was drenched and was on the phone with his production manager in Spain, who told him that Christie was packing and would leave for London the next morning. When O'Brien asked him what they were shooting the next day, he was told "a scene at the Russian train station with 5,000 dress extras and Julie Christie, and she wasn't going to be there. Oh, and David Lean didn't know, because they were afraid to tell him. If they did, they were sure he would walk off the film. O'Brien, wiping his brow with a now-soaking-wet handkerchief, looked at Bob Chartoff and me and said if Lean walked off, it would be the end of MGM. There was a stockholders' fight with the Bronfmans of Seagrams, and this would give them the ammunition to take over, and he would be fired. At that point I told O'Brien I wanted to talk to Nat Cohen in London, as I had a solution in mind. By now it was 4:00 P.M. in New York, 9:00 P.M. in London, and O'Brien's secretary reported that all the lines were down and she couldn't get through to London. O'Brien threw up his hands in despair and could only talk about the end of MGM (and his job). I told the secretary to call the production manager in Madrid, to have him call Cohen in London, and to have Cohen call me at O'Brien's office. Everyone looked at me, astonished, and I had to repeat to his secretary to please call Madrid. In just about ten minutes Cohen was on the phone from London, and I told him that rather than Christie flying to London to do the post work on *Darling*, why not do it in Madrid at night, and MGM would pay for it? Cohen was more than agreeable, O'Brien was thrilled, and only Melniker complained about MGM paying for *Darling*'s post work. O'Brien shut him up and said he had never seen anyone think on his feet like I did, and that's what he needed in Hollywood. He told Bob and me to find a script, and, if he liked it, he'd make us producers for MGM in Culver City.

A couple of days after the Julie Christie *Doctor Zhivago* affair, Russ Thatcher, head of the MGM story department in New York, called and had a script he thought would be a perfect vehicle for Christie. But he had a problem: Mr. O'Brien would only green-light films after he read (and liked) the script, and Mr. O'Brien had a big stack on his desk and just wasn't getting around to reading them. Their productions were almost at a standstill. However, Thatcher said, O'Brien wanted us to produce films for MGM, so he would give us their script, and if we liked it, we would give it to Mr. O'Brien. In that case there was a good chance he'd read it, and MGM would have a chance at making the film with Julie Christie. I read the script *Double Trouble*, didn't think it was very special, but with nothing to lose and figuring O'Brien would be eager for a Julie Christie film, I called him and pitched the script with the chance of Christie starring. He was receptive to reading it.

Bright and early the next morning O'Brien was on the phone, only he wasn't interested in making the film with Christie. He wanted to do it with Elvis Presley instead. I wasn't sure we were talking about the same script. I asked O'Brien if the script I'd sent him, *Double Trouble*, to star Julie Christie, was the one he wanted to do with Elvis Presley. He said, "Yes, what do you think of starring Presley instead of Julie Christie?" I gulped hard and told O'Brien that it was a great idea, the best idea I'd heard in a long time. He said we should do a quick rewrite, change the female lead to a young male rock singer, and have Elvis sing a couple of songs. He asked how quickly I could be out in Hollywood. I answered "pretty quick," but first he wanted Bob Chartoff and me to meet with his California production president Bob Weitman, who was in New York. Weitman looked at the two of us and asked which one of us was the director and which one was the producer. We blinked and both immediately chose producing, having an inkling of what that entailed but absolutely no idea about the skills directing might require.

CHAPTER TWO

Actually making movies, Double Trouble, *and a very tough*
Lee Marvin in Point Blank

STILL SHAKING MY HEAD in wonder and trying to figure out how a script starring a dramatic actress would be fashioned for Elvis Presley, I checked in at MGM to meet Presley's manager, "Colonel Tom" Parker (I don't know what he was a colonel of), an ex-carnival hustler who ran Elvis's career. When we met, he quickly dismissed me and my "New York" ideas and said MGM had hired a writer to rewrite the original script (no one bothered to tell me). Leaving Colonel Parker, I wandered into the MGM commissary for lunch and was greeted by the hostess, who asked what I did. I thought that was strange, so I asked her why; I just wanted a bite to eat. She explained that there was a table for the actors, another for directors, and a special private room for producers. When I told her that I was of the last category, she looked me up and down, surprised, and suggested I go to the very exclusive Lion's Den in the rear of the commissary, where they served Louis B. Mayer's mother's chicken soup. Seated at the round table were the producers of the great days of MGM and Hollywood: Arthur Freed, who produced the musicals *Singin' in the Rain, Gigi,* and *An American in Paris*; Pandro Berman, who produced all the Fred Astaire and Ginger Rogers musicals at RKO; Joe Pasternak, the producer of Deanna Durbin musicals . . . all legendary, but I immediately understood why Bob O'Brien wanted some young blood (Chartoff and me) at MGM. The trio greeted me with calculated silence only interrupted by Arthur Freed getting a phone call from Irving Berlin. I quickly and dutifully ate Mrs. Mayer's chicken soup and left.

As we prepared *Double Trouble,* I sat in on as many production meetings as I could find out about rather than sit in the fancy corner office I had been assigned in the Thalberg Building. No one seemed to know anything about me other than that I was sent out by the boss, Bob O'Brien. Because of my seemingly mysterious presence, Howard Strickling, the man in charge of MGM's publicity department going back to the MGM glamour days in the late 1920s, decided to give me an oral-history trip through the MGM lot. We began in Louis B. Mayer's office (which was kept as though Mayer was coming back to work that day, although he had been gone some fifteen years), with its ivory-inlaid desk that was mounted on a platform so visitors had to look up to Mr. Mayer. Strickling happily filled my ears with his reminiscences of a greater time as we strolled the streets of the historic studio.

After hanging around a couple of days I asked to meet the director MGM had assigned to *Double Trouble*. (I had no say; MGM and Colonel Parker were still operating as if this was 1935.) It was arranged, and I was to wait on the steps of the Thalberg Building at noon the next day.

I arrived at the appropriate time, and a car that was a bit old— probably a Buick, nothing fancy—pulled up, and the driver ran around the car and opened the passenger door for an elderly gentleman, whom he helped up the stairs. I was introduced to my director, Norman Taurog, who had started out directing silent films in the 1920s. He was the youngest director to win an Academy Award, in 1931, for *Skippy*. But that all was a long time ago. I was so surprised by his age and obvious infirmity that I was almost speechless. I mumbled how much I admired his Buick and his chauffeur too. He told me that he loved to drive, but, unfortunately, he was blind in one eye, and his other eye was going fast.

I realized that my foray into Hollywood was going to be with a famous male rock singer playing a dramatic role that had been written for a woman, a controlling, hostile manager, a story that took place in Europe and would be shot in Culver City, California, and a very nice director who could hardly walk up the stairs to meet me and who'd told me he was going blind. I knew right then that I'd better learn about producing pretty fast.

Elvis was always professional, on time, knew his lines, and was friendly to the cast and crew. He really got engaged when he recorded the music. Those sessions were always at night, and Elvis was gregarious, gracious, and in his comfort zone until, at Taurog's insistence, he had to sing the children's classic "Old MacDonald Had a Farm." (The rest of the songs were a lot more up to date, but none was outstanding.) There was plenty of beer and pizza at the recording studio but no drugs (that I saw). On the set Norman Taurog had meals served to him at a table with a linen tablecloth and napkins, fine china, and a rose in a crystal vase while everyone else ate at a communal table off the catering truck. That provided one of my early lessons in moviemaking—you don't get loyalty by being exclusive.

Irwin Winkler and director Norman Taurog
Double Trouble

There was one special day set aside for Elvis to do a karate scene. That day Elvis's family, his entourage, MGM executives, and Colonel Parker showed up just before lunch to watch as the crowd applauded and Elvis broke a wooden board in half with one swift motion of his hand. Although the wood was prepared to break if a strong wind came along, everyone congratulated Elvis, and off we all went to a catered lunch in the commissary.

I found it fascinating on the film set watching Antwerp being shot on Washington Boulevard and London shot on Lot 2 on Motor Avenue in Culver City. This was in contrast to MGM making *2001: A Space Odyssey* in London and *Doctor Zhivago* in Spain. Why the disconnect? Did Elvis Presley represent MGM unwittingly trying to hold on to the past? I would soon find out that Elvis himself was trying to hold on to the past. As he left the MGM lot, his two closest pals, Red and Sonny, would get into his car with him, and as they approached the MGM gate to leave, they would have Elvis get down on the floor of the car and throw a blanket over him so that the crowds outside the gate wouldn't storm the car to get a glimpse of their idol. The sad truth was, there was no one there. Did he know that the crowds weren't there anymore, or did he simply not want to know?

While I was learning about producing on the set of *Double Trouble*, Bob Chartoff was in New York running our talent management business. Bob asked me to cover the opening of one of our new acts at the Troubadour. The client was the Chad Mitchell Trio with John Denver as a lead singer (Chad Mitchell was in jail on a drug charge. Oh, the '60s). I hated the idea of going from producing a Hollywood movie to sitting in the back of a smoky nightclub watching an unknown singer. After John Denver's set, Margo and I went backstage, and I introduced myself to John and his wife, Annie. After some polite conversation he asked me how I'd liked his performance. I couldn't help myself, and instead of a polite "fine" or "great," I asked him if he'd done anything else (besides performing). John looked at me oddly and said, "What do you mean? I was a schoolteacher." The compulsion to be a movie producer, not a singer's personal manager, took over, and I told John, "That's what you should do, teach school." The next morning a call came from Harold Thaw, Denver's business manager, and—no surprise—he said Denver didn't want Chartoff-Winkler to manage him, and I quickly agreed. Bob Chartoff and I decided neither of us wanted to choose the management business over moviemaking, so Bob joined

A LIFE IN MOVIES

me in California, and we slowly gave up our clients and quickly started looking at producing films as our future.

POINT BLANK (1967)

I had learned quite a bit on *Double Trouble*, enough to know that, as nice as he was, Elvis Presley was not the future for Bob and me. Our partner in making *Double Trouble*, Judd Bernard, a Hollywood publicist with no film experience but some agency contacts and unlimited energy, knew that Bob O'Brien wanted us to make more pictures at MGM, so he brought us scripts that he unearthed, whether they were good, bad, or indifferent. Finally, one caught our eye: *Point Blank*, a screenplay written by Rafe and David Newhouse, based on a book by Donald Westlake (using the Richard Stark pseudonym). It was a tough look at a criminal who gets betrayed by his wife and best friend, gets shot, and is left for dead. We thought *Point Blank* interesting, as the Walker character was tougher and more abrasive than most bad guys in then-current films. Even when James Cagney or Humphrey Bogart played a tough bad guy, they wanted the audience to like them. Not the Walker character—he wants his revenge and payback, no holds barred and not a smile in sight.

Lee Marvin came to mind for the role, and although we called his agent, Meyer Mishkin, several times, we couldn't get him to return our calls. We learned that Marvin was working for MGM in London, starring in *The Dirty Dozen*. We had no way to get the script to him, much less get him to read it. Out of desperation we contacted British director John Boorman, whom we had a loose relationship with from our management days. Boorman had done some documentaries for the BBC and had recently directed a small film called *Having a Wild Weekend* about a British rock and roll group called the Dave Clark Five. It was a free-form semi-biographical film, very unstructured, and it had absolutely nothing to do with *Point Blank*, but we saw a talented director (who lived in London) and called Boorman and told him if he could find Lee Marvin, get him to read the script, commit to the movie, and, of course, agree to John directing him, he had a job (if we could get the studio to agree). When you think about it, pretty naïve and almost impossible.

Boorman chased down Marvin, had a drink with him, and, lo and behold, Marvin not only liked the script but said he would do the film only with Boorman directing! This was quickly confirmed by his ordinarily unenthusiastic agent, Mr. Mishkin.

We now had to deal with the internal politics at MGM, as the New York production people were very competitive with the Hollywood head of production, Robert Weitman. If we gave the script to Weitman and he liked it, he would give it to Bob O'Brien in New York, where his head story man, Russ Thatcher, would surely kill it because he didn't get it first. We decided to go to New York, see O'Brien and Thatcher, make our pitch, and do an end run around Weitman.

In New York, much to our chagrin, we found that Mr. Weitman was coincidentally also in town and was going to be seeing O'Brien the same day that we had scheduled our meeting. Our old management client Pamela Tiffin was starring in a play on Broadway, and Bob and I had planned to see her performance and have dinner with her afterward. But when we thought about Weitman meeting O'Brien, we realized we needed to get the script to him or else he was surely going to be negative when he got into O'Brien's office the next day. We left at the intermission of Pamela's play, slipping out a side door into a taxi, and went to our office on Sixth Avenue and Fifty-Fifth Street, to get the *Point Blank* script to give to Weitman. When we got to our office, the building was closed. The janitor didn't know either Bob Chartoff or me because we had both been in California for the past few months, and he wouldn't let us in. We persuaded him to call the owner of the building, who was home sick. After he described us on the phone to the owner, we were allowed in. We got a copy of the script, thanked the janitor with a $20 tip, got back into a cab, and ran over to the Regency Hotel on Park Avenue and gave the bellman $20 to take the script up to Weitman's room with a note explaining we were going to discuss the script the next day with O'Brien. We then got back into the cab, went back to the theater, greeted Pamela Tiffin as she came off the stage, and had dinner with her afterward, all smiles (she was very good in the first act, after all).

The next morning both Weitman and Russ Thatcher greeted us in O'Brien's office. Weitman said that he had stayed up late to read *Point Blank* and didn't get to the end but liked it a lot. Thatcher was even more enthused. Thatcher, I think, because he "discovered us" with *Double Trouble*. Weitman slapped Bob Chartoff on the back and remarked that he appreciated that we'd gotten him the script at the last minute.

O'Brien was so pleased that both his warring executives agreed on something, he didn't ask to read the script and was ready to commit. He said he liked what he saw of Marvin's work on *The Dirty Dozen* and wanted to know what it would cost and who would direct. We told O'Brien we could make the film for a bit less than $2 million (a guess), and we had this young, vibrant director, John Boorman. We were unsure if O'Brien would accept our recommendations. After all, we had made one not very good Elvis Presley film. Suddenly we were interrupted by a call from Stanley Kubrick in London, who was in some crisis on *2001: A Space Odyssey*. When O'Brien hung up, he turned to us and asked, "Now, what were we discussing?" We sheepishly told him we were talking about the budget and didn't mention Boorman. He asked again what the budget was, and Thatcher jumped in and said $2 million. "Go make the movie," a very happy O'Brien said. We got out of there as quickly as we could with a big hug from Weitman.

When we got back to California, Weitman absently asked, "Did we ever talk about a director?" I said, "Sure, John Boorman." Weitman recalled that we had mentioned his name, and that was that.

As we started to prepare for production on *Point Blank*, all the old MGM studio machinery and support came to work. Although we were in the post-studio era, some vestiges of the system remained. Before we could hire any key crew—cameramen, set director, production manager, composer—we had to go through the MGM key technical staff.

Luckily they were a talented group, especially our cameraman Philip Lathrop, who, just like in the golden MGM days, wore a jacket and tie on set. The casting started off fine, with Carroll O'Connor (before *All in the Family*) as the Mafia chieftain, but got difficult when Weitman found that we were hiring the beautiful and talented Rat Pack favorite Angie Dickinson for the lead opposite Marvin. Weitman called Bob Chartoff and me into his office and asked why we wanted to cast Angie Dickinson when he, to our great surprise, had already hired the actress Stella Stevens. He had hired her for the lead role without telling any of us, the old studio way. We told Weitman that we were committed to Dickinson, as were John Boorman and Lee Marvin. Weitman picked up the phone, called Meyer Mishkin, and told him that he was "thinking" of replacing Angie with Stella Stevens. Mishkin made it very clear that Lee would walk off, that there was no way he was going to do the picture with anyone other than Angie Dickinson. As we walked out of Weitman's office, two other young producers, Jerry Gershwin and Elliott Kastner, started in, and I kidded them, "I'll bet you guys are gonna cast Stella Stevens in your next movie." And, sure enough, Kastner and Gershwin ended up with Stella Stevens for their movie *Sol Madrid*.

Shooting started with a rather tight schedule, and Boorman was very much in charge. Hard to believe he was a first-time Hollywood director. Marvin played the tough Walker character to the hilt, and the actual locations, unlike the Culver City back lot used for *Double Trouble*, gave energy and realism to every scene. After the first week a frantic call came for Bob and me to see Weitman. By now we knew the way to his office by heart. Weitman had a problem with the dailies. Boorman, afraid of what MGM might do to the film in editing, "cut the film in the camera." That is, he shot just enough of each scene so that it had to be edited the way he wanted. There was almost no room to allow for an editor and certainly no extra film to change what was shot. Weitman was quite upset by what he saw in the projection room. Boorman, he remarked, had no idea how to direct a scene; all he saw in dailies were pieces of scenes. Weitman had prepared a list of directors who were available to take over from Boorman, and if Marvin disagreed, Weitman would shut down the picture and sue Marvin. The threat seemed ridiculous, but his determination seemed real. We convinced Weitman to have Boorman cut a few scenes together and screen them for him and MGM's chief editor, Margaret Booth (who had edited for Irving Thalberg). Boorman took to the task gladly and added some sound effects and music, and after the screening Booth congratulated us on a really fine, "very modern" movie. From then on Weitman was supportive and never complained, even when we were delayed a few days shooting in San Francisco.

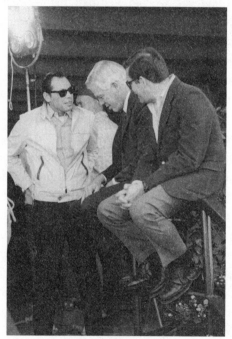

Irwin Winkler, Lee Marvin, Judd Bernard
Point Blank

The reason for the delay? Marvin, who got very drunk when we arrived in San Francisco to shoot the opening and ending scenes on Alcatraz Island, disappeared with the vocalist Ella Fitzgerald. We all scrambled to find something to shoot while we quietly looked all over San Francisco but found no sign of Marvin or the queen of jazz. In

22

frustration, Boorman destroyed his hotel room, and we took the frag-
ments of the furniture out of the hotel in our suitcases in the middle
of the night. Finally, a contrite but sober Marvin showed up, no worse
for his spree. He had done it before and would do it again. I certainly
would not make excuses for his drunkenness, but when sober he was
charming, fun, and really gave a great performance. Boorman brought
in two writers, Bill Stair and Alex Jacobs, to rewrite as we went along.
Although that could have brought chaos to the set, John had the complete confidence of the actors, the crew, and now the studio. With Stair
and Jacobs rewriting, much like the camera setups and the editing, the
dialogue was short and attacked the scenes. It was movement, Marvin's
character coming at you all the time.

Walker, getting shot in the opening scene by his best friend and
his wife, played "dead" on the ground with a furious single-minded-
ness to get revenge. After that scene he's seen emerging into the frame
and standing up as if he was a dead man reborn in his need for that
revenge. The conceit (I guess you could call it that) is that Marvin is
shot dead and for the rest of the film he is imagining his future as a
"man on a mission." The idea was intriguing if not rather fanciful.

Every scene had a reality to it. When Brewster (Carroll O'Connor
as a Mafia chief) arrives at his house with Walker waiting in the shad-
ows, Brewster complains about the pool not being taken care of. When
Walker confronts him about his money, he snarls that he's with a big
organization, and they don't keep cash around, suggesting that crime
is a big business, not a bunch of small-time crooks running around
holding up banks. The actor James Sikking assassinating another gang
member brings to mind Lee Harvey Oswald's assassination of President Kennedy only a few years before.

John Boorman edited the film quickly, and we hired the composer Johnny Mandel, who wrote an eerie score that played well with
Marvin's character.

After several successful screenings, with great anticipation we
took the finished film to New York to show it to O'Brien and the other
top executives. It was our first experience showing a film to the top

brass, and we had no idea how it would be received. It was received with silence, no congratulations, no handshake or head shake. We were devastated. O'Brien and company just got up and walked out of the projector room and into the elevator. Bob Chartoff and I followed and squeezed in after them, and Bob asked how they'd liked it. O'Brien loudly said, "Oh, fine, good picture." The elevator door opened, the MGM executives followed O'Brien into his office, and we got back into the elevator and repeated O'Brien's "good picture" as we hugged each other.

Lee Marvin's character, Walker, didn't die on Alcatraz at the end of *Point Blank*, and neither did the film. Some forty-five years later, in December 2014, I visited an art exhibition by Ai Weiwei at Alcatraz Island, and there at the gift shop was a DVD of *Point Blank*. I bought a copy and asked the saleslady if it sold well. She assured me that it did and added that she had seen it and thought, "It's really good—you'll like it."

CHAPTER THREE

A rebuff of Shakespeare, a welcome from Jack Warner,
and diversity

PLEASED WITH THE SUCCESS of *Point Blank*, Bob O'Brien welcomed us when we called about another movie to be directed by John Boorman. This was the Tom Stoppard play *Rosencrantz and Guildenstern Are Dead*. Stoppard brilliantly took two very minor characters from *Hamlet* and followed their journey, separate from Hamlet's. Bob O'Brien had his brain trust hanging around the office when Bob Chartoff and I arrived: his international sales manager, "Red" Silverstein; his legal counsel, Ben Melniker; and his domestic sales manager, Morty Lefkoe. When we pitched the idea of Rosencrantz and Guildenstern being characters in Stoppard's masterpiece, we knew by the shrugged shoulders that we were in trouble. Finally, Lefkoe, with a cigar hanging out of the side of his mouth, snarled, "You gotta change the title." Bob and I protested that it was Shakespeare. Lefkoe retorted, "I don't care who wrote it—to me it sounds like two guys from the dress business who had a bad season." That was that. Tom Stoppard directed his version of *Rosencrantz & Guildenstern Are Dead* in 1990.

In June 1967 I was invited, much to my surprise, for cocktails at the house of Jack Warner, the founder, with his brothers, of Warner Bros. Studios. We had just made *Point Blank* and thought we had "arrived" in Hollywood. Imagine being invited to Jack Warner's house for cocktails! Driving up to this magnificent estate (now owned by David Geffen), I was met by a golf cart to take me from the front gate to the house surrounded by massive trees and statues. In the den Jake Warner greeted me (not by name), and as I looked around, there were the leaders of Hollywood: Darryl Zanuck, Lew Wasserman, Jimmy

Stewart, Abe Lastfogel, Gregory Peck, and other assorted big shots. What was I doing there?

Warner brought the room to attention and announced that Israel was at war with its Arab neighbors, and it was incumbent upon all of us to support Israel financially. He called on Darryl Zanuck first, who pledged $250,000. Warner said that since Zanuck, who wasn't even Jewish, was giving $250,000, Wasserman, who, he needlessly reminded everyone, was Jewish, should give $500,000. Wasserman nodded his head, and so it went until Warner looked at me. I gulped and pledged $1,500, which was a good portion of our bank account at the time. Warner said, "Look at this kid. He doesn't have a pot to piss in, and he's giving $1,500. You should all double your pledges." I got a couple of pats on the back as I left to return to our small rented house and tell Margo. She smiled proudly and assured me that I had arrived in Hollywood.

THE SPLIT (1968)

After the minor success of *Point Blank* we understood that, even though we had a receptive studio in MGM and an invitation to Jack Warner's, we still had to have a script, a star, an opportunity, and a lot of luck to get a movie made.

Bob and I, searching for another movie, went back to the Donald Westlake library and dug out another Richard Stark novel, *The Split*. It had the same kind of intense character that Lee Marvin played in *Point Blank* but with a very different plot. This was about a group of criminals robbing a football stadium while the game is in progress, getting away with the loot, and then having it stolen and ending up fighting among themselves. We developed the script and thought it was good enough to cast with a star actor in the leading role.

We knew our way around Hollywood a little better now and had a relationship with a senior agent at William Morris, Phil Kellogg, who handled the directors Elia Kazan, David Lean, and Fred Zinnemann and some high-profile actors. We gave the script to Kellogg, who liked it and gave it to his client Steve McQueen, the biggest star in movies at the time. Kellogg soon reported that McQueen wanted to do it.

Before we got on the plane to New York to see our friend Bob O'Brien, I got a call from the agent Phil Gersh, who had given the script of *The Split* to his client, the great former football star Jim Brown. He had been in a couple of films in the past few years, some of which were for MGM. Gersh said that Brown had read the script and wanted to do the film. I thanked Gersh but told him we were going to New York to make a deal for Steve McQueen to star in the film.

We got to the MGM offices of Bob O'Brien, and the receptionist told us to wait a few minutes, as O'Brien was in a meeting with—of all people—Phil Kellogg. We waited awhile, and Kellogg emerged from the meeting all smiles and asked what we were doing in New York. We cheerily explained that we were there to pitch *The Split* with Steve McQueen to O'Brien. Kellogg said, "Oh, I forgot to tell you. Steve McQueen isn't going to do your picture. He's going to do *Bullitt* instead." At that moment the receptionist said, "Mr. O'Brien will see you now," and ushered us in. O'Brien asked what he could do for us. We said, "We've got this script called *The Split*." O'Brien then asked who we had to star in our script. Bob Chartoff looked at me, I took a deep breath, and I said, "We've got the great Jim Brown." O'Brien didn't hesitate. He said he liked Brown and was sure we would make another *Point Blank* for MGM.

Since a lot of the new, interesting films were coming out of England, our impulse was to follow John Boorman with someone who was not Hollywood. Gordon Flemyng, who had done *Great Catherine*, a good picture with Peter O'Toole, read the script and had some good notes. We were nervous about Jim Brown's acting and decided to surround him with as strong of a cast as we could. Donald Sutherland, Gene Hackman (in his first Hollywood film), Warren Oates, Jack Klugman, Ernest Borgnine, Julie Harris, Diahann Carroll, and James Whitmore supported Brown. It helped some, but Brown was still a bit stiff, except in the action scenes, when he moved like the great football player he had been. But strong performances by the rest of the cast gave the dramatic scenes substance. The actual robbery of the stadium when the football game was in progress had lots of tension, good editing, and a suspenseful score by the great Quincy Jones.

Irwin Winkler, Diahann Carroll, Jim Brown
The Split

Although the casting of an African American actor in a starring role was quite unusual at the time, Brown physically and emotionally was right for the part, and we never thought about skin color. Some of the critics did. Roger Ebert, discussing the act of Jim Brown pushing around his white gang members in the first thirty minutes of the film, wasn't sure whether it was exploitive or not, missing the point that, although the role was written for a white actor, it was played by a black actor with absolutely no change in character portrayal.

The Split came together as a solid thriller, no more, no less. Nothing to be ashamed of, nothing to be proud of, except the accidental casting that was groundbreaking. We decided to have a preview of the film up in Oakland, California, where we expected to get a positive response, since it would be before an African American audience. The film played well but not great, and it confirmed our feelings that it was not much more than an OK heist movie. At the end of the screening, as we realized that no one from MGM had bothered to come and the audience's meager response would influence the studio's marketing efforts, we decided to grab a bunch of audience preview cards and fill them out ourselves. Bob and I wrote *excellent* on as many cards as we thought we could get away with (a lot). We did get a surprised congratulations from the MGM marketing department when they computed the results of the screening. But to no avail. Even with a very favorable *New York Times* review, the film just wasn't good enough to capture an audience.

CHAPTER FOUR

From the college campus uprising, to decadence in London, to a
Hollywood dance marathon, to the Cannes Film Festival

THE STRAWBERRY STATEMENT (1969)

CLAY FELKER ALERTED US to a story he was about to publish in *New York* magazine. It was by a Columbia student, James Kunen, "The Strawberry Statement: Notes of a College Revolutionary," about the riots that led to the takeover of the school by a group of militant students in 1968. Kunen himself wasn't much of a militant—he was more committed to meeting girls than bringing down the establishment—but he was a pretty good diarist. When he came to visit us in Los Angeles, his girlfriend, who proudly wore a Students for a Democratic Society emblem, had a makeup case and enough luggage to fill an armored tank. Kunen's story nonetheless touched a political nerve, and we bought it immediately.

Bob O'Brien had gone, retired from MGM to a farm in Minnesota (don't all studio heads?). A friend from my William Morris days, Herb Solow, took over MGM at the behest of the new owner, Kirk Kerkorian. Solow was very encouraging, and we hired the New York playwright Israel Horovitz to adapt Kunen's story and to move it to the West Coast, since Columbia wouldn't allow us to shoot on its campus and that usual problem: budget. We wanted the film to be filled with the music of the period, which would help tell the story of the revolution playing out in America. We had good contacts from our management days and "cast" the music as well as the group of young actors led by Bruce Davison, Kim Darby, Bob Balaban, James Coco, and Bud Cort.

The film started off with Joni Mitchell's "The Circle Game" sung by Buffy Sainte-Marie and went from there to "Something in the Air" by Thunderclap Newman; "Helpless" by Crosby, Stills, Nash & Young; "Suite: Judy Blue Eyes" by Stephen Stills performed by Crosby, Stills & Nash; "Long Time Gone" by David Crosby performed by Crosby,

Bud Cort, Robert Chartoff, Irwin Winkler
The Strawberry Statement

Stills & Nash; "The Lover" and "Down by the River" by Neil Young. The film ends with a police riot as the students are peacefully protesting and chanting John Lennon and Paul McCartney's "Give Peace a Chance."

I had seen several commercials directed by Stuart Hagmann that were innovative and had the freewheeling style of the students and the atmosphere of the times. We hired Hagmann, and his signature pink glasses went well with my beads, beard, long hair, and the silk stripes down the sides of my jeans as we walked the streets of Sacramento and Haight-Ashbury in San Francisco.

The plot was simple enough—a naïve young student (Davison) on the rowing team becomes infatuated with a girl, Linda (Kim Darby), who is involved in the campus unrest. His interest in Linda leads him to activism and a close examination of himself, his fellow students, and the university establishment. Ultimately *The Strawberry Statement* is about the idealism and radicalization of the 1960s in America, a time of Vietnam, political unrest, youth rebellion, and a terrible violence by the establishment against change.

Because of Hagmann's directorial style, which involved a great deal of camera movement, the actors sometimes suffered from the crew's allocation of production time versus acting time. But they were game and young, though they required a lot of on-set communication by Bob and me. There are some good surprises in Israel Horovitz's script that played well, and the brutal ending, with our hero beaten to death by police, was somehow a foretelling of the incident the following year at Kent State University in Ohio when four young students in a peaceful protest were killed by the National Guard.

The conservative and pro-establishment and pro-Vietnam press, such as the *New York Times*, hated the film, but *The Strawberry Statement* stands out as an unflinching look at America at a time of great change.

LEO THE LAST (1969)

Leo the Last is surely a poster boy for the upheaval at the major Hollywood studios in the late 1960s. The script was based on a play by George Tabori, who was known as an adapter and screenwriter of Bertolt Brecht and several special films directed by the likes of Elia Kazan, Joseph Losey, and Alfred Hitchcock. Bob Chartoff and I met Tabori through his wife, the actress Viveca Lindfors, who had been a management client of ours. We didn't develop the script of *Leo the Last*—it came to us directly from Tabori, and we thought it a natural for John Boorman, who immediately committed and wanted Marcello Mastroianni for Leo. After turndowns by MGM, Paramount, Universal, and Columbia, we decided to go see David Picker, the head of production at United Artists. He was an affable man and had done some interesting films, including the initial James Bond, *Tom Jones*, and the Beatles' *Help!* and *A Hard Day's Night*. When we met, he asked why we were so passionate about *Leo the Last*, since he, and he guessed everyone else, had passed on it. We told Picker we believed the script was special, and so were Mastroianni and Boorman. That didn't seem to move him, so I took a shot and asked him how many movies he'd made in the last year, and he said, "Twelve or thirteen," and I replied, "How many were successful?" He hesitated. "Probably four." I asked if he liked all the scripts he had put into production. "Sure, or I wouldn't have made them." "Well, you're better off making our script that you don't like; the odds are a lot better." I was dead serious. He laughed, looked at Bob and me, and said, "Nobody ever said that to me. Go make the damn picture."

We got out of his office as fast as possible, had a good laugh, and set up a dinner in Venice with John Boorman and Marcello Mastroianni, who was shooting a film there. The purpose of the dinner was supposedly to get to know one another and talk about the script, cast, and locations, but really Bob and I wanted to see if Mastroianni could speak English well enough for George Tabori's dialogue. Dinner was on the terrace of the Gritti Palace Hotel, and as the sun was setting over the Grand Canal, a speedboat pulled up, and out stepped a young and beautiful Faye Dunaway and Marcello Mastroianni, as handsome as could be, dressed perfectly in a dark blue suit, crisp white shirt, and silk necktie. He was as charming as he was handsome. Marcello offered Margo, who was seated next to him (and all the ladies), a taste of his pasta, a sip of his wine, and a wide, seductive smile. After dinner the two lovers went back to their boat and waved gaily as they disappeared into the moonlit Venice night. The next day Bob and I looked at each other, and neither of us could figure out if Marcello could really speak good enough English for the film. However, we agreed that he was so charming, it didn't matter; he could get away with anything. He ended up doing the part phonetically.

When it came to checking out of the Gritti Palace Hotel, we were told they didn't accept credit cards, only cash. Our rooms and certainly our big dinner were way beyond the cash we had. What to do? Bob Chartoff was actually a pretty good gambler, and we borrowed some lira from Marcello's agent, who had flown down from Rome, and went off to the Lido. Bob played and won enough to pay our hotel bill. Very different from our gambling junket to the Victoria Sporting Club in London four years earlier.

Boorman, after rewriting (with Bill Stair) most of Mastroianni's dialogue, keeping every sentence very, very short, wanted a dark, moody look and, with our fine cinematographer Peter Suschitzky, shot most of the scenes in overcast London. Just the opposite of most films that shoot "cover" when it rains, we went to our cover sets when the sun shone. Needless to say, London was unusually sunny when we were shooting. Mastroianni played a European royal exiled to London. His opulent living is in sharp contrast to the slums that surround him. Leo, living with his unhappy wife (Billie Whitelaw), voyeuristically spies on his neighbors and becomes smitten with their young, beautiful, black, eighteen-year-old daughter. His actions change his life and his plans for the future. The film was meant to be a statement about the decline of the European upper class, but Mastroianni, as good an actor as any producer would want, couldn't overcome his own charisma, and the plot turned confusing. Still, when we showed it to David Picker and his boss, Arthur Krim, they were very congratulatory and thought it would play well in Europe and at film festivals. They were right about the festival part. John Boorman was Best Director at the Cannes Film Festival in 1970.

THEY SHOOT HORSES, DON'T THEY? (1969)

The first time I heard about They Shoot Horses, Don't They? it was a phone call (once again) from Edgar Scherick, the president of Palomar Pictures, a subsidiary of the American Broadcasting Company. The television network was going into the production of motion pictures, and he wanted to discuss the possibility of me and Bob Chartoff producing *They Shoot Horses, Don't They?*, a tough look at a group of desperate people in a dance marathon during the Depression. At lunch the next day he told us he had acquired the script, written by James Poe, and the rights to the book, written by Horace McCoy in 1935. Poe would also direct the film (his first).

After reading the script and the novel, we felt that the script needed a rather extensive rewrite, not so much in the characterizations but more in the structure of the last act and the events that led to the climax. A couple of days later we met with Scherick and Poe and told them we were enthusiastic about producing the film but were concerned about the script. We were even more concerned when Scherick told us the film had to be made for only $900,000.

Poe was extremely arrogant and seemed to think that we had been offered the job as some kind of aides-de-camp to him rather than as producers. He also told us that the script was perfect, didn't need a word changed. We politely told him it needed some careful thought and quite a bit of rewriting. He reminded us that he had won an Academy Award for his screenplay *Around the World in 80 Days* and that he had been the president of the Writers Guild of America West. We in turn reminded him that this was his first directorial effort, and it was a film with a very large cast, music, period costumes, and marathon dancing. He looked at us blankly and wouldn't discuss it. He also told us that, as far as he was concerned, the film was just about fully cast. Poe seemed unaware of the normal process of preparation, even though he'd been around movie sets for decades. We told him we had to get a staff, cameramen, locations, wardrobe, a casting director, financing budgets, script revisions, and probably a star to satisfy the financiers, and then we would start. It was a rocky introduction.

We soon found Scherick to be in a constant state of hysteria; he kept insisting that the film had to be made for $900,000, even after he had agreed to our deal, Poe's deal, and the rights to the book, which altogether came close to $200,000. Finally, we convinced him that the film would cost substantially more than he had originally committed to. Although Scherick and Poe never mentioned it, we discovered that there had been previous producers, who had been fired, after they made an offer for Faye Dunaway to star for $600,000 without Scherick's knowledge. When we brought up Dunaway as a possibility, Scherick's anger escalated to the point where he didn't want to discuss the possibility of her doing the picture for any price. We tried to convince him that his anger was misdirected, but to no avail.

We proceeded to look for a lead actress, and Mia Farrow expressed great interest. Scherick was enthusiastic until he called me on a Sunday and said that he and his wife had gone to a restaurant on Saturday night, and he had seen a young girl who looked exactly like Mia Farrow. After looking at that girl, he couldn't imagine paying Mia Farrow $500,000. After that there was no way to convince him that Mia Farrow was worth any more than that young lady he'd happened to see in a restaurant on Long Island.

After going through the list of other major stars and getting nowhere, we decided that we'd better start interviewing good actresses and not concentrate on star names. Surprisingly, a great many of the non-names turned it down as well. I suspected it might have been due to their meetings with James Poe. The name Jane Fonda came up, and we were all intrigued. The pictures she had done up to that point were light comedies (*Barefoot in the Park*) or unimpressive pictures she had made in Europe with her husband, Roger Vadim (*Barbarella*). Her films really didn't seem to bring her to the point of being ready for a strong dramatic role, but we were desperate. We called her agent, Dick Clayton, and asked him to send the script to Jane, who was living in Paris, and if she was interested, we would meet with her to discuss the role.

The problem was, this was May 1968, the same time the French student riots had started in Paris, and the whole city was in turmoil. No phone calls or mail were getting through, and there was no way to get the script to Jane Fonda. The production of *They Shoot Horses, Don't They?* seemed to be getting precarious as Scherick exerted more and more pressure on the budget and casting. Poe seemed to be more unhinged and was not eager to wait for Fonda. All he could think about was that he was going to start the picture in a few weeks whether we had any locations, crew, casting, or the money to shoot the film.

One evening, I was attending a meeting of the Indian Guides (a group like the Cub Scouts that I belonged to with my son Charles). One of the other members of the Indian Guides was the director Bud Yorkin, who was preparing to film *Start the Revolution Without Me*. It was a comedy that took place during the French Revolution, and Bud said he was determined to get to France to look for locations no matter what. I asked him if he would take our script and give it to Jane Fonda. He agreed, and despite the French protests Jane got the script, called Dick Clayton, and said she was interested. Faced with no other choices and a fairly reasonable price for Fonda, Scherick agreed to her deal, and an offer was made and accepted, all subject to our meeting. Jim Poe and I flew to Paris, then drove to the countryside, where Jane had a beautifully redone old farmhouse about forty miles from the city. We had lunch and talked quite a bit about the script, and Jane took a walk with Poe out in the garden and came back and said she was pleased with the meeting. She was pregnant, and we would schedule the film for after she gave birth.

With our lead actress set, we started casting the other roles and liked Michael Sarrazin for the male lead opposite Fonda. He was an up-and-coming actor who had tested for *Midnight Cowboy* and gotten the part, but because he was under contract to Universal and they asked for an enormous fee for him, the producers refused to pay it, and he lost the part to Jon Voight. We put Universal on notice that if we had the same kind of money problems as *Midnight Cowboy*, we wouldn't consider him. Sarrazin was obviously furious with Universal for losing *Midnight Cowboy* and made sure he didn't lose this role.

We kept asking Poe to rewrite the script based on the notes we had given him months earlier, and he kept assuring us we would get to it shortly. August turned into September, and we started getting more and more concerned about the script, and whatever little confidence we might have had in Poe, we lost completely.

The physical preparation of the picture, however, started to go forward on a more or less orderly basis. We hired the necessary key personnel, Harry Horner as the production designer, Phil Lathrop (who had done such a good job on *Point Blank* and could support Poe with his vast experience) as the cameraman, and Donfeld as the wardrobe designer. We checked the pier in Santa Monica to see if it was usable, as Poe wanted to shoot at the real location. Our sound experts informed us that the salt water had eaten away at the bottom of the pier, and it would be impossible to shoot there because of the acoustics. Poe stomped his feet, angry at the acoustic engineer and Bob and me for "making him" shoot on a stage. We then started to negotiate with the various studios for space to build the set. We got bids from MGM, Warner Bros., and Paramount and were able to finalize the most favorable deal with MGM. We told Scherick, who said he wanted to think about it but then flew to Los Angeles, met with Warner Bros., and made a deal at less favorable terms without discussing it with us. If we had any idea of how difficult things were to become, this kind of action assured it.

As shooting grew closer, we started hiring actors for some of the lesser parts. We got Scherick to understand that the film would cost $4 million, not the $900,000 he had envisioned. Surprisingly, he took that very well. We then moved over to Warner Bros. and started construction of the set. While this was going on, we found ourselves in daily communication with either Scherick in New York or the production manager in California, Ted Sills. One day, as the construction crew was putting down the ballroom dance floor, Scherick called, saying that we had finally gone too far, that he had only approved us putting up the walls and not the floor. I explained to him the impossibility of putting up walls without a floor to base them on, but it did no good, and he said that we had now reached the point where something had to be done.

The next morning at 6:30 I got a call from my attorney, Lee Steiner (yes, the same Lee Steiner who was Carlo Ponti and David Lean's lawyer in the *Doctor Zhivago* days), who had just come from a meeting with the ABC executives and Scherick, where he learned that Scherick was going to fire Bob Chartoff and me. Sure enough, about ten minutes later Scherick called and told me that he'd had a conversation with the ABC executives, and it was decided that they were going to ask us to step down. I told him that I would have to call him back and got off the phone before he could actually fire us. At about this time, Marty Baum, a former agent, had become president of the two filmmaking divisions of ABC, which meant that he was Scherick's supervisor. I knew Baum—he had been Pamela Tiffin's agent in our management days—and arranged to meet him to find out what was going on. He told us he knew about the decision to fire Bob and me and had gone along with it because he'd heard that we had made some remarks about him that were not flattering, that we thought he was stupid. We denied that we had said anything of that nature, and he blandly said, in that case Bob and I ought to go to New York and see Sam Clark, who was his boss. Baum called Clark and set up an appointment for us to meet him the following morning. We had a definite sense that there was a lot of manipulation on the part of Baum over Scherick. Margo and I had just moved to a new house that day, and I had to climb over packing boxes to get to her to tell her I was leaving for New York and to ask if the unpacking could wait. She looked at me and smiled (not her usual smile but a smile nonetheless).

We took the red-eye to New York and went directly to Lee Steiner's office, where he told us that in this matter he would be representing our interests and not ABC's, whom he also represented, and that he had spoken to Sam Clark the night before and he thought that everything would work out. We then went to Clark's office and were greeted rather warmly. We told Clark we couldn't understand what was going on, and he said he couldn't understand it either, and as a matter of fact he was very disturbed that this picture, which was a very ambitious picture for them, had a director who had never directed before, that Baum and Scherick had never made a movie before, and that the only experienced people involved in the film, Chartoff and Winkler, were being fired. We brought up the Warner Bros. studio deal over the MGM deal we'd negotiated, with the comparative final figures of both, and told Clark about the general problems we were having with Scherick over casting, budget, and construction. He then called in one of the ABC lawyers and had him send a telegram to Scherick advising him that if he didn't resign by the close of business that day, they would take action against him. He then called Baum and told him that Bob and I would be reinstated. Baum readily agreed and was thrilled that he'd gotten his way, getting rid of Scherick. It seemed that he'd used Scherick to get us fired, and when Sherick went along with it, he used that act to get rid of Scherick. Scherick was obviously caught up in a very well done Baum manipulation. We then spoke to Baum on the phone with Clark and made arrangements to meet him that evening.

We arrived in Los Angeles, and a car took us directly to Robert Aldrich Studios, where Baum was waiting for us. We screened Aldrich's *The Killing of Sister George* to see Susannah York's work; Baum wanted her to play the second female lead (the same role Poe wanted for the lady he was living with). We saw the film, were impressed with York's performance, and agreed that she would be our choice too. Baum told us that there were several roles he wanted our thoughts on. He "suggested" Red Buttons to play the sailor; we liked that idea a lot, and we agreed that Gig Young would be good to play the master of ceremonies. He then told Ted Sills to call Poe at home and tell him that Red Buttons was going to play the role of the sailor and to hang up immediately. Sills proceeded to do just that. Baum then told Sills to call him back and tell him that Gig Young was going to play the role of the MC and then hang up. At this point we said this was a terrible way to treat Poe, that he was the director of the film and the man who wrote the script and was involved in the project long before any of us. In all decency we should have a meeting with him, and if Poe was going to be fired, which none of us was against, it should be done in a decent and proper manner. We pointed out that if we fired Poe, we would have to get an extension from Jane Fonda on her start date, and although she didn't have a formal approval of the director in her contract, it would be impossible to go forward without her consent.

We arranged to have breakfast with Poe and told him that the situation was very serious and the film was going to be cast the way the studio and we thought best. That he'd had months to cast the film and, except for Fonda and Sarrazin, we had no real cast lined up. To our surprise Poe said he thought the casting ideas were quite good and he could live with them. When we approached Jane Fonda's agent, he told us that there was no way Fonda would accept a substitute for Poe. It seemed we had no choice but to stay with Poe, but we still couldn't get him to rewrite the script. We told Poe that the actress (his girlfriend) he wanted for the second lead role would not be as good as Susannah York and that we were going to make a deal with York. He just looked at us fish-eyed and said fine and walked out of the office. He made no argument for any of the actors he had insisted on casting for many months. Poe then, however, became hard to find, and when he showed up, he was often drunk. I kept telling Fonda that Poe was more and more unreliable and we should get another director, but I got nowhere.

As we got more and more frustrated with Poe—no rewrite, his absence, his unreliability—I used the casting of the actress Bonnie Bedelia to not only test her but also to show Fonda (and us) how Poe would direct a dramatic scene. Of course Jane would be acting in the test, and I'm sure she knew this was a test of the director too. On the set Jane asked Poe questions about the blocking of the scene, why she moves in one direction rather than another, why in front of a sofa rather than behind it, etc. She was asking very basic questions an actor asks a director. He couldn't answer her questions and told her to talk to the cameraman. I left the set, and twenty minutes later Jane came into my office and said, "OK, let's find another director." I asked her why it had taken her so long, and she said that she realized finally that Poe had no idea about how to direct an actor or how to shoot a scene. The test had made it clear to her that he was no John Ford!

I told Baum that we were finally in a position to replace Poe and that we would meet later that evening to talk about directors, and Jane agreed to give us as much time as we needed. We then had the unpleasant task of telling Poe that neither the financiers, the producers, nor the actors had any faith in him as director of this ambitious film. In the best interest of all concerned he was going to be replaced, he would be paid his money in full, but he would not be directing the movie. Poe never said a word. He just walked away. I never saw him again.

The next morning, I prepared a list of the various directors who were immediately available. Sydney Pollack was someone we had been in conversations with about another picture several years before, and we were very interested in him. Billy Friedkin, whom I was very high on and who had just directed the Harold Pinter picture *The Homecoming*, was available, and his agent said he might be interested in directing *Horses*. There were several other lesser candidates, and Baum came up with his primary candidate, Jack Smight, who had just directed a film with Rod Steiger, *No Way to Treat a Lady*. I thought Smight was not nearly up to Pollack or Friedkin. I met with Baum at his house and discussed Pollack and was turned down flat. Baum said that Pollack had directed *The Slender Thread* with his clients Sidney Poitier and Anne Bancroft, and he didn't like Pollack's work at all, and that the picture was a disaster at the box office. There was no way Pollack would direct *They Shoot Horses*. I impressed upon Baum the need for a quick decision, and he agreed that we would meet later that evening to discuss it further. As I walked out of his house, I heard his wife telling him that they were going to make their vacation trip to Acapulco the next day, and there was no way she was going to cancel. I realized that this was the opportunity to lock up a director of our choice. When I got home, I called Friedkin's agent. I knew that Freidkin had gotten $75,000 to direct *The Homecoming*, which had just opened in New York to very good reviews. But that was an art house film, and he'd obviously worked for short money. Friedkin's agent, Tony Fantozzi at William Morris, said that he wanted $200,000 for Friedkin. I told him that I wanted Friedkin but that price would kill Friedkin's chances. He wouldn't budge. I felt that Freddie Fields, the agent for Jack Smight, would try to cash in on our difficult situation. I also knew that Baum was afraid of being taken advantage of and that, although Smight's real price was in the area of $100,000, Freddie Fields could not bear but to give it to Baum and try to grab a lot more. I then called Joe Wizan, who was Pollack's agent at the William Morris Agency, and worked out a tentative deal with him for $150,000 and told him to call me at Baum's house at ten that evening. After dinner I went back to Baum's, told him that Freidkin and Smight were available, and said that I feared Freddie Fields was going to try to take advantage of us. Instead of asking $100,000 for Smight, he would ask for $250,000 and that he was putting it to us. Sure enough, Baum called Fields and Fields asked for $250,000, and Baum hung up the phone. Baum said, let's go with Friedkin. I agreed, but Friedkin's agent wouldn't take less than $200,000. Baum was outraged and wouldn't discuss it any further. The phone then rang, and it was Wizan, Pollack's agent. I told him to hold on and said to Baum, "Listen, we don't have a director, we've got to start right away, Pollack is the only one who is available who's in our

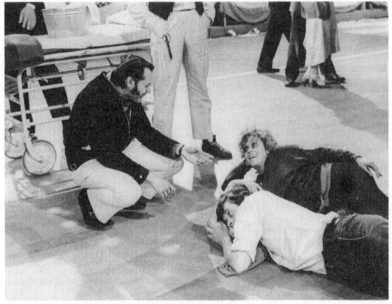

Irwin Winkler, Jane Fonda, Michael Sarrazin
They Shoot Horses, Don't They?

price range, he'll take it for $150,000." Baum, still outraged by Fields and Fantozzi, said OK, lock him up. I told Wizan that he had a deal. Baum flew off to Mexico. I went home.

I tried to reach Sydney Pollack the next day to no avail and then found out that Wizan had locked up the deal and never confirmed it with Pollack, who had some second thoughts. I finally met with Pollack the next day. He thought our casting was excellent and about as good as he would want it; however, he had serious doubts about the Poe screenplay. I told him we had wanted to do a rewrite for months and that we would get a writer of his choice and start rewriting. He reluctantly agreed to go forward. Jane proved to be no problem in approving Pollack. His personality was such that everybody had great confidence in him. The preparation at that point went along on a very professional basis with very few problems, and Pollack worked on the new script with a Horace McCoy expert, Robert Thompson.

The final cast was assembled with Jane Fonda, Michael Sarrazin, Susannah York, Red Buttons, Gig Young, Bonnie Bedelia, and Bruce Dern as the principals. The deals were all set, everybody seemed happy, and I spent a quiet weekend at home with Margo and my three boys playing a little tennis, good family time. That is, up until Sunday night. At about 9:30 that evening Pollack called and said he had just gotten a call from his new agent, Freddie Fields (yes, Jack Smight's agent), who told him that he represented Susannah York and that unless she got a stop date that ensured her leaving the production at a specific date, whether or not her part was completed, she wasn't going to start work the next day. I called Fields and told him I couldn't understand why at this late date he was asking for a stop date, since the deal had been negotiated a long time ago and nobody had ever said a word about it. He told me Susannah York's cousin had written a screenplay and wanted her to play the female lead opposite Peter O'Toole and that some months ago Susannah had been in Scotland with her cousin and O'Toole, and they'd all agreed to do the picture. She saw her cousin off after the meeting, and as he drove away, he got into an automobile accident and died. She felt an obligation to her dead cousin, MGM had now agreed to finance the picture, and O'Toole wanted to start on a specific date, and therefore she was insisting on the stop date. I told Fields I could certainly understand her commitment to her dead cousin but I couldn't understand why the MGM picture, which was just now being set up, couldn't start at some later date that would assure her completing her part, and we just couldn't allow her to leave with a partially completed role.

Since we were starting the next day and couldn't replace her on such short notice, I told Fields he'd better make sure that Susannah York showed up for work the next day, and I would try to settle her problems. The set call the next morning was for the full cast and quite a few extras and a full orchestra. While Pollack was setting up the shot, he and I discussed the possibility of replacing Susannah York. We thought that if we could find an immediate replacement who was acceptable to us, it would be better to do that than have an unhappy actress on our hands. As it turned out, York showed up but announced she was not going to leave her dressing room until she got her stop date. Pollack then told me that his own casting agent said Sally Kellerman (of *M*A*S*H* fame) was available and wanted to play the part. I thought that was a good idea and called Baum in New York, and he said it was fine with him. I started to negotiate a deal with Kellerman's agent, when I got a call from Baum saying he had discussed it with his bosses and they wanted York and would not accept any replacement whatsoever. I then called Herb Solow at MGM and told him that by giving a start date to the other picture, he was causing us a great deal of difficulty on our film. He was very cooperative and said that he wouldn't do anything that would injure us and would advise the producer of the O'Toole picture that they should push back their start date. By this time the whole company was ready to shoot and was just standing around waiting for York. I went to her dressing room and told her I had spoken to MGM and they would not go ahead with the other picture as long as it interfered with her performance in *They Shoot Horses, Don't They?* After about a half hour of hysteria, she finally agreed that she would perform under the terms of her contract, but now she was too embarrassed to come out of her dressing room and face all the other people in the company after she had kept them waiting so long. I told her that I would walk out with her and everything would be fine. After a few minutes, she got herself together, took my arm, and out we went, arm in arm like two best friends.

From the first day of shooting I was convinced that we had something special going. Red Buttons, who had made his reputation as a borscht belt comedian and in a couple of dramatic films, was totally committed and set an example to the other cast members by never complaining and never avoiding the harsh physicality of the dance marathons. Bruce Dern, Bonnie Bedelia, and Susannah York were all living their parts. Best of all was Jane Fonda. She lived up to the Fonda name.

I was impressed with Sydney Pollack's ease on the set. He never seemed to be working very hard and yet was able to get marvelous performances out of the actors. Everybody in the company adored him. I asked him how he kept so calm, what with the pressure of all the actors, the many, many extras, and the complicated camera setups. He said, "Oh, it was really quite easy." That afternoon we were standing and chatting during a camera setup, and he just fainted. We called the medics, and they said there was nothing wrong with him, that he'd simply fainted from nervousness.

The ABC executives, including Leonard Goldenson, the president, saw whatever film we had cut together and were very supportive in spite of the fact that we were losing more and more time as the film progressed. Part of the delays were due to Pollack and Thompson's new scenes, which we felt were necessary and pushed the schedule. By the time the film was completed, the final cost was about $4,700,000, which was quite a distance from the first meeting we'd had with Ed Scherick, when he wanted the film to cost $900,000. But, just like Poe, I never saw Scherick again.

When the film was completed, we previewed at the Northpoint Theatre in San Francisco to a packed house. The film seemed to play quite well, but near the end, when Jane Fonda took out a pistol and asked Michael Sarrazin to shoot her, the audience seemed to think it was the funniest line they had ever heard in the movies. We were all obviously distraught. However, that preview did not include a series of flash-forward sequences that were placed strategically throughout the film, scenes of Robert (Sarrazin) being arrested and imprisoned in very short cuts that prepared the audience for that murder/suicide scene. Without those flash-forwards, the audience obviously couldn't deal with the reality of what they were about to see. We managed to cut those scenes back into the film for the Saturday-night preview in Palo Alto. The film never played badly again.

York was so embittered about what had happened, and although she realized she'd given a great performance, she sent instructions that she wanted no publicity or no campaign for her to get an Oscar nomination. As it turned out, she was nominated, flew to Hollywood for the Academy Awards, and apologized to me and everyone else involved. She said that it was one of the finest performances she ever gave and she was really quite proud of it.

They Shoot Horses, Don't They? was one of very few films that got nine Oscar nominations but not Best Picture.

PART II

THE 23RD CANNES FILM Festival took place on the sunny shore of the Mediterranean Sea in May of 1970 with more glamour than Margo and I had ever witnessed. Women in expensive gowns and jewelry, men all in black-tie, just to see a movie. Well, not just any movie. The films chosen to be screened at the Palais were carefully selected from hundreds, if not thousands, submitted from countries all over the world.

Bob Chartoff and I arrived with three films. *They Shoot Horses, Don't They?* was honored with the closing-night gala screening. Horace McCoy's novel was a well-known and respected classic in France, and the Festival assured us it would be well received. *Leo the Last*, starring Marcello Mastroianni after his great success in Federic Fellini's *La Dolce Vita* and *8½*, was a Cannes favorite. *The Strawberry Statement*, depicting the youth revolution in America not unlike the one France lived through in 1968, when the Festival itself was disrupted and cancelled due to the student riots in Paris, was our third entrant. One day Bob, Margo, and I went to a couple of screenings and suffered through them—I don't know if it was because we had too much sun that afternoon or too much Blanc de Blancs during lunch. Another afternoon we were once again enjoying a bit too much of the wine and sun when Gig Young, who'd won an Oscar for his performance in *They Shoot Horses, Don't They?* suggested that Margo, Sydney Pollack, a young actress who had starred in another film playing in the festival, and I take a short boat ride with him across the bay from Cannes to the Hotel du Cap in Antibes. I walked over to a man with a small motorboat, gave him some francs, and the five of us continued our afternoon of sun and wine on the terrace of the du Cap. When we'd had enough, our little boat took us back across the bay to our hotel. We all squeezed into the small elevator, and when it stopped at Gig Young's floor, he got out, looked up and down at the pretty young actress, smiled, and said, "What do you think?" The actress hesitated for a couple of beats, smiled back at Young, and said, "What the hell!" and stepped out of the elevator and down the hall with Young.

M*A*S*H won the Palm d'Or for Best Picture that year. The Strawberry Statement shared the Jury Prize, and Leo the Last won Best Director for John Boorman.

When Bob Chartoff and I left the film festival, we knew we were in a different movie world than the one we had stumbled into four years earlier. We had gotten into Hollywood through a series of almost unbelievable lucky breaks, and once there we just plowed straight ahead, and as we looked around, there didn't seem to be anyone to stop us. In those four years we produced Double Trouble, Point Blank, The Split, Leo the Last, The Strawberry Statement, and They Shoot Horses, Don't They? Three films in the very prestigious Cannes Film Festival all honored, and Point Blank a box office and critical success. Six films in four years. With those films under our belt and our reputation coming out of Cannes, Bob and I jumped on the changing boundaries of film production. The great directors of the golden era of Hollywood were, sadly, just about gone. No more great Vincente Minnelli musicals, no more George Cukor romances, no more John Ford Westerns. The loss of these great talents through age or changing times was sad but inevitable. In their place came a new breed of directors who encouraged a new audience. Martin Scorsese with Mean Streets, Peter Bogdonavich's The Last Picture Show, Steven Spielberg's Jaws, Billy Friedkin's The French Connection, and Francis Ford Coppola's The Godfather. In those years we worked with a mixture of old school and some newer young directors, some very good, some not as good as their reputations. In spite of a mixed bag, Bob and I were known in the "new" Hollywood as producers who worked hard, knew good material, and could get pictures made.

CHAPTER FIVE

Starting a long friendship with the great actor Bob De Niro,
the 1970s drug culture, and two different looks at the
Los Angeles Police Department

THE GANG THAT COULDN'T SHOOT STRAIGHT (1971)

WE HAD ALL THE elements for a very good comic gangster film in 1971 with *The Gang That Couldn't Shoot Straight*. Good source material, the novel by Pulitzer Prize–winning *New York Daily News* columnist Jimmy Breslin; a screenplay by Waldo Salt, the Academy Award–winning writer of *Midnight Cowboy*; and an incredibly talented cast led by Robert De Niro, Jerry Orbach, Jo Van Fleet, and Lionel Stander.

So what went wrong?

We got a big pitch from an agent to consider Francis Ford Coppola, who had read Breslin's book and Salt's screenplay and was eager to direct a Mafia film. I dutifully screened his musical *Finian's Rainbow* and the coming-of-age film *You're a Big Boy Now* and decided there was no reason to think Mr. Coppola could direct a gangster film . . . no reason at all. After telling the agent I wasn't interested, I received a letter from Coppola, in script form. The pages set a scene where a young film director is having dinner (with his Italian mother cooking pasta, no less), and the young director is telling his mother why he wants to direct *The Gang That Couldn't Shoot Straight* and how he would do it. Pretty clever, but I was not moved.

We were impressed when we screened the Paul Newman and Joanne Woodward film *Winning*. It was a very good car racing drama with great performances. We had several meetings with director James Goldstone and felt that since he was good enough for the great actors

Newman and Woodward, he would be good for *The Gang That Couldn't Shoot Straight.*

The background of Breslin's book is the New York Mafia, when the Young Turks are trying to take over from the old Mafia dons. The Young Turks use every crazy device to bring down the dons, even resorting to a leashed lion walking through the streets of the neighborhood to make trouble. Breslin used the mobster "Crazy Joe" Gallo and the Colombo family as the centerpiece of his book, and Salt's comedy played to their ineptitude. Salt was a rather interesting man, blacklisted in the 1940s after an excellent early career and returning in the 1960s as an important screenwriter. My friendship with Salt was unique. With my family living in Los Angeles, I flew home every Friday, and Salt generously drove me to the airport. I was joined on one flight by Salt's daughter Jennifer, who laughed when I told her how much I appreciated her father driving me. She said her father hated to write and found any reason to avoid it, and I (the producer) was providing the perfect excuse. From then on I took cabs.

On one trip Salt told me what it was like to write for studios in the glory days of Hollywood. He had been hired out of college by MGM in the 1930s when the studio's output was close to fifty films a year, just about one every week. To support that number of films, they had scores of writers and large story departments and lots and lots of executives who all had to express an opinion. Salt wrote very fast but would be criticized when he turned in a script too quickly; how could it be any good if it was written so fast? He also felt that the criticism of the scripts was quite arbitrary. In order to control the rewrite, before turning in the script he would remove three or four pages from the first act, blend in the gap, and do the same in the last act. The story department would quickly point out the holes in the script, and Salt would have those pages in a desk drawer, ready to deliver a rewrite based on "their" notes.

We cast Al Pacino, who had just done *The Panic in Needle Park,* for the starring role of an illegal Italian immigrant bicycle rider who is just as crooked as the Mafia characters he gets involved with. Jerry

Orbach, who had made his reputation as a Broadway musical star in *The Fantasticks* and *The Threepenny Opera*, was quickly signed and did his research by spending time with "Crazy Joe" Gallo, the real-life Mafia killer. An unlikely friendship developed between the mobster and the musical comedy actor; the actor "found" his character and also found a friend for life. I never understood it, but Jerry Orbach was one of the nicest people I've known, so there must have been something about Gallo that he saw and no one else did. As fate would have it, in 1972, Jerry and his wife celebrated "Crazy Joe's" birthday with Gallo and his wife at the Copacabana nightclub in New York. Afterward the Orbachs went home, but Gallo continued his celebration at Umberto's Clam House until a gunman burst into the restaurant and Gallo was shot dead. The killer was Frank "The Irishman" Sheeran, whose story I would return to forty years later.

Margo Winkler, Irwin Winkler, Robert De Niro
The Gang That Couldn't Shoot Straight

Trouble on *The Gang That Couldn't Shoot Straight* started even before the first day of shooting. While the company was rehearsing, the agent David Begelman (later convicted of check forging) called and told me the "iffy deal we had for Al Pacino" wasn't binding, and Pacino would be leaving the set immediately to star in, yes, Francis Ford Coppola's *The Godfather.* We had a signed contract, but Pacino very quickly left, and we looked for a replacement. I had heard about an actor who had done a couple of independent films, *The Wedding Party* and *Greetings,* directed by Brian De Palma. Bob De Niro came in, and we instantly wanted him to play Mario. He agreed but said he wanted to go to southern Italy to research the character he was to play. I told him we didn't have the budget to send him to Italy. "No problem," he said, he'd pay for the trip out of his (small) salary. De Niro came back a week later with a tan, the clothes, the props, and his character. I knew right then that Bob De Niro was a special actor and a special person. I didn't know that we would be friends for the next fifty years.

Breslin's book had quite a few great comic sequences: our lion walking through a car wash, a mobster sending his wife out to start his car before he drives off to make sure there's no bomb planted in it, a killer's gun blowing up in his face when he tries to shoot a Mafia boss. Those sequences should have been showstoppers. They weren't. Bob De Niro and Jerry Orbach gave terrific performances, but many of the other actors—Leigh Taylor-Young (who became an ordained minister in a religious cult), Jo Van Fleet, Hervé Villechaize, and Lionel Stander—kept asking Goldstone for direction, only to find he was more interested in keeping to the schedule than working with the actors. These "comic" scenes fell flat, and the film in editing couldn't make up its mind whether to be funny or dramatic. It ended up being neither.

Months after *Gang* had come and gone (quickly), the breach-of-contract lawsuit MGM had filed against Paramount and Pacino came to deposition. Paramount hired Sidney Korshak to represent them. Korshak was well known as the tough lawyer for the Teamsters Union. While I was giving my deposition, I was called out by a phone call from the president of MGM, Frank Rosenfelt, who told me the matter was settled. It seems Korshak had called Kirk Kerkorian, the owner of MGM, who was building a hotel in Las Vegas. Korshak remarked to Kerkorian how much the Teamsters in Las Vegas, who were working on the new hotel, were upset that Kerkorian was picking on the kid Pacino they all liked. Kerkorian got off the phone with Korshak and immediately instructed Rosenfelt to withdraw the claim against Paramount and Pacino. Al went on to great acclaim as Michael in *The Godfather,* but I saw the real "Godfather" in action. His name was Sidney Korshak.

I haven't seen *The Gang That Couldn't Shoot Straight* since 1972, and I see *The Godfather,* directed by the man I couldn't imagine directing a gangster film, every chance I get.

BELIEVE IN ME (1971)

When television executive James Aubrey, known as "the smiling cobra," died in 1994 from a heart attack, those who knew him doubted that diagnosis. He'd never had a heart, was their feeling.

Margo Winkler, Irwin Winkler, Gail Sheehy, Clay Felker, Maura Sheehy
Believe in Me

By the time Bob and I produced *Believe in Me,* we thought we were pretty well established in Hollywood. We had made some good pictures in our few years in Hollywood. But not according to James

Aubrey, who had never made movies but had made his reputation with the television show *The Beverly Hillbillies*. He was the man the gambler/financier Kirk Kerkorian brought in from CBS to run the film studio.

We had bought Gail Sheehy's *New York* magazine piece "Speed Is of the Essence," based on Sheehy's heartfelt story of her sister's descent into drug addiction. Bob Chartoff and I put together the same writing/directing team from *The Strawberry Statement*: Israel Horovitz to adapt the story and Stuart Hagmann to direct. MGM had agreed to finance the film and arranged for us to shoot *Speed Is of the Essence* in New York, with New York actors. Bob Chartoff was working in London, and I headed to New York with Margo and our very young sons. We rented a large apartment on Park Avenue, and before we could unpack our bags, Jim Aubrey was on the phone. He said he had good news. He had engaged Michael Sarrazin and Jacqueline Bisset for the leading roles. The two were excellent actors and were romantically involved. But what bothered me was not the casting, as they were two really fine actors, but that Aubrey didn't even ask me as the producer or Stuart Hagmann as the director what we thought about the casting. It showed a lack of respect for our opinions and judgment; after all, we were the ones making the film. I told Aubrey that I would discuss it with Hagmann, and his reply was, "That is the casting, and if you can't make it work, you can leave the film." Faced with a lease on the Park Avenue apartment, no return ticket to Los Angeles, no place to go back to in Los Angeles, as I had lent my home to a recently divorced friend, and with Bob Chartoff in London, with very little (very little) money in the bank and the prospect of no producing fee, I swallowed my pride and agreed to stay with the film, as did Hagmann.

The shooting in New York went well, as did the performances. Remy (Sarrazin) is an intern at a hospital who is caring and well liked. The problem, not uncommon in the early 1970s, is that he initially uses speed as a recreational drug (even if he has to steal it from the hospital) and ends up addicted. Pamela (Bisset) is a children's book illustrator who falls in love with Remy and ultimately follows him down the path to addiction. In the very realistic spiral both Bisset and Sarrazin

give excellent performances. I have heard that the great French director François Truffaut hired Bisset to star in his film *Day for Night* after
seeing her in our film. Stuart Hagmann captured the 1970s New York

Stuart Hagmann, Irwin Winkler, Jacqueline Bisset
Believe in Me

City grittiness, and the bleak climax *of Believe in Me* was a warning for
anyone wanting to take "just one pill."

We were all pretty satisfied with the finished film. Jim Aubrey
was not. He hated the film (and the casting) and wouldn't release it
and disregarded (once again) the director and producers. He demanded
(yes, demanded) that our counterculture film with our hero ending up
an addict be another *Love Story*. *Love Story* was the huge box office hit
starring Ryan O'Neal and Ali MacGraw with the tagline "Love means
never having to say you're sorry." Hadn't Aubrey read our script? Apparently not!

Aubrey demanded reshoots but not with Stuart Hagmann.
We decided to protect as much of the film as possible and convinced

Aubrey that John Avildsen would be right for directing the reshoot. John had directed *Joe*, a gritty film that we admired. Avildsen did a very good job in the three-week shoot, but the final film was a mishmash of styles, story, and ideas.

We liked working with Avildsen, and a couple of years later, when we were looking for a director for Sly Stallone's script of *Rocky*, we remembered John's work on *Speed Is of the Essence* reshoot. Oh, yeah, James Aubrey changed the title to *Believe in Me*.

THE NEW CENTURIONS (1972)

Although *The New Centurions* could be categorized as an old-fashioned cop story, it is anything but that.

The New Centurions was based on Joseph Wambaugh's fourteen-year experience as a Los Angeles policeman, and Wambaugh wrote it while still working as a detective. Wambaugh's policemen in *The New Centurions* were the "street cops" who rode in squad cars and dealt with prostitutes, local robberies, domestic violence, drug dealers, and every-day crime. The title of the book refers to the army that was brought in to protect the declining Roman Empire. Of course the "new" refers to the army of police that protect the "mean" streets of Los Angeles.

With *Dirty Harry*, starring Clint Eastwood, a big hit in movie theaters, Wambaugh's book was a hot property in the hands of the top agent in Hollywood, Irving ("Swifty") Lazar. Lazar's nickname came from how quickly he would make a deal, and in our case, he lived up to the nickname. Bob Chartoff and I had just settled into a "first look" deal with Stanley Schneider, the newly installed president of Columbia Pictures. (The "first look" deal was a new concept for producers in Hollywood. The studios would guarantee the producer a substantial amount of money, and the producer was obligated to submit whatever properties he/she intended to develop into a film; if the studio didn't want to go forward, the producer was then free to take the script else-where.) Some years later, still under that first look deal, we were given the manuscripts of *The Towering Inferno* and *Jaws* by Ben Benjamin, an agent and the father of Jeff Benjamin, who worked for Chartoff-Winkler. We quickly submitted them to a Columbia executive, Robert Litman (whom I persuaded Stanley Schneider to hire), and he turned both down. In no time Zanuck/Brown hired Steven Spielberg, and Irwin Allen made a massive hit movie out of *The Towering Inferno*. So much for "first look" deals.

We met Lazar's price for *The New Centurions*, and at the last minute "Swifty" said he would only close the deal with us (rather than peddle it to other studios) if we gave Wambaugh $1,500 for every week the book was on the *New York Times* Best-Seller list. We settled for $1,250, and Wambaugh got an additional $40,000. That was "Swifty."

The New Centurions featured the rookie cop Roy Fehler (Stacy Keach), who joins the Los Angeles Police while he tries to complete his

Stacey Keach, Hal Polaire, Charles Winkler, Irwin Winkler
The New Centurions

law degree; the ex-Marine Sergio Duran (Erik Estrada), who wants to conceal his Latino heritage; the middle-class, slight, suburban Gus Plebesly (Scott Wilson); and the veteran Andy Kilvinski (George C. Scott), who spent his life as a police officer and is now being forced into retirement. We had the screenplay written by the Academy Award–winner (*In the Heat of the Night*) Stirling Silliphant and set Richard Fleischer to direct. Fleischer had some really good, tough films like *Che* and *Compulsion* to his credit, and some not-so-good films like *Doctor Doolittle* and *Tora! Tora! Tora!* He worked in all genres, and his most recent film was *The Last Run* starring George C. Scott. We wanted Scott for the Kilvinski role and knew we needed help getting him after his starring roles in Stanley Kubrick's *Dr. Strangelove* and his renowned portrayal of General George Patton. Fleischer was able to convince the hesitant actor to accept the secondary role of the veteran cop. Scott, one of the industry's most independent actors, always chose his parts carefully. He showed his independence when he was the first actor to refuse the Oscar after he was awarded Best Actor for *Patton* in 1970, but he liked Kilvinski (and Richard Fleischer).

We signed Scott for six weeks, and Fleischer, through good scheduling and economic shooting, finished the Kilvinski role in three weeks. Bob Chartoff and I were not going to have this great actor sit around (or go home) for the remaining time on his contract. We decided we would add additional scenes to his part. Stirling Silliphant was off writing another film, but luckily Robert Towne had a couple of weeks free. Towne was very expensive (we paid him $200,000 for two weeks' work), as he had done some excellent last-minute writing for Warren Beatty on *Bonnie and Clyde* (uncredited) and several other very good original scripts (the Academy Award–winning *Chinatown* was upcoming). We were very anxious to get the scenes from Towne, as every day we waited was one fewer day to use George Scott. Towne went missing for several days, and we got pretty frantic; it turned out his dog had wandered away, and Towne spent the time locating his pet. In short order, however, we got several really good new scenes. We were enthusiastic, scheduled them for shooting, completed them quickly, and still got Scott out a few days early. In one new scene, hardly a word is spoken when Kilvinski understands that, without his uniform and gun, he has no life. After a brief phone call with his ex-partner, he calmly and slowly puts a gun to his head. It's a very short scene, confidently directed and beautifully acted. In 1999, almost thirty years later, Scott, while acting as Rocky Marciano's father in Charles Winkler's film *Rocky Marciano*, fondly remembered his suicide scene from *The New Centurions*. This from the actor who had so many memorable parts in a forty-year career in film, television, and theater.

The New Centurions had the hard edge of the 1970s. Not only does Kilvinski die by his own hand, but Roy (Stacy Keach), our lead character, is shot and senselessly killed at the end of the film. We wanted the film to reflect Los Angeles just six years after the famous Watts riots, when approximately fifty people died and large areas of East Los Angeles were burned to the ground. A somber reminder of how tough it was to be a "new centurion."

For the early 1970s, the biracial relationship between Roy and Lorrie (Rosalind Cash) was unusual. Yes, there was *Guess Who's Coming to Dinner*, but that was about the potential for a mixed marriage (which was groundbreaking in 1967). The relationship in *The New Centurions* between the white cop and black nurse was written (and played) without comment. The racial differences are not part of the relationship, and all the characters around Roy and Lorrie take it as normal. But there was to be no happy ending to *The New Centurions*. It ends with a picture of the police that only a policeman who spent so many years protecting the streets, Joe Wambaugh, could tell.

BUSTING (1973)

Busting was a very laid-back Los Angeles cop film, just the opposite of *The New Centurions*. While *The New Centurions* dealt with the life and death of street cops, *Busting* was more about the fun side of two vice cops played by Elliott Gould and Robert Blake. Fun until they run into corrupt cops and politicians. The two actors couldn't have been more different. Gould six feet two, bulky, shaggy, and sloppy; Blake five feet three, muscular, neat, and serious. Yet they made a perfect pair. Gould was born in Brooklyn in 1938 and came to fame with a 1968 Oscar-nominated role in *Bob & Carol & Ted & Alice* and Trapper John in the Korean War comedy/drama *M*A*S*H*, the 1970 hit directed by Robert Altman. Robert Blake came from a very, very different background. Born in New Jersey in 1933, Blake was cast in MGM's Our Gang series in 1938 when he was five (yes, that's five years old). He starred in Our Gang films for another five years and then went on to play Little Beaver in the Red Ryder Western series. He worked through his teens in film and early television and gained fame in 1967 in Truman Capote and Richard Brooks's *In Cold Blood*. In that film, the docudrama of two murders in the town of Holcomb, Kansas, Blake brilliantly played the ex-con Perry Smith. Coincidentally Scott Wilson, who starred in *The New Centurions*, played Perry's partner in the murders, Dick Hickock. *In Cold Blood* was a landmark film, as was Capote's book. In the strangest "movie killer becomes real-life killer" series of events, Blake was

Irwin Winkler, Elliott Gould, Robert Blake
Busting

accused of murdering his wife Bonnie Bakley in 2001. He was found innocent by the jury in a trial that made headlines all over the world.

The difference in the two styles of acting was fun to see. Elliott Gould was chewing gum, carefree, always confident, while Robert

Blake played serious with a chip on his shoulder. Both cops are about their jobs and not much else.

Strongly influenced by Billy Friedkin's 1972 *The French Connection*, the writer/director Peter Hyams managed some very fine action scenes. A long chase through the historic Grand Central Market ends on a serious note when an innocent bystander is shot and killed (in the movie), a disturbing, realistic result of cops shooting at villains in a public place. With a very low budget we managed a chase scene between two ambulances that stands up to the chase through the streets of San Francisco in the classic *Bullitt*.

Busting has the look, feel, and attitude of sunny, glittering Los Angeles and the dirty, dark alleys behind it all, with the prostitutes, dope dealers, small- and big-time gangsters, and small- and big-time cops.

Allen Garfield is the corrupt businessman Gould and Blake have to bring down, and the man has a family that he cares about as much as he cares about his "business" (Margo Winkler played his wife).

Elliott Gould is remembered for outstanding performances not only in *M*A*S*H* and *Bob & Carol & Ted & Alice* but in many, many other roles he played over the last forty years. As with most good actors, some performances stay with them. Case in point: one morning in January 2018 my phone rang, and it was Elliott wanting to discuss, of all things, *Busting*. He thanked me for introducing him to Peter Hyams and reported that Hyams told him that I didn't approve Gary Marshall (the director and sometime actor) for a small role in *Busting*. Gould said, had he known this at the time, he would have insisted we hire Marshall, because he felt his performance would have been even better alongside Marshall than it was.

Busting is virtually unknown today, but not to Elliott Gould and not to me.

CHAPTER SIX

From Africa with Barbra Streisand to Charlie Bronson and a fine
script that went sour

UP THE SANDBOX (1972)

BACK IN 1965, BOB Chartoff and I went to see borscht belt comic Sammy Shore at a small Greenwich Village nightclub. Shore was the star of the show and the closing act. The opening act was a girl singer on a stool wearing an outfit that could only have come from a second-hand shop. But the voice, that was by no means secondhand. Not only was she a great singer with a great voice, but on that stage she was also a fine actress. In the years that followed, Barbra Streisand came to Hollywood and, in her very first film role, won an Academy Award for *Funny Girl*. Bob Chartoff and I thought, why not have Streisand do a drama with a political message, as she had always been involved in women's causes?

We had bought *Up the Sandbox*, Ann Roiphe's novel about a female character who dreams and fantasizes about breaking away from the boredom of being a housewife. She's pregnant and in Roiphe's story starts to rebel against her mother, society, and middle-class culture. After all, it was a time of reinvention in America, and rebellion was in the air.

Barbra liked the book and wanted it to be her first film with First Artists Company, a star-based film production company that she owned with Dustin Hoffman, Steve McQueen, and Sidney Poitier. First Artists had complete control of the creative and business affairs and no interference from its financial backer, Warner Bros. We liked

Paul Zindel's Pulitzer Prize–winning play *The Effect of Gamma Rays on Man-in-the-Moon Marigolds* and had him adapt Roiphe's book.

Zindel's screenplay was quite good, and Barbra and we felt it was on the right track for us to bring in a director. Streisand, appear-

Barbra Streisand, Dick Clayton, Irwin Winkler
Up the Sandbox

ing onstage in Las Vegas, asked me to join her and discuss potential directors. I sat at a front table by myself, admiring (as did everyone else) Barbra's talent, and met her for dinner in her dressing room between shows. We discussed the script and agreed on a short list of directors, and then she had to get prepared for her second show. I went to my room, and as I fell asleep, my phone rang. It was Barbra, who had finished her show and had ideas about the script and wanted to go over them with me. Sleepily I got dressed and met her back at the club; we went through the script and, while doing so, decided that Irvin

Kershner, whom we both knew and who was interested in directing the script, was a good choice and that I would meet with him. When does Barbra sleep, I said to myself when I got back to my hotel bed.

When next we met, it was in San Francisco at the Huntington Hotel, where Barbra stayed while she was shooting *What's Up, Doc?* When Kershner and I arrived in her suite, Barbra greeted us warmly, ready to hear Kershner's plans for the script changes he had worked on for the past two months. As soon as Kershner enthusiastically told us his initial thoughts, Barbra went from sitting to supine on the sofa and had room service bring hot tea. As Kershner went on, his ideas became more and more obscure and had nothing to do with the Zindel script. Barbra actually started to cough and wheeze and soon was covered with a blanket. At that point it was obvious that if Kershner continued, Barbra might end up in the hospital. We quickly wrapped things up, and Kershner asked if I would go back with him to Los Angeles on a late flight. I declined, thinking it best to give Barbra some moral support. Kershner went to work with Paul Zindel's script and, I must say, improved it quite a bit once he focused on what we all liked.

We had a very good shoot in New York with Gordon Willis, our director of photography, and a good supporting cast. The fantasy sequences, especially a fight under a dining room table with Barbra's mother, were classic. The idea for the intensity of the fight came from Barbra and her difficult relationship with her own mother. Less classic were the remote locations in Africa to shoot Barbra's fantasy in which the women are the warriors and the men are the housewives.

On the night flight to Nairobi I was awake and noticed a single light over Kershner's seat. He was working on the script and looked me in the eye and said, "The African scenes can't work; they're awful." I reminded him that we had had a second-unit crew in Kenya for the past month preparing the action sequences. He was adamant that he couldn't shoot the scenes that were written (he had written them). When we landed, we arranged for two small planes to scour the African plains for locations, one with Kershner and Willis, the other with our first assistant director "Hawk" Koch and me. We managed to find sequences to shoot in Samburu while holed up at the incredible Mount Kenya Safari Club. Streisand was no star to the Samburu natives—they'd never heard her sing—but she became quite friendly with the wife of the chief and never complained about the heat or the occasional intrusion of a snake. I'm not sure if the Africa sequences we shot were that special, but they did serve the character Margaret (Streisand) and the world she imagined.

The editing went well, and Barbra worked tirelessly in the editing room with Kershner and had excellent suggestions. Billy Goldenberg wrote a wonderful score, and we had a couple of friends-and-family screenings that played well. We showed the film to the Warner Bros. executives (all rich white middle-aged males); they scratched their heads, since they'd never expected a film about a "women's issue." Still, they were respectful.

Barbra didn't make any other films for her First Artists Company, and shortly thereafter Warner Bros. decided to cease their financing. I give Barbra a great deal of credit for using her company to make a film about an issue she (and we) cared about.

Up the Sandbox was well received, and Pauline Kael, the critic for the *New Yorker*, wrote that "Barbra Streisand never seemed so radiant as in this joyful mess . . . The picture is full of knockabout urban humor." She got it!

We got an R rating from the Motion Picture Association of America for a scene of Barbra fantasizing about going into an abortion clinic. Although it was the 1970s and revolution was in the air, the motion picture executives and the theater owners were still in the 1950s.

BREAKOUT (1975)

Unlike the working trip to Africa with *Up the Sandbox* in July 1974, the Winkler and Chartoff families were enjoying a vacation in Kenya and Tanzania. One of the high points of the trip was a stop at the

Ngorongoro Crater on a mountaintop off the wide Tanzania plains. The crater was famous for the animals that had wandered into it over many years and, because of the steep hills, were unable to climb out. The animals ending up spending the rest of their lives in the crater.

Taking a break in the lobby of our hotel, I was approached by a porter asking me if I was Mr. Winkler or Mr. Chartoff. He said he had an urgent radio message: "call your office." Here we were, in the middle of the Serengeti; the radio in the hotel was only used for reservations and emergencies, and we were politely told it wasn't available to us. Bob and I had to figure out what our office wanted to speak to us about.

Bob and I had bought the book *The 10-Second Jailbreak: The Helicopter Escape of Joel David Kaplan,* and Columbia Pictures committed to finance the film if Charles Bronson starred in it. Bronson had a big hit with *Death Wish,* and we had made the successful thriller *The Mechanic* (and two more sequels decades later) with Bronson. Michael Ritchie (*Downhill Racer*) had come aboard as director after Bronson signed on.

The script, written by Elliott Baker (*Luv*) and Howard Kreitsek (*The Ilustrated Man*), was a thriller and posited an unusual character for Bronson. A bush pilot hired to fly a helicopter into a Mexican prison to free an American serving time for a murder he didn't commit, Bronson had gotten rid of the scowl he'd been famous for and had a light, comedic touch. That comedic touch turned back to a scowl when talk of any actress other than his wife, Jill Ireland, came up to play a small part in the film. Our director, Ritchie, was adamant that she shouldn't be in the film. Bronson's agent, Paul Kohner, told us in no uncertain terms that if there was "No Jill, no Charlie."

Before Bob and I left for our trip, we (and the Columbia executives) met and explained to Ritchie that without Bronson there would be no *Breakout,* and without Jill Ireland there would be no Bronson.

A small charter plane was due to pick us up that afternoon and fly us to a campsite on Mount Kilimanjaro. We wrote a note and asked the pilot to send a telegraph to our office when he returned to his home base in Dar es Salaam, Tanzania: *Hire Ireland, fire Ritchie.*

When Ritchie decided he'd rather not make the film with Jill Ireland, we brought in Tom Gries (*The Hawaiians*) to direct *Breakout*. We cast Robert Duvall, who had just played (brilliantly) Tom Hagen in *The Godfather* and *The Godfather Part II*, John Huston, who had played Noah Cross in *Chinatown*, and a very young Randy Quaid dressed in a skirt as a Mexican prostitute. Charles Bronson, comfortable with Tom Gries (and Jill Ireland), gave one of his best and most unusual performances in a long career, and Jill Ireland also turned in a very good performance playing Robert Duvall's character's wife.

Bob and I weren't very high on the finished film—we thought it was mildly entertaining—but Columbia Pictures thought they had a big hit and introduced a "saturation booking" plan: have the film open in 1,300 theaters. This was a first. Most films in 1975 would never play in more than 300 to 400 theaters. The studio also spent $3 million on television ads, again a first (the average television expenditures for a movie opening in 2018 is $20 to $30 million). Saturation booking is now the standard for all films after *Jaws* followed *Breakout* to be (a well-deserved honor) one of the top-grossing films of all time.

I'll always remember Bob Chartoff and I finding an answer to the request to "call our office" on the mountaintop in Tanzania as we watched the animals circling in the crater below. "Just like Hollywood," I remarked to Bob.

PEEPER (1974)

Peeper was the final title of a movie we produced based on the book *Deadfall*, by Keith Laumer. It was a film that started off ambitiously with a script by W. D. Richter that was a clever takeoff on Dashiell Hammett and Raymond Chandler. We were lucky to get Michael Caine to play the private eye and then hired Peter Hyams to rewrite Richter's script and direct the film. Hyams had done *Busting* for us, and he brought a comic element to the film. We were fighting the seriousness of the *Deadfall* book and Richter's original script, wanting to bring in a lighter tone.

Natalie Wood agreed to costar opposite Michael as the femme fatal. I had had a strange relationship with Natalie back when I was starting out in the late sixties. We had a script, *Very Special People*, that was written by Joe Heims of *Double Trouble* fame (and, no, we weren't going to star Elvis) that Natalie liked a great deal. She was in London, having just married agent Richard Gregson. MGM suggested I fly to London and discuss available directors for the film. I arrived and called Natalie as I unpacked and suggested I come by her apartment to talk about directors. She told me, "Oh, Irwin, I'm packing. I'm going away." I reminded her that I'd just flown in from California to meet with her and she knew I had been coming. She said she was sorry but she was leaving the next day for a ski vacation and just couldn't see me, and she didn't know when she'd be back. It was pretty devastating. I then called the head of MGM in Los Angeles, Robert Whiteman, and told him I didn't want to hang around in London waiting for Natalie without any idea of when she'd be back. I explained that my wife was pregnant in Los Angeles, and I was going to leave. Whiteman asked if my wife was capable of traveling, and if she was, he'd arrange to have her come and stay with me until I was able to meet with Natalie. I called Margo, she got a babysitter, and she got on a plane that night. We stayed in London until Natalie came back the following week, when we met and talked about the script and, of course, about directors. We somehow never made the movie, but Margo and I had a great time in London. Humphrey Bogart said to Ingrid Bergman in *Casablanca*, "We'll always have Paris." Well, Margo and I will always have London. Thanks to Natalie Wood.

When we were preparing the budget on *Peeper*, Natalie told me that she had to have a diamond bracelet. She explained that when she did *Rebel Without a Cause* with James Dean, she broke her wrist, and it was now slightly deformed, so she needed a bracelet to hide the deformity. I told her the prop department would make her one. But she said it had to be real diamonds. I increased the budget by $10,000 to cover up this so-called deformed wrist that I never once noticed. When the studio asked for the bracelet back at the end of the shoot, it was nowhere to be found.

Making the film with Michael Caine was special. Michael was not only a wonderful actor, but he and his wife, Shakira, were great company, and we became lifelong friends. Our crew took over a ship, and we shot and sailed the Caribbean for ten days. Not a bad way to make a movie.

NICKELODEON (1976)

Some movies are terrible failures but bring good fortune through peculiar circumstances. Over the years I became intrigued with the history of filmmaking. How did it all start, and who were the pioneers in the career I'd chosen? As I researched the obvious—Cecil B. DeMille, Charlie Chaplin, Mack Sennett—I found an even earlier group of silent (short) film directors like Allan Dwan, who directed films going back to 1911 in the hills around Los Angeles. I knew I wanted to make a movie about that ragtag bunch of actors, directors, and producers who fled to California for the long days of sunshine and to avoid the royalty the Edison Company, who owned the patents on the camera, had demanded. These "filmmakers" were from all walks of life and professions: accountants, lawyers, photographers, carnival workers, and even some hobos and drifters. Several who came to the land of sunshine were "blue" filmmakers from small studios in New Jersey whose work would make Deep Throat blush.

Bob Chartoff and I had worked on a couple of films in the past with W. D. Richter, and he was willing to write a script for my movie on spec, meaning no money up front but with the promise of a big check to come if the script sold. It was a good deal for Richter and Chartoff-Winkler. We gave Richter the idea, worked with him on the script, and if we sold it, he got all the money, and we would produce. If we didn't sell it in a prescribed time, all rights (and our work) would belong to

Richter with no obligation to us. When Richter finished the screenplay, we titled it *Starlight Parade*, and we were so pleased, we decided to auction it off to the studios, get Richter a big payday, and then get a director and cast.

It made for an interesting weekend. John Calley of Warner Bros. called first thing Saturday morning and was interested but wasn't ready to make an offer. Mike Medavoy at United Artists said his boss, Arthur Krim, was very interested but was at Lyndon Johnson's ranch in Texas and didn't have convenient access to a telephone. No actual offer came in until David Begelman, CEO of Columbia Pictures, made a substantial offer that he would withdraw if we didn't accept immediately. We were pleased but didn't trust Begelman, who was notorious for double dealing and who, years before, had pulled Al Pacino out of *The Gang That Couldn't Shoot Straight* in spite of a signed contract. We insisted that we receive a bank check for the full amount of the sale by Monday morning. Surprisingly Begelman came through with the payment as promised. Why so quick? The agent Sue Mengers (who once worked for Begelman) had slipped it to her very hot director client Peter Bogdanovich, who wanted to direct. Or so we thought. That afternoon Bogdanovich had Begelman, Bob, and me drive across town to his office, where he sat behind a desk (slightly raised) and arrogantly told us that he would direct the movie but hated the script. His version had no resemblance to our story and seemed totally arbitrary. As we left Bogdanovich's office, we told Begelman we didn't want to go ahead with a director who hated our script. Begelman answered that he had bought the script and believed in Bogdanovich, claiming he was a genius.

A few years later, in 1977, it was discovered that Begelman had forged a series of checks while president of Columbia Pictures. He was convicted of fraud but got off with probation and a fine. Later it was discovered that the check forging was only part of Begelman's criminal activities. He was accused of embezzling funds from his client Judy Garland, and he inflated budgets of films he produced and pocketed the difference. A couple of years later his bank put a lien of $90 million on his new company's assets. In spite of this activity, Kirk Kerkorian had him run MGM for a while, but his tenure was short (no reason given). When he formed yet another new production company, Begelman got into trouble with the Hollywood guilds for his failure to pay residuals and was personally embarrassed when it was discovered that he had lied about going to Yale.

On a hot summer day in August 1995, Begelman checked into the Century Plaza Hotel, had the concierge hand deliver a personal note to five of his close friends, had sex with an old girlfriend he invited to his room, meticulously hung up his clothes, took a shower, got into bed, put a pistol into his mouth, and pulled the trigger.

Bob and I were bothered by Bogdanovich's attitude and stayed on Begelman to replace him. Begelman was adamant. A day or two later Mike Medavoy, the production head of United Artists, called to tell us that his boss Arthur Krim was very upset at Bob and me for not giving him a chance to bid on *Starlight Parade*. We explained that Begelman had made a preemptive offer and we had an obligation to make sure Richter got paid for his screenplay, and in any event we'd never heard back from Krim. Shortly thereafter Medavoy heard that I was going to New York and asked if I would have lunch with Krim and his New York staff. At lunch I asked Krim why in the world he wanted to buy me lunch since he was upset at the *Starlight Parade* deal. Krim surprised me by saying, "Yes, I was upset, and I don't want something like that to happen again." He wanted Bob and me to sign an exclusive contract to develop scripts and produce films for United Artists. I hesitated, but Bob in Los Angeles suggested a deal that allowed us to force United Artists to finance a film under certain conditions (called a "put" picture).

The new script that Bogdanovich wrote had very little to do with our *Starlight Parade*, and Bogdanovich enjoyed complete freedom from Begelman. He cast Ryan O'Neal, whom he had worked with on *What's Up, Doc?* and *Paper Moon*, and O'Neal's daughter, Tatum (who won an Oscar in 1973 for her role in *Paper Moon*, at ten years old the youngest actress ever to win an Academy Award). Bogdanovich was frustrated when his longtime live-in girlfriend, Cybill Shepherd, turned down the female lead (he blamed it on the studio, said they wouldn't approve her) but did cast Burt Reynolds, whom he had worked with in *At Long Last Love*, opposite Ryan O'Neal.

Bogdanovich told Begelman he wanted to shoot the film, just like the early silent shorts, in black-and-white. Begelman's sales force convinced him the film would lose its value on television if it wasn't in color, and for a change Bogdanovich reluctantly agreed. In 2008 at his own expense Bogdanovich made a black-and-white print and showed it at the Castro Theatre in San Francisco. It was well received.

When we visited the set in Modesto, California, we were met by a group of very unhappy actors and Bogdanovich directing on horseback. I had never seen or heard of a film director riding a horse on set, but Bogdanovich told me that John Ford directed on horseback (but of course Bogdanovich was no John Ford). Jane Hitchcock, who had the misfortune to replace Cybill Shepherd, was a bit inexperienced and couldn't get beyond the director's disappointment at the loss of Shepherd. Burt Reynolds complained to me that Bogdanovich had him do extremely difficult stunts and was trying to get him killed. Reynolds ignored me when I reminded him that Hal Needham was doing all the stunts (Reynolds later made a film, *Hooper*, directed by Needham, in which a character played by Robert Klein imitates an arrogant film director very much like Peter Bogdanovich, with an enormous ego. That director puts his star in danger and even makes a speech about filmmaking being "pieces of time," a line right out of *Nickelodeon*). The O'Neal father-and-daughter pair, however, seemed to be having a good time and were joined by Griffin O'Neal, one of Ryan's sons. Bob and I kept trying to find our *Starlight Parade* script on film. Instead we got a film that had no surprises, very old-fashioned gags and pratfalls, and every punch line telegraphed beforehand. Bogdanovich was imitating the movies of seventy-five years earlier, but what had worked then didn't now.

There was, however, a moment at the end of the film that was very moving. As the director and his actors pass a big glass stage one night, they see it all lit up with a group of soldiers marching, and Leo (Ryan O'Neal), choking up, says, "Look, they're making a movie." That to me was very personal. Even though I've been on movie sets all of my adult life, I still marvel at the process, and when I walk by a company shooting in the street, I stop and smile.

When Bob Chartoff and I were invited to see the edited film in Peter Bogdanovich's living room, we were dismayed but not surprised. The film was just a series of pratfalls, bad jokes, and forced attempts at comedy. And it was very, very long. As we started to give Bogdanovich notes, his mother walked into the living room and in front of us told him, "Don't listen to what they say; it was people like them (pointing to Bob Chartoff and me) who ruined your father's life." We were shown the door.

At the world premiere we decided we would charge a nickel to see the film to imitate the price the early nickelodeons charged. Unfortunately, it gave one critic the opportunity to remark that the movie wasn't even worth the nickel.

I recently reread our original script of *Starlight Parade*. It's wonderful, nostalgic, warm, funny, and moving. Someday I'll make it.

CHAPTER SEVEN

To quote Rick in Casablanca, *"This is the beginning of a beautiful friendship."*

NEW YORK, NEW YORK (1976)

The theater in San Francisco was packed for the first screening before a "civilian" audience of the big-band musical *New York, New York*. The audience screamed and applauded when Liza Minnelli sang the title song "New York, New York," and Bob De Niro, Liza, Marty Scorsese, the editors, the United Artists executives, and Bob Chartoff and I left the theater buoyant with the reception after a long production and editing process. We had a hit!

I had grown up in the big-band era listening to Frank Sinatra, Bing Crosby, Peggy Lee, the Dorsey Brothers, Harry James, and Benny Goodman. I had cut school to see and hear a very young Frank Sinatra at the Paramount Theater in New York. I hung on to those early memories as the big bands fell away and the 1960s brought Elvis Presley, the Beatles, the Rolling Stones, and Bob Dylan.

Musically, however, I never left the big-band sound behind and thought about our managing Felicia Sanders, a vocalist at a small hip nightclub called The Bon Soir in New York. Sanders had a couple of hit records and television guest shots. Her husband, Irving Joseph, who accompanied her on the piano, was a very good jazz musician who let his wife take the bows. (I always wondered about his feelings about his wife being the headliner in the spotlight, with him in the background in spite of his considerable gifts.)

I met a young and inexperienced but talented writer out of Dartmouth College, Earl Mac Rauch, who liked my idea of a film based on the Bon Soir couple and was willing to write a script on spec with a big payday if we got it made. While Earl was researching (and writing), I saw *Mean Streets* at the New York Film Festival and had a drink with Marty Scorsese, who liked *Point Blank* so much, he used our poster in a scene in *Mean Streets*. We talked about working together, and he told me he was eager to direct the Nikos Kazantzakis book *The Last Temptation of Christ*, so I never thought of mentioning *New York, New York*.

In an interview with the columnist "Army" Archerd of *Variety*, I had mentioned that I was planning to make our musical *New York, New York*. To my surprise, Marty's agent called and said that Marty had seen the article, was interested in the subject, and wanted to read the script. I was surprised, as *Mean Streets* was a brilliant, tough character study of a group of young men growing up violently in New York's Lower East side. No reason whatsoever to think Marty would want to direct a romantic musical. Meanwhile I had met with Gene Kelly, the iconic MGM musical star who wanted to direct *New York, New York* but soured me on the idea, as he had some very traditional ideas. We were also in touch with Bob Fosse and Jerome Robbins; both had expressed interest but had lots of commitments in the theater. So why Marty Scorsese? The script of *New York, New York* was pretty conventional. Girl meets boy, girl falls in love with boy, they marry, her career rises, his falls, and so does the marriage. The film needed a director who was respectful of the genre and yet could make the characters contemporary. When we met again, I found that Marty had the same love of the MGM musicals that I had. We talked about our mutual favorite director, Vincente Minnelli, who had made *An American in Paris*, *Gigi*, *The Band Wagon*, *Meet Me in St. Louis*, as well as some great tough dramas and one of my favorite films about Hollywood, *The Bold and the Beautiful*.

I didn't hesitate, and neither did Marty. We decided to make the film together, and United Artists was eager to finance it. We talked about actresses/singers and agreed that Liza Minnelli was perfect. Not only had she won an Academy Award for *Cabaret* a few years before, but it tickled us that she was the daughter of Minnelli and Judy Garland. Liza was enthusiastic about the script, Marty was enthusiastic about Liza, but Liza wasn't enthusiastic about Marty directing her. That changed quickly when I screened *Mean Streets* for her and she spent some time with Marty. For the aggressive, talented jazz saxophonist,

Liza Minnelli and Irwin Winkler
New York, New York

Bob De Niro was perfect. He had two great screen successes already with Marty directing him in *Mean Streets* and *Taxi Driver*, and they were very close friends. Bob, who liked the character, had one major concern: could he learn to play the saxophone and be as good at it as the character he was playing? We hired a jazz saxophonist from the era, Georgie Auld, who'd had his own band in the 1940s and was part of the great bands of Benny Goodman and Artie Shaw, to tutor Bob. Bob soon went from holding the sax and fingering the keys to learning notes and playing actual passages. After weeks of intensive lessons, one afternoon Georgie's wife came into the living room where they were rehearsing and complimented Georgie on a particular riff she had heard from the next room of their apartment. It was Bob who was playing. That sealed it.

Because of Liza's great success in *Cabaret*, we brought in the *Cabaret* songwriting team of John Kander and Fred Ebb to write special material for the film, including and most specifically a big dramatic song "in a major key" that De Niro's Jimmy writes for Liza's Francine. When we all met in New York, Kander and Ebb played the material they had worked on (including a special ten-minute "Happy Endings" number—more on that later) that we all liked and then the song "New York, New York" in a minor key rather than the major key we were expecting. They explained that they didn't want to compete with the Leonard Bernstein, Comden and Green song "New York, New York" from the play *Wonderful Town*. We reiterated it was imperative that we have a song in a "major key," and a week later I received a package with a tape recording of Kander and Ebb at the piano singing "New York, New York" in a "major key." Marty, Liza, Bob, and we all had exactly what we needed.

We put together a crew with Boris Leven as production designer (*Sound of Music, West Side Story*), director of photography László Kovács (*Easy Rider*), and editors Irving Lerner (*Studs Lonigan*) and Marcia Lucas (*American Graffiti, Taxi Driver*). We shot at the old MGM studio lot in Culver City where Judy Garland and Vincente Minnelli had made their legendary musicals. On those stages we shot our first sequence as a tribute to Judy Garland. Kander and Ebb wrote "Happy Endings," a ten-minute musical sequence within the film that follows a theater usherette (Liza) in her dream of movie stardom. She sings, she dances, and she falls in love—very much like Judy Garland's "Born in a Trunk" segment in *A Star Is Born*. (After we opened, Marty and I sensed that the length was a problem for the audiences, so we cut the "Happy Endings" sequence. We restored it for later theatrical release and the home entertainment version).

De Niro and Marty's improvisational style slowed down the pace of production, but it also brought spontaneity to the characters and the shooting. In one scene Jimmy impulsively decides to marry Francine, has a cab driver take them to a justice of the peace, where he knocks on the window of the door, and the glass breaks. Marty loved the realism of the broken window, and we had the prop man at 7:00 P.M. find

Irwin Winkler and Robert De Niro
New York, New York

breakaway glass. He then had to replace and clean up the broken glass after every take (it took about a half hour each take).

I loved the realism of it too, but at the twentieth take (at 11:00 P.M.) I told Marty we would not be able to shoot the next day (it was an outdoor location, and the actors had a twelve-hour turnaround) unless we finished at once. He replied that in the last take he saw a tear in the corner of Liza's eye when De Niro proposed marriage. Did I want to go for the tear or stop? Of course we went for the emotion.

The long days took a toll on Marty, the actors, and the crew (the producers too). Some took pills to stay awake and alert and ended up with the opposite effect. The studio executives were anxious until they saw a scene where Jimmy, just out of the army, sees a sailor and his girl dancing under a streetlight to the sounds of a subway train; it was magical, and the studio was supportive from then on.

Ultimately Liza playing a sweet band singer and Bob playing an aggressive, unconventional jazz saxophonist who ends up owning a saloon was a tough mix for the audience. They wanted desperately for the two lovers to stay together just like in the Judy Garland, Mickey Rooney MGM pictures. That wasn't to be.

Marty staged the song "New York, New York" in a nightclub setting with a large audience and Jimmy, Francine's estranged husband, in attendance. Francine sang not only to the crowd but to Jimmy. She had made it (he hadn't). It was the climax of the film, but, in fact, it wasn't. Jimmy goes backstage to see his son (played by my son Adam)

Sylvester Stallone, Irwin Winkler, Hal Polaire, and Robert De Niro
New York, New York

and to congratulate Francine. They chat uncomfortably and make a date to meet later. She starts to go to him but turns back, and he waits, turns, and walks away, and we end the film with Jimmy realizing she's not coming. We hear a very somber instrumental version of the "New York, New York" song. It was a realistic ending but not a very satisfying one. We couldn't get airplay for Liza's version of "New York, New

Martin Scorsese, Adam Winkler, and Robert De Niro
New York, New York

York," and it faded from public attention quickly. Two years later, Frank Sinatra, who at the time was not at the "top of the heap," asked Liza if he could cover it. She gave him the OK, and it became the powerful theme of New York City, one of Sinatra's biggest hits, and it renewed his career, but it was too late to help the film. The song, considered one of the most popular to ever appear in a film, was ignored by the Academy and didn't even get a nomination for Best Song.

We had shot a lot of film and had a five-man crew in the editing room led by Marcia Lucas (Irving Lerner had passed away), who joined us after editing her husband's film *Star Wars*. Our first cut was long, and we had screenings for and advice from Vincente Minnelli and George Cukor. When we showed a four-and-a-half-hour version to the Italian director Bernardo Bertolucci (*The Last Emperor*), he told us not to cut a foot. "It's a great opera," he said.

We mixed the sound at the Samuel Goldwyn studio, and after a couple of weeks Marcia Lucas asked me if her husband could impose on us. It seemed he had run over his allotted time for mixing *Star Wars*, so could he use our facilities at night after we finished our day's work? I couldn't say no to Marcia, so George and crew would be waiting every evening for us to finish so they could complete their work on *Star Wars*. When they did, George invited Margo and me to be among the first ones to see the just-finished film. The screening halted a couple of times, as the machinery was overused, and George constantly apologized. He need not have. We were dazzled by the unique storytelling, the visual effects, and the characters Lucas had created. Of course John Williams's score brought our thrills to another level. When we congratulated George, he seemed surprised by our effusive response. I bought stock in 20th Century Fox studios (the *Star Wars* distributor) the next morning.

VALENTINO (1977)

Rodolfo Alfonso Raffaello Pierre Filibert Guglielmi di Valentina d'Antonguella—that was the name Rudolph Valentino was born with. Figuring out what the name meant could be a movie in itself.

The silent-screen star was credited with (or accused of—take your pick) being a taxi dancer, gigolo, bigamist, Latin lover, jailbird, you name it. We thought Valentino's life would certainly have enough drama for a movie and bought the book *Valentino: An Intimate Exposé of the Sheik* written by Chaw Mank and Brad Steiger. We asked Mardik Martin, whom we had met through Marty Scorsese and who worked on rewrites of *New York, New York*, to adapt the book. Mardik came up with the concept of starting with Valentino's funeral. No ordinary funeral, though. Pandemonium reigns in August of 1926 in New York City as 100,000 shrieking, crying, grieving fans (mostly women) break through the police barriers to get one last glimpse of the famous movie star laid out in a coffin. The story of Valentino's life is then told in flashbacks by the women who shared his life, all of whom are just as hysterical as the fans.

Now to get a director. Ken Russell had done some groundbreaking biographical films in the 1960s and '70s. His films about Tchaikovsky, *The Music Lovers*, and Mahler, *Mahler*, and his *Tommy* and *Lisztomania*, starring Roger Daltrey, were all fresh and interesting and quite outlandish. When he expressed interest in Martin's script, we were (we thought) on the way to a most interesting filmmaking experience.

To play Valentino, we wanted a new face, someone who would be able to hold the audience much the same way Valentino had. The romantic and exotic actor had had great success with the dashing Latin lover in *The Sheik* and the heroic lover in *The Four Horsemen of the Apocalypse*. The great Russian ballet dancer Rudolf Nureyev had,

Rudolf Nureyev and Irwin Winkler
Valentino

in 1961, been one of the first artists to defect from the Soviet Union (under the nose of the KGB, who were trying to kidnap him from Paris back to Russia). He caused an international sensation and toured with great success in Europe. He fit the role of Valentino perfectly. Born and raised in Italy, Valentino had a sexy look that was different from that of American leading men in Hollywood. Nureyev had a Slovak, sexy quality, and since Valentino was a dancer early in his career, we could show off Nureyev's talents dancing the tango and other popular dances of the period.

We set the production in London for budgetary reasons, and Bob Chartoff spent quite a bit of time traveling back and forth as the picture got under way. He was concerned after the first couple of weeks that Russell was going overboard. Looking at dailies in Los Angeles, I was too, and I joined Bob in London. We sat Ken Russell down, and he accepted our criticism and assured us he was "only experimenting" and was shooting enough film to protect the scenes as written (he had done a rewrite of Mardik Martin's script). It was hard for us to ignore some of Russell's innovative talent (and the great talent of Nureyev in a ballroom scene with the dancer Anthony Dowell playing Vaslav Nijinsky, and in a boxing-match scene that played to Nureyev's grace). But back in Los Angeles, I was appalled (as was Bob in London) by a scene we felt was staged by Russell to not only show the humiliation of Valentino but to embarrass Rudolf Nureyev as well. Valentino is arrested for bigamy and must spend the the night in jail. Russell had the cell built as a cage in a zoo. The drunk and nasty prisoners are all crowded together and taunt Valentino about his masculinity, and one prisoner simulates him masturbating. Then when Valentino is refused the toilet by a cruel guard, he pisses all over himself. When Russell showed me the film in Los Angeles, I told him he *must* cut that scene. A couple of hours later I was delivered by special messenger the scene actually cut from the film in a Beverly Hills Hotel laundry bag, with a note saying, *Here's the scene you don't like.* We had Russell make some cuts, and, very reluctantly, we kept most of it in the film at his insistence. I don't think there was one reviewer who didn't take exception to that prison scene.

The excess, however, was evident throughout the film; just about every scene was over the top. At a dinner one night in London after a day's shooting, I asked Rudolf how he managed the disrespect

and cruelty from his director. He laughed and said it was nothing com-
pared to what the KGB would do if they had caught him and sent him
to Siberia.

Princess Margaret, Robert Chartoff, and Irwin Winkler
Premiere of *Valentino*, 1977

I've often been asked what is my favorite or best film. No one has
asked me what was my least favorite or worst film. I'll answer that one
now: *Valentino* by a large margin.

CHAPTER EIGHT

From Rocky *to Oscar*

ROCKY (1976)

IN 1976, AMERICA HAD gone through a decade of unrest, chaos, and disillusionment. Watergate, the Vietnam War, the murders of Dr. Martin Luther King and Robert Kennedy, the violent confrontation between the police and peaceful protestors at the Democratic Convention in Chicago, and the killing of four innocent young students at Kent State in Ohio by the National Guard.

Along came a film that said forget your past, believe in yourself, and you may be a million to one shot.

That was *Rocky*.

A relatively unknown, out-of-work actor, Sylvester Stallone, came into the Chartoff-Winkler office for an interview at the insistence of a young man who worked with us, Gene Kirkwood. We had no intention or desire to spend an hour in idle conversation with an actor who had had only a few small parts in a couple of movies. No interest whatsoever. Stallone told us about his background and education—nothing much to interest us, as we weren't casting a film. As he left our office, Stallone turned to Bob Chartoff and said he had written a screenplay, and would we read it? We were curious, as he certainly didn't talk like a writer (although what does a writer really talk like?), and we read the screenplay. It was *Hell's Kitchen* (later *Paradise Alley*), and we thought the writing was quite good, with well-defined, unusual characters, but it wasn't something we wanted to produce. When we told Sly that, he immediately offered up another idea about an unlikely fight between an unknown second-rate fighter and a Muhammad Ali–type world champion. We liked the idea, and at the time we were trying (unsuccessfully) to get the rights to another fight picture (*Body and Soul*). We agreed that Sly would write the script based on his pitch, for no payment, with the understanding that if we wanted to go ahead and make the film, Sly had to be the star. Sly very quickly wrote about a third of the script. We gave him our notes (not that many, as we liked the pages), and when he delivered the finished script, we thought it was a nice, small film about an interesting character and an unusual love story. Nothing more.

We had made an exclusive producing deal with United Artists and had a "put picture" clause. That gave us the right to make UA finance (not necessarily distribute) any film (except X-rated) with a budget of $1.5 million or less *if* we hadn't made a film for them in the first nine months of our exclusivity. Just our luck, we hadn't made a film in that period of time.

When we brought the *Rocky* script to Arthur Krim, CEO of UA, he wanted to know why they should finance a film about a broken-down fighter who falls in love with an ugly duckling, gets an unlikely match with a world champion, and loses that fight, and we wanted as a star . . . Sylvester Stallone? No, they wouldn't make *Rocky*. We then said it would be a "put" picture under the terms of our contract. To get around the "put," UA budgeted the film at $2 million in spite of our budget of $1.2 million and declared it was outside our $1.5 million put picture clause. We told the head of production, Mike Medavoy, that we'd make it for $1 million and that Bob and I would personally guarantee any costs over the $1 million. It was within our contractual rights. In that case, he said, he would OK the picture, and we insisted he call Arthur Krim in New York to confirm it. He did, and Krim reiterated that he didn't want to make the film, but if his production head made the commitment, he would stand by it. But, Krim wondered, would we consider other casting, say, Burt Reynolds, Ryan O'Neal, James Caan? We said it had to be Stallone.

UA (to this day I don't know who) offered to buy the script from Stallone for $250,000, I suspect with no intention of making the movie but just to get us out of their hair. To them, $250,000 seemed a lot cheaper than $1.5 million, plus a couple more in marketing costs. Sly, who was broke and had a wife and small child, refused their offer and said that Bob Chartoff and I promised him that he would star in the film, and he refused to sell the script.

Arthur Krim wanted to familiarize himself with our star, so we set up a screening for him and the rest of the New York UA executives. *The Lords of Flatbush* was the best (and only) film that Sly Stallone had to show his acting. It costarred Henry Winkler (no relation) and Perry King. At the end of the screening Krim was quite pleased with Perry King and assumed that he was going to be the star of *Rocky*. It wasn't until he saw our finished film nine months later that he realized he'd made the movie with the wrong guy.

When Bob Chartoff and I were looking for a director, we remembered John Avildsen, who had done a three-week reshoot on *Believe in Me*. Bob, Sly, and I ran Avildsen's film *Joe* and met with him and felt he was the right director for our little film.

Casting started with turndowns by Carrie Snodgress (our choice for Adrian), Lee Cobb (for Mickey), and Ken Norton (Apollo), all because we had very little money, even though they liked the parts. Instead we engaged Talia Shire, Burgess Meredith, and Carl Weathers as our second (or third) choices (and they turned out to be a lot better than we could have imagined).

Avildsen led the rehearsals, and it became clear that this was Sly's film. To his credit, Avildsen acknowledged Sly's importance not only as the star of the film but also for his authorship of the screenplay and his knowledge of the boxing ring and what happens in it. Every aspect of Rocky's character was Sly—even the turtles, Cuff and Link, and his dog, Butkus (whom we didn't have the money to ship from LA, so Sly spent three days in a small train compartment with Butkus— who, Sly reported, had flatulence problems—on the way to Philadelphia, where we'd be filming).

Our budget caused us to economize in every area. We used one truck, a Cinemobile that carried our generator, camera, grip, and electrical equipment. We used one small camper for Sly's dressing room, production office, producers' office, wardrobe, and honey wagon (toilet). No catered meals—we would find a convenient restaurant for spaghetti, Philly cheesesteaks, or a pizza.

Luck found us in Philly too. We didn't have the manpower to shoot the training sequences and certainly not Sly running up the stairs at the Philadelphia Museum of Art. We were approached by a local cameraman who showed us a rig he had invented that would solve our problems. Garrett Brown's rig was called a Steadicam. It was a camera secured to the operator's body and had very little movement because of a stabilizer. We used it in Philadelphia and in the fight scenes when we moved to Los Angeles. Since its use in *Rocky*, the Steadicam is standard equipment on just about every movie or television show in production.

Just as in rehearsals, Sly was all over every scene, every shot, every piece of vocabulary, every location. So much so that we asked Sly to direct *Rocky II* and then *Rocky III*, *Rocky IV*, and *Rocky Balboa*.

We got more movie luck after the production moved to Los Angeles. Rocky and Adrian's first date was written to be played at an ice skating rink. We didn't have the money for ice skates, let alone ice skaters, the number of extras, or shaving the ice after each take. For alternatives to skating we considered a restaurant (too expensive), a bowling alley (too noisy), or a movie (too dark). We came up with the solution: since the scene was set during Thanksgiving, why not have an ice rink empty for the holiday (really unlikely), and Rocky gives a couple of dollars to the janitor to let them skate in the empty rink. It was magic.

How do you fill the Sports Arena with extras? Nowadways you could use computers, but not in 1975, and certainly not on our budget. We had to find a way to make a world championship boxing match look like the event it was supposed to be. We made a favorable deal with the extras union for twenty-five extras per day (they had to be seated close to the ring) and filled the rows with people from nearby assisted-living facilities. We were able to keep the old folks attentive and following instructions (cheer, boo, clap) by auctioning off TV sets every hour and by having a plentiful supply of snacks. We had to bus them back home by late afternoon to get their meds but kept the union extras until we finished. That's how we filled the arena, but don't look too closely; the fight fans you see might be dozing at some very exciting moments.

Most "small" films shoot in about forty days. Our shooting schedule was twenty-nine days. We didn't build sets (money!) but used real locations for the interiors all over Los Angeles and Philadelphia, including the meatpacking plant where Rocky trains by pounding the sides of beef. This again was a bit of movie luck, as we were shut out of another location and found the meat locker at the last minute.

We wrapped, and as we edited, our sound editor, Frank Warner, built the effects for the fights, with the gloved hits being their own distinctive sound made from animal grunts, gunshots, trees falling, and train crashes. Warner found or made a unique selection for us to use. We met with several composers (all good but not within our budget), when our editor recommended Bill Conti, who had been performing in a piano bar in Venice, Italy, when he did some work for "Paul" Mazursky on the film *Blume in Love*. We had $18,000 in our budget, a ridiculously small amount for music, and Conti agreed to not only compose the score but to pay for its performance, including the musicians, the studio, and the tape that it was recorded on. Conti played a sample version (on a piano) of his score against the training sequence, and we knew right then it was special. Conti brought in lyricist Carol Connors, who wrote "Gonna Fly Now," which was not only responsible for the audience reaction to the training sequence, but it became the most motivating music for sports events and political candidates as well.

By coincidence Clay Felker was staying with us, and we asked him to attend an early screening we were having for a few close friends. We didn't know what to expect (you never do), and we were stunned when people got up and yelled at the screen, asking for Creed to stay down when he's hit and Rocky to get up when he's down. I looked over, and to my amazement I saw my friend, a very sophisticated New Yorker, standing with the rest of the crowd yelling at the screen. That all changed with the very last scene, when Rocky and Adrian, with the camera at their back, glum and defeated, walk out of the dirty arena. Although the rest of the film played great, it lost its energy in that very last scene. We felt it needed a more upbeat ending. Even though Rocky lost the fight, he was triumphant, but we did not have the triumphant moment. Sly then rewrote a new ending where Adrian runs through the crowd, climbs into the ring, and is embraced by Rocky as Conti's music soars.

We proposed the new ending to UA, who told us they were fine with the ending we had and that if we wanted to shoot a new one, it was our problem, that Bob and I would have to pay for it ourselves.

So we did!

We hired a dozen extras and had them bring hats and coats. As we see Adrian going from the rear of the auditorium to the front of the ring, we moved the extras from the back to the front or middle, had the ones with hats remove them and come to the front, had some with coats remove them and move to the back. We managed to make a dozen extras look like a hundred with Rocky telling Adrian "I love you" and Bill Conti's very simple but emotional music in the background.

By now UA was enthusiastic, so I was surprised and dismayed when I got a Dear John letter from UA president Eric Pleskow, who wrote that they liked *Rocky* but wanted to remind Bob and me that UA had no obligation to release the film in theaters and might sell it directly to television with no theater release. Was he just annoyed that a film he didn't want to make and was forced to make was that good? It seemed so. We had asked for *Rocky* to be released in theaters for Christmas and the Academy Awards. We were told there were no theaters available, and UA's Academy Award picture was the Woody Guthrie biopic *Bound for Glory*.

We arranged a screening of the finished film for the New York UA executives at The Baronet, a small theater on the East Side. We secretly invited the buyer for the Loews theater chain, Bernie Myerson, and the owner of a number of independent theaters, Don Rugoff. Margo was seated next to Arthur Krim, who fell asleep after the first fifteen minutes and stayed asleep through a good deal of the film. After the screening the UA people said they liked the film (and the new ending), but it didn't change anything. No theaters were available. Both Myerson and Rugoff disputed UA and said they would give us the theaters we needed. After a bit of a nasty confrontation, UA agreed to release *Rocky* in a few theaters with no advertising campaign.

Irwin Winkler and Sylvester Stallone
Rocky, opening day, 1976

We opened the film on a Sunday at the Cinema III on Third Avenue in New York. The crowds were good all day, and I waited for the review from Vincent Canby at the *New York Times*. If we got a great one, by the time we opened in the rest of the country, all the reviewers in those cities would have read the *Times* and happily followed the leader. Canby's review was awful. He said that Stallone was a bad television actor and the film wasn't worth seeing. I was standing in front of Cinema III reading this review and feeling crestfallen when the actor Peter Falk came out and congratulated me. I didn't understand how he could congratulate me, given the *New York Times* review. Falk laughed and told me not to pay attention to the review, to just go inside the theater and have a look. Because inside the theater the audience was standing and cheering.

In spite of Canby, the reviews in the rest of the country were excellent. Later on we shared the Best Picture Award from the Los

Angeles Film Critics with *Network*, and when it was announced, I put out my hand to congratulate the *Network* writer, Paddy Chayefsky, and he responded, "I hope you die." Competitive?

Irwin Winkler, Sylvester Stallone, Robert Chartoff
Best Picture Oscar, 1977

Rocky got nominated for ten Academy Awards and won for Best Picture, Best Director, and Best Editing. When it was announced, I pulled Sly up from his seat, and he joined Bob and me in accepting the Oscar. He deserved it.

PART III

THE DAY AFTER WE won the Oscar for *Rocky*, Margo and I took our three boys to Los Angeles International Airport for a vacation in Hawaii. We checked in at the American Airlines desk to get our boarding passes. The agent looked me up and down and asked if I was the Irwin Winkler who had won the Oscar for *Rocky* last night. I nodded, and he said he was proud to meet me, and there were three seats free in first class, and he would upgrade us from our economy status. So the benefits of winning an Academy Award were immediate: our three sons went from Los Angeles to Honolulu first class.

Being bumped to first class wasn't the only change after *Rocky*. The whole landscape of the film industry was changing, and *Rocky's* success was part of the onslaught of the "new" Hollywood that started with Robert Altman's *M*A*S*H*, Billy Friedkin's *The French Connection*, Mel Brooks's *Blazing Saddles*, Peter Bogdanovich's *The Last Picture Show*, John Boorman's *Deliverance*, Bob Fosse's *Cabaret*, Sydney Lumet's *Serpico*, Hal Ashby's *Shampoo*, Sydney Pollack's *The Way We Were*, Woody Allen's *Annie Hall*, Francis Ford Coppola's *The Godfather*, Arthur Penn's *Bonnie and Clyde*, Roman Polanski's *Chinatown*, Steven Spielberg's *Jaws*, Marty Scorsese's *Taxi Driver*, and Alan Pakula's *All the President's Men*, to name a few (quite a few).

By the time *Rocky* finished its theatrical run, most of the great stars of the golden era of Hollywood would have made their last film: John Wayne in *The Shootist*, 1976, Gary Cooper in *The Naked Edge*, 1961, Humphrey Bogart in *The Harder They Fall*, 1956, Barbara Stanwyck in *The Letters*, 1973, Ginger Rogers in *Harlow*, 1965, Greer Garson in *The Happiest Millionaire*, 1967, Edward G. Robinson in *Soylent Green*, 1973, Marilyn Monroe in *The Misfits*, 1961, Esther Williams in *Magic Fountain*, 1963, Judy Garland in *I Could Go On Singing*, 1963,

Spencer Tracy in *Guess Who's Coming to Dinner,* 1967. These stars were replaced by a new group of actors, more ethnic and many from New York: Robert De Niro, Al Pacino, Sylvester Stallone, Robert Duvall, James Caan, Jack Nicholson, Bill Murray, Jane Fonda, Meryl Streep, Diane Keaton, Debra Winger, Goldie Hawn, Robert Redford. The great British actors Laurence Olivier and Vivien Leigh were also replaced with the "working-class" actors Michael Caine, Albert Finney, and Peter O'Toole.

New screenplay writers Robert Town, William Goldman, Paul Schrader, Paul Mazursky, and Lorenzo Semple Jr. were now center stage, replacing I. A. L. Diamond, Ernest Lehman, Clifford Odets, Dudley Nichols, Ben Hecht, and Charles McCarthy.

As we headed into the 1980s, there was a new set of rules. Directors, having shown great box office clout, were given much freedom:

The Godfather (1972)
Domestic: $134,821,952
+ Foreign: $133,533,589
= Worldwide: $268,355,541
In today's dollars: $1,598,461,781

The Exorcist (1973)
Domestic: $232,906,145
+ Foreign: $208,400,000
= Worldwide: $441,306,145
In today's dollars: $2,475,182,056

Jaws (1975)
Domestic: $260,000,000
+ Foreign: $210,653,000
= Worldwide: $470,653,000
In today's dollars: $2,179,818,203

Close Encounters of the Third Kind (1977)
Domestic: $135,189,114
+ Foreign: $171,700,000
= Worldwide: $306,889,114
In today's dollars: $1,261,437,250

Of course George Lucas's:

Star Wars (1977)
Domestic: $460,998,007
+ Foreign: $314,400,000
= Worldwide: $775,398,007
In today's dollars: $3,187,196,564

And

Rocky (1976)
Domestic: $117,235,147
+ Foreign: $107,764,853
= Worldwide: $225,000,000
In today's dollars: $984,954,784

The directors' new freedom didn't always mean great pictures, but it did give all of us filmmakers, directors, producers, and writers a chance to take a chance. If a one-in-a-million film like *Rocky* can bring in close to one billion dollars, anything is possible, as in the *Rocky* story itself.

CHAPTER NINE

A very different fight film

RAGING BULL (1980)

WHILE WE WERE SHOOTING *New York, New York* in 1976, Bob De Niro asked Bob Chartoff and me to read *Raging Bull: My Story* by Jake LaMotta. The book was a memoir of the former boxing champion of the 1940s who had made his reputation as a fearless fighter who could take (and seemed to enjoy) punishment from his opponent as few boxers do.

De Niro was fascinated with the book, always carrying a copy around, and when there was an occasional break in the shooting of *New York, New York*, he would be reading some part of Jake LaMotta's story.

I read the book and saw not only a fight film (we had just done *Rocky*) but a look into the soul of LaMotta and what the violence in the ring had brought to his life outside the ring.

I told De Niro that Bob Chartoff and I would be interested in producing *Raging Bull*. He then told us that there was a problem: the rights belonged to the Italian producer Dino De Laurentiis (*8½, Serpico, Barbarella*). I thought, well, that's that. Why would De Laurentiis give it up? Somehow De Niro persuaded de Laurentiis to turn the rights over to Chartoff-Winkler, and we agreed to develop a screenplay.

On the *New York, New York* set Bob De Niro pointed to Scorsese and said he wanted Marty to direct *Raging Bull*, and there was no one else, period. I was surprised, because Marty had told me he'd never liked boxing, and although he liked *Rocky*, it just wasn't his passion. His passion was the book he was carrying around, *The Last Temptation of Christ* by Nikos Kazantzakis, and he asked if Bob Chartoff and

I would produce *that* film. *The Last Temptation of Christ* was about as far away from *Raging Bull* as one could imagine, as LaMotta was a man who had very human obsessions: jealousy, rage, and violence. *The Last Temptation of Christ* was about a humanized Christ figure and the temptations all people, even Christ, have. Bob and I had worked with many talented people in the past, but Scorsese and De Niro represented a whole new way of approaching filmmaking with a passion that was infectious. We went to work on both projects.

Screenwriter Mardik Martin, who had gone to New York University with Scorsese and had worked on *Mean Streets* and *New York, New York*, went to work on a draft of *Raging Bull*. Martin was pretty much on his own, as Scorsese, after the long editing period on *New York, New York*, directed *The Last Waltz*, his documentary of the last performance of The Band, and directed the musical play *The Act* starring Liza Minnelli; he was not yet up to working on *Raging Bull* full time.

De Niro, Bob Chartoff, and I were disappointed in Martin's *Raging Bull* draft. It was a pretty standard biographic film script: LaMotta as a youth (getting into trouble), starting to fight (losing, winning, losing, winning), meeting women (marriage, divorce, marriage), and not much of the passion the character needed and De Niro insisted on.

In September 1978, Marty Scorsese had collapsed on a trip to the Telluride Film Festival and was hospitalized in New York and very ill. De Niro, was who was visiting with me in Los Angeles, flew to New York and spent time in the hospital, where the doctors told him Scorsese was in danger of a brain hemorrhage. As Marty recovered, Bob held his hand and talked to him about the most important thing in Marty's life, directing movies. Marty slowly recovered, and his passion for *Raging Bull* took over and soon matched De Niro's.

Paul Schrader, who had written the great script of *Taxi Driver*, agreed to write a new draft of *Raging Bull*, which he completed expeditiously. It was very filmable, it went back and forth in time, but it was ultimately "cold." We thought the best way to proceed was to have Marty and Bob go off and do a draft themselves based on Schrader's work and LaMotta's book. They went to the La Samanna Hotel in St. Martin, worked for four weeks, and came back with an exciting new draft. Where Schrader's draft was cold, Marty and Bob's draft was passionate, dramatic, and unconventional.

Now that we had a script that all of us liked (an understatement), we set about getting United Artists on board to finance the film. The studio had gone through a management change, and the executives we had dealt with making *New York, New York* and *Rocky* were gone. A new group had taken over, and those execs were preoccupied dealing with a crisis on the big-budget troubled film *Heaven's Gate.* Two new executives, David Field and Steven Bach, were hired to run United Artists, and their first call was to tell me and Bob Chartoff that they definitely would not finance *Raging Bull.* I didn't tell Marty or Bob, and I arranged a meeting at Marty's apartment for Field and Bach to meet with De Niro, Scorsese, and me. I met the UA executives in the lobby of Marty's apartment building, and Bach said he didn't know why we were meeting, as they had told me quite clearly that they had absolutely no intention of making the picture. I told Bach and Field that I wouldn't accept that position and that they should hear Bob and Marty's take on the film. As the meeting started, Field said he not only hated the script, but he also hated Jake LaMotta, saying, "He's no better than a cockroach." De Niro was furious, and I asked Field and Bach to leave. I then told Bob and Marty not to worry, we would be making *Raging Bull,* and it would be with United Artists.

Bob Chartoff and I went to work on "Andy" Albeck, the new CEO of UA (and Bach and Field's boss) who had a background as UA's international finance executive with close ties to Transamerica, the insurance company that owned UA. We made it clear to Albeck that there would be no *Rocky II* if there was no *Raging Bull.* We were serious; it was not a bluff.

We got the green light for *Raging Bull,* and UA got *Rocky II* as well as *Rocky III, Rocky IV, Rocky V, Rocky Balboa,* and, years later, *Creed* and *Creed II.*

The uplifting family drama made the darker masterpiece possible.

Bob De Niro started preparing, and just as he'd had to be an expert with the saxophone to play Jimmy Doyle in *New York, New York*, he had to learn to be a great fighter to play Jake LaMotta. Jake trained De Niro for months, to the point where Bob was so good that Jake had him fight a couple of professional fighters (Bob was so muscular and so trim, the fighters never recognized him as the movie star). He lost two of the bouts but gave a pretty damn good showing as a prizefighter.

Marty saw Joe Pesci in an independent film, *The Debt Collector*, and he was sure he was a natural for Jake's brother, Joey. Pesci then mentioned that he knew a maître d' at a local Italian restaurant, Cathy Moriarity, who, although she had never acted, would be a good Vikki LaMotta (Jake's second wife). We tested Cathy and never looked at the film. Bob De Niro, Marty, and I knew while we were shooting the test that she'd be perfect, and she was. Her lack of experience was handled patiently in Marty and Bob's hands, and she gave a realistic, tender, dramatic, and sexy performance. Joe Pesci, who apparently had some very distant relationship with mob guys, was inventive, tough, and very believable.

UA, because they were concerned with the problems they were having on *Heaven's Gate*, stayed far away from *Raging Bull*, giving us an opportunity to make it in black-and-white and cast it exactly how we wanted. It was one of those rare instances that a studio was hands-off from all creative and financial decisions once they approved our budget.

The shooting of the early scenes took place in Marty and De Niro's old neighborhood on the Lower East Side of New York. Although it was twenty-five or thirty years after LaMotta had lived there, it maintained its authenticity; the neighborhood swimming pool where kids met, the small apartments, the shops, the restaurants, and the streets all were familiar to Marty. The meeting/dance hall where Jake meets the neighborhood priest and goes off with Vikki was the same one Bob had hung around in as a teenager. The storefront Mafia hangout was still where it was when Marty was growing up. Bob De Niro and Marty were in constant communication. They were closer in spirit and action than any director and actor I had ever seen; they would finish each other's sentences or nod or look at each other sometimes without a word and understand what the other person was thinking.

The early scenes with Jake and Vikki meeting, dating, and falling in love were calm, quiet, and subdued, except for a passionate scene before a fight when Jake poured ice water on himself to cool his "ardor" (that was a new one for me). The later scenes between the two of them, with Jake's irrational jealousy, brought a whole different dimension to the film. Some of it was in the script, and Marty and Bob enhanced that part of LaMotta's character so that he was just as violent toward the people he loved as the opponents he fought in the ring.

Although I had been at rehearsal, I was shocked when Marty started shooting the scene where Jake confronts Vikki in a jealous rage, slaps her around, and, as she walks down the street, accuses her of fucking his brother. She runs from him, he continues to beat her, and she taunts him with, "I fucked all of them. What do you want me to say? I fucked all of them: Tommy, Salvy, your brother, all of them. Yeah, I sucked your brother's cock. I sucked his cock and everybody else's on the fucking street. You're nothing but a fat pig, selfish fool!"

Jake then goes to his brother's house and beats him viciously in front of his brother's wife and children. No film out of a major Hollywood studio allowed for the language that was exchanged in these scenes. No one at UA saw our dailies, so no one complained, and once again the filmmakers enjoyed a tremendous amount of freedom. Was our good luck based on United Artists' preoccupation with *Heaven's Gate*, or did they simply trust Bob Chartoff and me because of the success of *Rocky*? I don't know to this day.

Jake LaMotta was around for the Los Angeles shoot. He was very helpful and had a surprisingly good recollection of each fight. Marty was determined not to repeat himself, and each fight had to have its own individual story. Marty also found new ways to shoot the punches and the fighters receiving the punches. That caused the shooting to be slower than the norm while makeup, "blood," and props were reapplied. The effect was stunning and was made even more authentic by the black-and-white film.

After we finished the fight sequences, we shut down the production for ten weeks to allow Bob to gain the forty pounds he needed to play the older LaMotta. Bob and I had discussed the possibility of him wearing a "fat suit" and prostheses rather than risk the health problems of adding and then losing the weight in such a short period of time. Bob felt strongly that the additional weight would affect all aspects of his character: body movement, breathing, and even his voice. In the long run the weight gain contributed to the great performance.

While the production was in hiatus, our editor, Thelma Schoonmaker, put together a couple of sequences, and we were knocked out by the rhythm of the quiet dialogue scenes followed by an explosive, passionate scene. We knew we were on to something very, very different.

We were now prepared for Bob's return from his "eating" trip in Europe. His diet was mostly very rich foods, and he stayed away from physical activity. It worked so well that one day the door to my office opened, and a big, heavy man walked in and gave me a smile (more like a laugh), and it took me a couple of beats before I recognized a man I had known for ten years! It was the heavier, older Jake LaMotta. It was Bob De Niro.

As we prepared the Miami sequences, the construction department came to me and needed specific instructions on how to build the jail cell Jake is thrown into after he's arrested for soliciting minors for sex. They knew from the script that he punches the wall, but having been around the set and seen the intensity of Bob's performance, they wanted to be careful not to make the wall he punched too hard (or too soft). After rehearsals, I told them that in order for Bob to perform (act), it had to be as real as possible. They didn't soften it very much, and when Bob screams, "I'm not an animal!" and pounds the wall, I really thought he'd break his hands. The "I'm not an animal" line came from Bob, and it has echoes of the first scene in the picture where an offscreen voice shouts, "What are you, an animal?" In Schrader's script he had Jake masturbate in his cell, but Bob and Marty nixed that and brought Jake's rage out by pounding on the cell wall. We finished the shoot in Los Angeles with a very different Jake LaMotta. Now that he wasn't fighting, the violence in LaMotta's character was contained.

On the return to New York to complete the filming, we shot in the very same nightclub where Jake was the MC/bouncer years before. In a beautifully awkward scene Jake finally embraces Joey, whom he had been estranged from since Jake attacked him in front of his family.

A few months later I flew to New York to see Marty's first cut (Bob Chartoff was preparing another film in Europe). It was long (aren't all first cuts?), but the force of the film was evident even at this early editing stage. A couple of weeks later Marty had me return to

Martin Scorsese, Irwin Winkler, and Robert De Niro
Raging Bull

New York. He had made changes in the structure and cut about ten to fifteen minutes, and the film really flowed. Marty wasn't sure about the use of *Cavalleria Rusticana* opera music that one of the assistants had

cut into the opening credits by mistake. He felt it might be too romantic. But finally Marty kept it in and enhanced it with the slow-motion
shot of Jake LaMotta warming up in a boxing ring. The combination
of the beautiful melody and the grace of De Niro's warmup was a stunning opening sequence for the movie.

Our sound editor, Frank Warner, had done an exceptionally
good job for us on Rocky, but he didn't want to use anything from that
film. He set about to make new punches, and every conceivable sound
ended up in the boxing ring. Just like after Rocky, Warner was so committed to originality that he destroyed most of the original ring effects
after we finished our sound mixing so they could not be used again.

The complicated sound mix with the original grunts, punches,
dialogue, and music went on for months, sometimes seven days a
week. As we neared our release date, we had to deliver the film to the
laboratory on a Sunday night the week before our opening. By then,
the crew and all of us were exhausted, and I was starting to question
my hearing. I told Marty that we had to wrap that midnight and the lab
was staying open for us to deliver our tracks. We were to open in New
York that Friday. We had one scene left to mix. It was in the Copacabana
nightclub, and the coauthor of LaMotta's book, Peter Savage, playing an
anonymous customer, asks for a drink, a Cutty Sark. After raising the
volume on the sounds of the glass, gulps from other customers, and
music in the background, Marty said that he couldn't hear the words
"Cutty Sark." I replied that all of us were stone deaf at this point and
probably would never be able to hear it clearly. We were going to wrap
and turn everything over to the lab. Marty said, "In that case, Raging
Bull is no longer a Marty Scorsese picture, and I want my name off."
I said, "Fine," and it went to the lab for printing. That's Marty's commitment to his work and every detail. When Marty presented me with
an award at the Chicago Film Festival several years later, they played
excerpts from many of my films and included the Copacabana scene.
Marty smiled and said now he could hear "Cutty Sark."

When we showed the film to Andy Albeck and the rest of the UA
staff, there was not a sound in the screening room when the film ended

and the lights came up. Albeck walked to Marty, shook his hand, said, "Young man, you are an artist," and left.

We opened in New York on November 13, 1980, at The Sutton on Fifty-Seventh Street. Marty and I stood in the back of the theater and were dismayed by the bad sound. I complained to the manager, who angrily informed me that he had bought six new speakers at $49 each at Radio Shack just for *Raging Bull*. We, of course, had spent about a million dollars to get the sound right.

Raging Bull received mixed reviews initially but got eight Academy Award nominations. Bob won for Best Actor and Thelma for Best Editing. The Best Picture Oscar went to the very *Ordinary People*.

Raging Bull is considered one of the finest movies, if not the finest, in modern filmmaking. The film has been deemed "culturally, historically, and aesthetically significant" by the United States Library of Congress and was selected for preservation in the National Film Registry in 1990. It has been recognized by the American Film Institute as one of the 100 Greatest Movies of All Time. *Time* magazine named it as one of the All-Time 100 Movies. *Variety* named it as one of their 50 Greatest Movies. The National Society of Film Critics named it one of 100 Essential Films, and the Motion Picture Editors Guild listed it as the best edited film of all time. The critic Roger Ebert named *Raging Bull* one of the 10 Best Films of All Time.

Even though the executives at UA had looked at De Niro, Marty, and me and said no one would want to see a movie about a cockroach, what they never understood was that De Niro and Scorsese were capable of making Jake LaMotta, in spite of his flaws, a man you understood and sympathized with, a man with a soul.

CHAPTER TEN

De Niro and Pacino have The Right Stuff

TRUE CONFESSIONS (1981)

HOLLYWOOD HAS HAD A fruitful history with films that picture the Church through a rose-colored lens. *Going My Way*, with singing, baseball-playing priest Bing Crosby and a very grandfatherly "father" played by Barry Fitzgerald, enjoyed great box office success in 1944. It won seven Academy Awards including Best Picture, Best Actor for Bing Crosby, and Best Supporting Actor for Barry Fitzgerald. Paramount followed it up with Bing Crosby again playing a priest (opposite Ingrid Bergman) in *The Bells of St. Mary's*, and that rather mediocre film did a great deal of business.

Bob Chartoff (Bob was back from Europe) and I were looking for something very different after *Raging Bull* when we read John Dunne's novel *True Confessions*. It was no *Going My Way* by any means, and there were no singing priests. The Roman Catholic Church in Dunne's novel was about ambition, money, secrets, gold rings to kiss, and gold vestments to wear.

Set in post–World War II Los Angeles, *True Confessions* is about two brothers, one a very ambitious monsignor of the Roman Catholic Church and the other a cynical homicide detective.

Although John Dunne was reluctant to adapt his book, saying he was finished with the subject when he finished the book, we persuaded him and his talented wife, Joan Didion, to write the screenplay when we explained that there was no screenplay writer who could capture John's cynicism and humor. Also we would pay them handsomely. John smiled, as he always liked to be in on a deal (and friendly gossip about it).

Considered two of the greatest actors of the time, Robert Duvall had won an Academy Award for *The Great Santini* and was nominated for *Apocalypse Now*, and Robert De Niro won for Best Supporting Actor

Irwin Winkler and Robert Duvall
True Confessions

in *The Godfather Part II* and of course for Best Actor in *Raging Bull*. They had for a long time wanted to work together. De Niro, after reading the script, felt that the priest character, Desmond Spellacy, should be a bit plump, soft-spoken, and deliberate, about as far away from Jake LaMotta as imaginable. Duvall liked the idea of playing Tom Spellacy, the tough homicide detective, as it too was different from the quiet lawyer/consigliere to Marlon Brando's Godfather.

Bob Duvall had worked on Broadway with the director Ulu Grosbard in Arthur Miller's *View from the Bridge* and recommended that we meet. Although Grosbard liked the script, he was hesitant about leaving his successful Broadway career to direct a movie. His last movie, *Straight Time*, had starred Dustin Hoffman, who was also the *Straight Time* producer. Although they had worked together successfully previously on Broadway, Hoffman had taken over *Straight Time*, shut

Grosbard out of the editing room, and "betrayed" him. I believe our relationship with De Niro and Duvall and the talent and charm of John Dunne brought him around, and he committed to direct.

The plot was pretty grim. A young woman's body is found horribly murdered, dissected, and bloodless in a vacant lot, not dissimilar to the tabloid-famous Black Dahlia murder some years before. In *True Confessions* she is called "the Virgin Tramp." The murder is never shown in the film, but the results of it are even more violent. Tom, investigating the crime, finds the murder scene, a pornography studio with a blood-soaked bathtub and rooms full of discarded, ugly, sex and

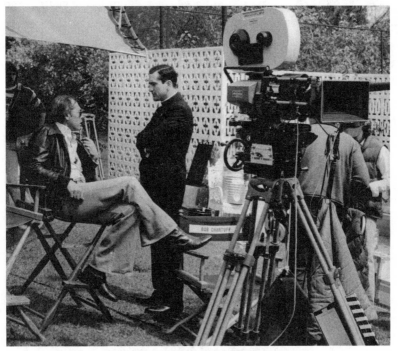

Irwin Winkler and Robert De Niro
True Confessions

murder tools. He goes through the room with the harsh, glaring sunlight coming through the filthy windows as an almost religious experience. That crime scene is in sharp contrast to the gold and glitter of the Catholic Church.

Both De Niro and Duvall's characters were complex: Duvall as the uncompromising cop who covers up for the church when he finds a priest dead in a whorehouse, while Des sweetly sends his cranky but dedicated teacher (Burgess Meredith) out to pasture when he's too outspoken in his criticism of the church. The LA Police have no compunction about accepting small bribes, and the Cardinal has no compunction about accepting big donations from crooked parishioners. The Cardinal, played with dignity by Cyril Cusack, looks away and covers up the financial corruption, which is a precursor to the cover-up of the sexual molestation that rocked the Los Angeles Diocese years later, with the church paying hundreds of millions to the victims and the forced retirement of Cardinal Mahoney in 2012. Desmond Spellacy operates as the church fixer with charm and great manipulation.

Joan Didion, Bob Chartoff, John Dunne, Irwin Winkler
True Confessions

Tom Spellacy, on the other hand, deals with corruption with violence and anger.

Both actors (as they always do) prepared vigorously for their roles. Duvall rode with the LA police, participated in a stakeout of a crime in progress, visited a murder site, and monitored a lie detector test. De Niro wanted a scene that would show his character's complexity, that in spite of being in the company and companionship of the LA rich and powerful, he was still a humble priest. John and Joan wrote Des coming home from a golf game into a tiny, stark room with nothing but a small cot, dresser, and open closet. De Niro patiently undressed, very carefully folded his clothes, meticulously hung up his trousers as he prepared for bed, and never said a word. It was a lesson in acting (and writing and directing).

The performances of all the actors were praised by the critics, and the two Bobs shared Best Actor Awards at the Venice Film Festival in 1981. The *New York Times* review called *True Confessions* "quite simply . . . one of the most entertaining, most intelligent and most thoroughly satisfying commercial American films in a very long time." But it never, however, achieved much of an audience. Was it too tough, too cynical?

AUTHOR! AUTHOR! (1982)

In the summer of 1981 Margo and I wanted a change. I had gone from film to film for fifteen straight years. Not that that was a hardship— most of the films were fun and satisfying. Our boys were grown and pretty self-sufficient. Bob Chartoff and I decided we would only make the Rocky films, *True Confessions*, *The Last Temptation of Christ*, and *The Right Stuff* together, as, after seventeen years, Bob wanted to spend most of his time on philanthropic endeavors, and I was still keen on making movies.

When shooting films in New York I had managed to attend a night course on Shakespeare at NYU, and when in Los Angeles I had studied Shakespeare at UCLA. I had studied, read, and watched plays by Shakespeare all my adult life. There was a Shakespeare course at Oxford in England. I applied, was accepted, and Margo and I rented a small cottage near the school. I had fondly thought of Oxford from the films set there that I saw growing up and that left a deep impression on me, but I was very different from the seventeen-year-old I had been when I was starting out at New York University in Greenwich Village.

At Oxford I was assigned to read the Shakespearean romances. The class was small, and we not only studied the plays but were asked to act out different scenes. I was better at reading than acting and found myself getting bored. There was, of course, no Internet in 1981. Not many American newspapers or magazines were available, and British television left a lot to be desired. The town had many pubs and one or two decent restaurants. I was not only bored but disappointed.

A couple of weeks into our stay, I got a very welcome call from Sherry Lansing, who was the president (first woman) of 20th Century Fox. A year before I had worked on a screenplay with Israel Horovitz titled *Author! Author!* about the trials and tribulations of a Broadway playwright who lived with his extended family in Greenwich Village. Horowitz had written scripts for me in the past (*The Strawberry Statement* and *Believe in Me*) and was a very successful playwright (*The Indian Wants the Bronx*, starring a then-unknown Al Pacino, won an Obie Award for Best Play in 1968). Sherry Lansing was calling about *Author! Author!* I was quite surprised when she told me she liked the script and wanted to make the movie. I was surprised because I hadn't given her the script and it had been developed at a rival studio, United Artists. It didn't take long for Margo and me to pack our belongings and leave the bicycle-riding faculty and students of Oxford behind. Little did I know what was in store for me.

Back in Los Angeles, I found that *Author! Author!* had been given to Sherry Lansing by the director Arthur Hiller (I never found out how Hiller got it). Hiller had directed some very good movies (*The Americanization of Emily*, written by Paddy Chayefsky) and some not so good (*Love Story*, a big box office success). His last film, *Making Love*, was groundbreaking, its plot innovative for the time: a happily married man finds his passion not for his wife but for another man. It was buried with a very limited release after Nancy Reagan told the new owner of Fox Studios, Marvin Davis, that she and Ronnie hoped "He didn't make those kinds of movies." Hiller was a pleasant, low-key, kindly man who loved working and wanted to cast and start *Author! Author!* quickly. That was OK with me; I was happy to be back.

Al Pacino, with a string of great roles behind him (*Godfather, Godfather II, Serpico, Dog Day Afternoon*) and his success with Horovitz in *The Indian Wants the Bronx*, was a natural to play Ivan. Al responded to the idea of playing a Broadway playwright with an extended family of children. He wanted to get away from the grim characters of Michael Corleone and Serpico to play the intelligent and sweet but troubled Ivan.

The story was right out of Horovitz's playbook. Ivan has problems at home: his wife, Gloria (Tuesday Weld), is having an affair and is leaving him and not taking her children. She lets him know that they are his to take care of. *His* girlfriend, Alice (the leading lady in his play, Dyan Cannon), wants to move in with him but doesn't like children. Ivan can't come up with a second act for the play that pleases him (and his director).

If Ivan is in trouble, it didn't compare to Al Pacino's relationship with *his* director, Arthur Hiller. Rehearsals in New York started off polite but not particularly warm. Hiller and Pacino danced around each other the first couple of days. By the end of the first week, with everyone seemingly comfortable, Pacino asked Hiller about how he thought he should play one potential scene. Hiller told Al that Jack Lemmon (whom he'd directed in *The Out-of-Towners*) could do the scene and wouldn't need to discuss how. I was as surprised as Pacino was by Hiller's reaction. From that moment on I felt as if I was holding my hands out trying to prevent two high-speed trains heading toward each other from colliding. The animosity continued, and after the second week of rehearsals Hiller was so upset with Pacino (and Tuesday Weld), he asked me to fire him. When I asked him why he didn't just quit, he told me that if I fired him, he would get paid; if he quit, the studio would probably sue him, and he certainly wouldn't get paid. I didn't fire him and he didn't quit, and once we started shooting, most active hostility stayed in the background. Horovitz was on set, and Pacino and Hiller had him frequently rewriting scenes, which caused lots of schedule changes. We kept shooting, and the dailies looked quite good as Pacino showed how well he could be funny and vulnerable. To catch the winter atmosphere, we flew to Gloucester, Massachusetts, for a climactic scene between Ivan and Gloria. Hiller set the scene in the bright winter sun, and Pacino, being delayed in makeup, was late on set. When Hiller blocked the actors to their places, Pacino was looking into the sun. He asked Hiller to restage the scene, as he was squinting, was uncomfortable, and it was affecting his performance. Hiller refused and told Pacino that if he had been on time, the sun would not have been shining in his eyes. Pacino calmly apologized for his delay, but Hiller would have none of it. Rather, he brought his anger from rehearsals and the coldness between him and Pacino into a full-blown, angry confrontation. Finally, Pacino walked off the set and into his camper.

Al Pacino and Irwin Winkler
Author! Author!

I tried to calm Hiller down, but he was not to be placated. It was embarrassing for not only Pacino and Hiller but the entire crew, who wished they were somewhere (anywhere) else. The 20th Century Fox representative who had flown in from California to spend a couple of pleasant days on the set (yes, the same David Field from the UA *Raging Bull* days) saw what was going on and stepped into his car and was driven back to New York before we knew he was gone. I spent the next few hours back and forth between Hiller and Pacino's campers. Pacino's position was that he had been embarrassed in front of the crew, and if Hiller apologized in front of the crew, he would return to work. Hiller refused, and the crew, just standing around, got an early lunch. Finally, Pacino suggested he would return to work but wouldn't talk to Hiller and didn't want Hiller talking to him. Hiller liked the idea of not talking to Pacino and agreed that Pacino and Hiller would talk to me, and I would be the voice of both Pacino and Hiller, with Hiller saying to me, "Ask Al to do it again," and Al saying to me, "Tell him OK." After about an hour *I* walked off the set, telling them both I was going to New York and they had better find a way to finish the film. They did.

There are some good and some bad circumstances in making most films. A very good one on *Author! Author!* was that we cast the actor/comedian Alan King in the role as the play's producer. He was a fine actor, funny, professional, and helpful on the set. We became friends for life. Alan was a performer who could hold the audience in the palm of his hand whether in a nightclub, on a stage, or at dinner. In May 2004 Alan came to Los Angeles to do a part in a film in spite of his being diagnosed with an advanced form of prostate cancer. He stayed at our guesthouse with his wife, Jeanette. Margo and I had some friends over for dinner, and Alan was very weak. On the short walk from the guest quarters to our house, he was bent over and needed Jeanette's help to take the few steps. When he approached the dining room where the guests were seated, Alan became "Alan King." He thrust his shoulders back, held his head high, and met our friends as if he had never been sick a day in his life. Alan and Jeanette went back to New York the next day, and, sadly, he died a week later. At Alan's memorial, Jeanette asked me to speak. Jay Cocks helped me write my short comments, and I followed Billy Crystal (no easy task). I thought of all the good times with Alan and the tough circumstances of our meeting and making *Author! Author!*

After Sherry Lansing stepped down as president of 20th Century Fox in 1982, I was asked to run the studio. Marvin Davis even invited Margo and me to dinner, seating us next to Frank Sinatra. That was pretty great, but I declined, remembering a meeting in Lansing's office when we decided to reshoot the ending of *Author! Author!* and I went off to New York to supervise the shoot and how Sherry told me she hated going back to her office and *not* making the movie.

THE LAST TEMPTATION OF CHRIST (1982)

On July 23, 1982, I was invited to lunch by a young Paramount Pictures motion picture executive. Jeff Katzenberg was looking for movies. I told him we had one project, but I doubted that he'd be interested. It was a script written by Paul Schrader (*Taxi Driver, Raging Bull*) based on Nikos Kazantzakis's controversial novel *The Last Temptation of Christ*, depicting a very troubled Jesus Christ faced with human temptations much the same as modern men and women face every day.

Marty Scorsese, who had asked Bob Chartoff and me to produce the film of the novel in 1975, had been committed to directing the movie version. Marty was given the book by the actress Barbara Hershey when they were doing *Boxcar Bertha* in 1972. With a religious Catholic upbringing, Marty has always been deeply committed to exploring the complexity of his religion and beliefs. We knew *The Last Temptation of Christ* would be very different from the biblical dramas of Cecil B. DeMille. Marty's film would be as far away from *The Ten Commandments* as one could imagine.

From *New York, New York* in 1976 through *Raging Bull* in 1980, we acquired and maintained an option on *The Last Temptation of Christ*. When *Raging Bull* was completed, we moved aggressively toward production of the film. Of course, we needed a screenplay. Although we were hesitant, because of his Calvinist upbringing, Paul Schrader was a natural to adapt the book. Paul could give the film the structure it needed, and Marty would bring the passion. We started talking to Paul in March of 1981, and he delivered a very thoughtful, daring outline in October 1981 and the script in March of 1982. Marty Scorsese, Bob Chartoff, and I were pleased but, of course, somewhat apprehensive now that we had to actually go out and get the financing and *make* the film. That's when the invitation to lunch came from Jeff Katzenberg.

Katzenberg, to my great surprise, actually wanted to make *The Last Temptation of Christ*. The next step was for Marty and me to meet in New York with Michael Eisner, Jeffrey, and their boss, Barry Diller. On October 11, 1982, we met in Diller's office and went over the budget and casting, and Marty presented his plans for directing the film. At the end of this very candid meeting, Diller said, "OK, let's make the movie." Interestingly, at lunch a week later Diller told me he wasn't that happy with the script of *The Last Temptation of Christ* but was going ahead based on his enthusiasm for Scorsese and that halfway through our meeting he'd known he wanted to make the movie.

With the surprisingly quick go-ahead from Paramount with no immediate demands for casting, we set out for Israel, as we wanted the locations to be as authentic as possible (or at least to see what those original locations looked like). When we arrived at Ben Gurion Airport, there was a press conference waiting for us that the Israeli government had arranged. They were totally prepared for our visit, as was Israeli film producer Arnon Milchan.

We didn't have much time to catch our breath, as the next morning we met with the mayor of Jerusalem, Teddy Kollek. He was helpful to the point of indecency, leaving his office with us as we headed to our first location scout. When our mini-bus got caught up in a traffic jam, the mayor got out of our van and directed traffic to make sure we didn't waste any time. It didn't take long to visit several sites with Roman ruins, most of which could work for the film. We stopped off for a quick lunch with one of the Knesset members who headed the Economic Committee and continued on our day of scouting. The following day we started at 7:15 A.M. and walked for miles through ancient hills covered with either endless piles of rocks and sand or olive trees that seemed to be as old as the land itself. To make the next day's scouting more efficient, the government had a helicopter take us from one end of Israel to another, making me realize how small the country was. The pilots looked like teenagers and for security had their names on their uniforms blacked out. When we flew over Masada, they cheerfully brought the helicopter down on the open plain and brought out a basket of sandwiches—a picnic on one of the most famous sites in the Holy Land.

After another day of scouting we were all ready to have a quick meal and be off to bed. That was not to be. We had time to shower and change our clothes, and then it was drinks with President Yitzhak Navon and dinner with Teddy Kollek. The next day Marty Scorsese was

Martin Scorsese, Irwin Winkler, Margo Winkler, William Chartoff, President Yitzhak Navon
The Last Temptation of Christ location scout, Israel

waiting in the lobby of the hotel at 6:00 A.M. for that day's scouting; his enthusiasm was contagious, and no one minded the long days. We were taken to Solomon's Stables, an underground structure built by

King Herod to hold the platform of the second Temple. We were told we could shoot there with the permission of the Muslim authorities, and I was surprised by the cooperation between the Israeli and Muslim officials. As we left for another site, Bob Chartoff remarked how much better this was than sitting around the Russian Tea Room *talking* about making movies.

A final dinner with the Israeli film community and we decided to cancel our scouting trip to Tunisia, as we were certain we were better off in Israel because of the location, availability of crews and cast, and cooperation. Costs could be a problem, however.

Our next stop was Paris, where we were met by United Artists executives who told Bob and me that they had a full afternoon of press set up for us to promote *Rocky III*. Just what we needed! Afterward Bob Chartoff left Paris. Marty and I stayed on and had dinner with the director Bertrand Tavernier and a discussion about *New York, New York* and the Jimmy Doyle character Bob De Niro played in that film.

Once back in Los Angeles, Bob and I faced myriad problems on *The Right Stuff*. We were having problems with NASA and Senator John Glenn and budget disputes with The Ladd Company. We felt that *The Last Temptation of Christ* was in a very good place with Paramount, the Israel location, and the very good producer Barbara DeFina, who'd worked with us on *The Gambler* in 1974. We discussed our situation with Marty and turned over all our rights to his company. We had worked on *The Last Temptation of Christ* for the past six years and very intensely for the last two, but we couldn't give the film the attention it needed and deserved. Shortly thereafter Paramount changed management, and *The Last Temptation of Christ* was put on hold until Universal Studios agreed to finance the film in 1987 in exchange for Marty directing *Cape Fear*.

The Last Temptation of Christ, for its originality, brilliance, and passion, is a masterpiece, but its picture of Jesus Christ as a man was attacked viciously by many groups. In protest, the filmmaker Franco Zeffirelli shamelessly withdrew his film *Young Toscanini* from the Venice Film Festival in 1988 when *The Last Temptation of Christ* was invited. Other religious groups were much more forceful in their criticism. When *The Last Temptation of Christ* played at the St. Michael Cinema in Paris, the theater was set on fire, with several people seriously injured. In Mexico, Argentina, Turkey, the Philippines, and Chile the film was initially banned, and in the United States the theater chain General Cinema refused to show it. Blockbuster Video refused to carry the home movie version in their stores. Universal was offered $10 million by a church group, the Campus Crusade for Christ, if they would burn all copies of the film.

THE RIGHT STUFF (1983)

In 1964 Bob Chartoff and I met the author Tom Wolfe at the behest of Clay Felker after he published "The Girl of the Year," a cutting-edge story of New York celebrity "Baby Jane" Holzer. Clay thought it could be a vehicle for his then-wife, the actress Pamela Tiffin. We all met at Felker's triplex on Fifty-Seventh Street, and after several meetings Tom wrote a film treatment of his magazine piece. It was quite good, but at the time, Bob and I had no experience in putting together a movie, and we weren't able to turn Tom's work into a film. We did, however, keep in touch socially, and Tom asked us to produce a film of his nonfiction book *The Kandy-Kolored Tangerine-Flake Streamline Baby*. Unfortunately, we couldn't figure out how to make that great book into a movie either. Luckily that was not the case when he gave us *The Right Stuff*.

Bob and I read the manuscript and saw a sprawling, epic story of the American space program where the hero was not so much one of the much-heralded astronauts but the unknown test pilot Chuck Yeager. Our experience with an unknown becoming an American hero had been very successful with *Rocky*, and we told Tom's literary agent, Lynn Nesbit, we were interested in making a film of *The Right Stuff*. Chartoff and I were driving back from Lake Tahoe, where Bob was buying a home, when we stopped off at a gas station to call our office (this was in the days before cellphones) and were told that Universal Studios had also seen the manuscript for *The Right Stuff* and had offered $350,000 for the film rights. We didn't hesitate; we matched the offer and thereby prevented John Belushi from doing it as a broad (did he do anything other than broad?) comedy à la *Animal House*.

When our friends at United Artists got wind of our purchase, they asked to finance the development. And development it was. Evarts Ziegler, a literary agent, asked us to meet with his star client William Goldman, who at the time was the most successful and most expensive screenwriter in Hollywood (*All the President's Men, Butch Cassidy and the Sundance Kid*). He liked the book but said he couldn't find a handle on the structure for a screenplay, since Wolfe's book covered not only the space program but the early test flights of Chuck Yeager, which broke the sound barrier. After several meetings with Goldman and discussions about who in the book had "the right stuff," Goldman enthusiastically agreed to write the screenplay for a million dollars.

When Goldman turned in the script, we were surprised and quite disappointed. In spite of all our discussions, Goldman had left out the character who had the "right stuff," Chuck Yeager, and had just written (rather well) the story of the astronauts.

UA, on the other hand, loved Goldman's script and did a quick (too quick) budget of $16 million and announced they were prepared to green-light the film. We informed UA that we wouldn't go ahead with the current script and wanted Goldman to deliver his two contracted rewrites, this time featuring Yeager's character. Goldman refused, saying it was his job to write a script that the studio green-lighted, he had, he had his million, and he would not write another word. Bob and I knew we needed a writer who was not so traditional. We met with Phil Kaufman, who had written the original story of *Raiders of the Lost Ark* and had directed some very good films; one, *The White Dawn*, shot in Antarctica with Eskimos as actors under the harshest conditions, really impressed us. He, as a director, had to have some of the "right stuff" to pull off *The White Dawn*.

Phil loved Tom's book and said he would direct the film if someone else wrote the screenplay. We told Phil that we wanted *him* to write the screenplay, that we didn't want another writer's version and then a director's different version. He reluctantly agreed and wrote an excellent forty-page treatment that we were sold on and that he then quickly turned into a very good screenplay.

We told UA that we were now ready to make *The Right Stuff,* but they still preferred William Goldman's version. Reluctantly UA agreed to let us shop the script, and we quickly got a lot of interest from Michael Eisner at Paramount and Alan Ladd from his new company. Ladd, who had left 20th Century Fox after the great success of *Star Wars,* seemed a natural. He wanted to "see" the film before OK-ing it at a $20 million budget, so Phil made an elaborate presentation showing Ladd the characters, their interactions, and the plot. Ladd, impressed, said he could now "see" the film and would finance it, but he didn't want to spend money for expensive actors and cut the budget to $18 million. The budget restrictions gave us the impetus to look for fresh faces, and we found some excellent actors with little film exposure. We tried to put together a coherent group and make sure no two astronauts were too alike, as, in fact, they were all very clean-cut, WASP, career air force officers. We cast Ed Harris as the very proper John Glenn, Fred Ward as Gus Grissom, Dennis Quaid as Gordon Cooper, and Scott Glenn as Alan Shepard. The casting of Chuck Yeager was the most difficult. Bob and I felt the Yeager part was so much the center of the film, we could get a big star to play the role (we were thinking of Bob Redford) for little money. Phil listened but wanted the sometime actor/playwright Sam Shepard. We kept pushing, and Phil kept resisting (little did we know that Sam didn't really want to do the part). Finally, when we were close to our rehearsal date, we told Phil we couldn't wait any longer and to go with Shepard. Phil then stalked/ talked Shepard into playing Chuck Yeager. Boy, was he right.

Tom Wolfe had intended his book to cover the Mercury program in the early 1960s to Apollo in 1975, but he found Yeager so interesting, he went back to the 1940s with the breaking of the sound barrier and the great test pilots of that era. Tom never got around to writing about the Apollo program. When he finished with the Mercury program and was ready to move on to the later heroics, his wife, Shelia, said "I've got great news for you." Tom asked what the great news was, and she told him he had just finished his book. It was time to move on and pay some bills (even great art has to pay the bills). In this case it was Shelia Wolfe who had the "right stuff."

Haha

Defining the quality of the "right stuff" was never easy. Although Tom Wolfe used his great talent to describe it in literary terms, on film Sam Shepard takes on the laconic quality Gary Cooper played so well throughout his career: the loner who goes out and does his job, so sure of himself that he never looks for praise and never has to boast of his achievements.

Ed Harris, playing John Glenn, the first astronaut to circle the earth, had to be (as Glenn was) high-minded, clean-living, outspoken, and, in the end, courageous enough to go into space in a "sardine can." By the time we were preparing to shoot the movie, Glenn was a very influential United States senator who didn't like Tom Wolfe's portrayal of him. After we got NASA's vital permission to use their facilities, he pressed NASA into withdrawing their OK. That would have been a financial and practical disaster for the film. Bob Chartoff flew to Washington, met with a very reluctant head of NASA, and persuaded him to rescind his order in spite of Senator Glenn's pressure. Sometimes it's an unheralded bureaucrat who has the "right stuff."

Dennis Quaid with a grin of confidence played Gordon Cooper, who was one of the first test pilots to join the space program. At a lunch I had with Gordon Cooper before we started shooting, I asked him who was the best pilot to ever fly. With the same grin Quaid had assumed, Cooper hesitated a beat, looked at me, and said, "Of course I am!" We used it in the movie.

The most difficult part to portray went to Fred Ward playing Gus Grissom, the astronaut who was accused of "screwing the pooch" or panicking and prematurely opening the space capsule after it landed in the ocean, causing it to sink and for him to almost drown. Grissom claimed it was an accident, and most people believed him. It was a tough role for Fred to play, as Grissom was an American hero who was killed in 1967 when Apollo 1 caught fire during a pre-launch test at Cape Kennedy.

Phil Kaufman, who lived in San Francisco, used a cadre of local artists he had known or worked with before: Caleb Deschanel, the

Sam Shepard, Levon Helm, Irwin Winkler, Philip Kaufman
The Right Stuff

cinematographer for George Lucas's first film, *THX 1138*, and Francis Ford Coppola's *Apocalypse Now*, and Walter Murch, Coppola and Lucas's sound editor. Phil chose to shoot many of the locations in San Francisco, as he had excellent access there (we were able to close down streets for our reenactment of John Glenn's heroic ticker-tape parade after his flight). We were also able to shoot for two days on the aircraft carrier USS *Coral Sea*, to the chagrin of Margo, as they wouldn't allow women on the ship in 1983. Edwards Air Force Base was absolutely essential to our early test-pilot sequences, and through Chuck Yeager we had unlimited access. Yeager even offered to give me a ride in an F-14. I foolishly declined.

The limited budget made us find ways to produce unusual visual effects on the cheap. The special-effects team used some very old-fashioned tricks to show Yeager's X-1 climbing into the atmosphere

Irwin Winkler, Chuck Yeager, Margo Winkler, Charles Winkler
The Right Stuff

and in freefall after engine failure. Our Special Effects supervisor, Gary Gutierrez, dropped the X-1 model from the roof of a highrise in downtown San Francisco, then simply reversed the film to show its climb into the atmosphere.

With so much to cover between the intimate story of the astronauts and their training, Chuck Yeager breaking the sound barrier, the political atmosphere under President Johnson, the German scientists brought to America, the press, and the Russian space program competition, the shooting took a lot longer than anticipated, which caused concern at the Ladd Company. We knew the film was special, so we had our team of editors put together a very rough version to show to the Ladd Company. It was met with enthusiasm. When we had a cut of the film at three hours and eleven minutes that represented what we thought of as final, we arranged a screening at the Northpoint Theatre in San Francisco. Alan Ladd insisted that two or three scenes we had cut for time be reinstated. It was brave of Ladd and certainly unusual, as I have never before or since had a studio executive suggest adding scenes to an already long movie.

After John Barry and Phil Kaufman couldn't agree on the tone of the score for *The Right Stuff*, we went looking for a composer. I happened to be in Paris, and the composer Vangelis, who had won an Academy Award for his score for *Chariots of Fire*, met me for dinner at the small bistro L'Ami Louis. In probably one of the most unusual "auditions" ever, Vangelis played the score for me on a number of water and wine glasses, some half, some quarter filled, some filled. He manipulated the sounds with his fingers, rubbing the rims of the glasses, and actually "played" his proposed score. In fact, Vangelis couldn't come to California to meet with Phil and/or work there, but I've often wondered how that wineglass score would have sounded on a piano or played by a full orchestra. We were a couple of weeks from our final mix, time was running out, and Bob Chartoff and I wanted Bill Conti, obviously because of *Rocky*. Bill asked what our thoughts were, and that was easy: something between Holst's *The Planets* and Dvořák's *New World Symphony*. Conti took the idea of those two pieces (and whatever else gave him inspiration) and won the Oscar for Best Score.

On October 16, 1983, we had an afternoon reception for Washington's political elite and a flyover by the U.S. Air Force. That night at the Kennedy Center, *The Right Stuff* had its first public screening. It really wasn't very public: only Washington's biggest players were in attendance (Henry Kissinger sat behind me). The film played great (as it always did). The *Washington Post* called it "a great American movie in a new epic form"; *Newsweek* had a cover picture of Ed Harris as John Glenn with the caption *Can a movie help make a President?* (it didn't); *Time* magazine, when magazines had massive circulations and influence, had a ten-page spread glowing about *The Right Stuff*. The audience at the Kennedy Center was cheering the ending of the film to the patriotic score, when Dennis Quaid as Gordon Cooper lifts off for the solo flight of the Mercury program.

I couldn't wait for the opening day. *The Right Stuff* was sure to be a box office hit: great reviews, great media coverage, great characters, funny, moving, and patriotic to boot! I drove to Grauman's Chinese Theatre on Hollywood Boulevard to watch the crowds storming into the theater and to see and hear their great reactions to the film, just as we had gotten in our screenings. When I got to the theater, my expectations diminished quickly when there were no crowds, no lines. I thought the theater manager had let the large crowds in early to avoid a riot. But inside the Chinese Theatre the audience was sparse (at best). By now, deep down I knew we were in trouble. Did the *Los Angeles Times* have the wrong time in its listings? Of course they didn't! I got back into my car and drove to Century City, where *The Right Stuff* was also premiering. Same . . . no one there. Later that afternoon my son Adam, who was a student at Beverly Hills High School near Century City, told me his teacher had arranged with the theater that her students could see *The Right Stuff* for free instead of going to school the next day. Adam, puzzled, said, "Dad, no one signed up."

When your son's high school classmates would rather go to school than see your movie, you know you're in trouble.

The Right Stuff was ultimately nominated for eight Academy Awards, including Best Picture, but lost to *Terms of Endearment*, a not very good tearjerker (Debra Winger dies of cancer at the end). Bummed at the loss of the Best Picture Oscar, Margo and I passed up the Governors Ball and all the after-parties and took our three sons in their tuxedos and a long, long limousine to our own after-party at Fatburger.

PART IV

THE 1980S ONCE AGAIN brought a wave of change to the Hollywood studios. With the success of the blockbuster films of the previous decades, the studios were no longer for sale at a discount. Now, new blood was coming in and wanted to invest and build. No more Kirk Kerkorian to sell off the assets. Now the new owners wanted to invest and grow.

In 1982, the Coca-Cola Company bought Columbia Pictures. Also in 1982 Texas oilman Sid Bass brought in Michael Eisner to run the sleepy but asset-rich Walt Disney Company. The Japanese electric company Matsushita bought MCA and Universal Studios in 1990, and Marvin Davis, a Denver oilman, bought 20th Century Fox in 1981.

For filmmakers, it was a time of growth, when content was king. George Lucas shepherded *Star Wars: The Return of the Jedi* and *The Empire Strikes Back*. Steven Spielberg directed *E.T. the Extra-Terrestrial, Raiders of the Lost Ark,* and *Indiana Jones and the Temple of Doom*. Stanley Kubrick directed *The Shining* and *Full Metal Jacket*. There were comedies: *Tootsie, When Harry Met Sally,* and John Hughes's *Sixteen Candles, Ferris Bueller's Day Off,* and *The Breakfast Club,* and Robert Zemeckis's *Back to the Future*; and the political films *Platoon, Good Morning, Vietnam,* and *Born on the Fourth of July*. Bob Chartoff and I produced *Rocky II, Rocky III, Rocky IV, The Right Stuff, True Confessions,* and *Raging Bull,* and I, with the aid of my sons Charles and David, produced *Revolution, Author! Author!, Round Midnight, Betrayed, The Music Box,* and *Goodfellas*. As we headed toward the end of the century, the future looked bright. Not only was content king, but the theaters changed from small or very large stand-alone theaters to conglomerate multiplexes with comfortable stadium seating and excellent sound systems. Yes, going to the movies became an event.

CHAPTER ELEVEN

The Cold War stars in one movie, the Revolutionary War in another, and one very fine movie doesn't get made

REVOLUTION (1985)

The Stinkers Bad Movie Awards
Stinker Award (Winner) 1985
Worst Picture (*Revolution*)
Irwin Winkler (Producer)

I'M USUALLY PLEASED WHEN one of the films I produced or directed gets an award. I'm not sure about the one *Revolution* got: the "Stinker Award for Worst Picture." I wonder who runs The Stinkers Bad Movie Awards and who the runners-up are.

In 1985 I spent four months in the damp, cold rain of King's Lynn, Norfolk, England, watching *Revolution* being shot from a script I loved and had worked on with a very fine writer, Robert Dillon, only to be awarded the Stinker Award. It wasn't that bad, was it?

I had always been curious about the American Revolution. Sure, I knew about the Boston Tea Party, Benedict Arnold, Nathan Hale, and George Washington. I didn't, however, know much about the men and women from the working class—the farmers, shopkeepers, and clerks—who fought the war. So I thought I'd find out. One of the best parts of making movies is the development: taking an idea, studying it, researching it, and finding the characters and incidents that make a movie. Books, newspapers, magazines, and very often old films are a pleasurable source of inspiration.

Some very good films had been made on the subject; D. W. Griffith's *America* (1924) and John Ford's *Drums Along the Mohawk* (1939) stand out but somehow aren't about the men in the boat looking up at the distinguished (and very well dressed) figure of General George Washington as they crossed the Delaware in the cold winter of 1776.

Coincidentally, I read an article about a Vietnam farmer who went to a nearby village with his young son to sell his small crop and finds his son missing. He discovers his son was taken forcibly to serve in the Vietnamese army. The farmer enlists in the army himself and spends years searching for the young man. I believed that we could use that story as a way to dramatize some of the events that went on in the Colonies from 1775 to 1783. Robert Dillion was able to turn such an incident into a personal story set against the epic battles that took place between the well-equipped, highly trained British redcoats and the poorly armed civilian fighters opposing them.

Warner Bros., where I had a first-look deal, was skeptical about a period costume drama, as they had financed their own costume drama, Stanley Kubrick's *Barry Lyndon*, starring my old friend from *Nickelodeon* Ryan O'Neal. They were on the fence but liked our script and would distribute the film and advance some of the budget if I got a partner. They suggested Goldcrest Films, an English production company, that had had a great success with the Academy Award–winning film *Chariots of Fire*. I promptly met in London with their CEO, Jake Eberts, who also liked Dillon's script, and he in turn suggested I give the script to Hugh Hudson, who had directed *Chariots of Fire*. It all seemed so easy. Hudson wanted to direct *Revolution*, Goldcrest would finance the production if we shot film in England, and Warner Bros. would distribute. I should have been suspicious, with everyone involved liking the script. I was apprehensive about shooting the American Revolution in the country America had fought, but they convinced me that England had a lot of hamlets, wide-open areas, and houses that hadn't been changed in two hundred years. According to Goldcrest, there were stacks of costumes, rifles, cannons, and props from the period available and cheap (available, yes, cheap, no). And, oh, by the way, a group of dentists in Norway were putting up some of the financing, so we'd have to shoot one or two scenes there. So now we were going to see the Americans defeat the British with British money, a British director, British crew, British locations, and throw in Norway too! I should have run back to the safe shores of New York right then. But I stayed the course (just like the early patriots, but they won).

CAA pitched both Michael Douglas and Robert Duvall for the Tom Dobb role, but Al Pacino's name came up, and Hugh Hudson and Goldcrest and I were very enthusiastic. I liked Al, had worked with him on *Author! Author!* and believed he could bring realism to Tom Dobb.

Irwin Winkler and Al Pacino
Revolution

Donald Sutherland, Joan Plowright, Nastassja Kinski, Steven Berkoff, and the singer Annie Lennox rounded out the rest of the (mostly British) cast. Actually Al Pacino and I were just about the only Americans looking after the Colonies.

The weather in the north of England was terrible as we started the shoot. It rained so heavily, we had to stop shooting constantly to allow the actors to dry off (and have a hot cup of tea). Getting some of our heavy equipment moving, as the mud was very thick, was a time-consuming, expensive, daily undertaking. Because of the size of the production, the costumes, props, and the sets, we had no cover (standby scenes the production can shoot if weather cancels out shooting), so we were forced to just stop until the weather cleared. When the grip department had to move heavy cannons in the mud, we found our crew insufficient and had to bring in extra crew from London (hard to find and very expensive at the last minute), and some of the nonprofessional locals who were used as background players quickly left when they were asked to stand in the rain while a shot was being slowly, slowly set up (we rounded up some other locals who didn't care or were too desperate to care). That last group was happy to get a hot meal from our canteen.

Hugh Hudson, who had a great visual sense, spent much of his time involved in the movement and placement of the dress extras, the cannons, equipment, and the battlefield. He barely had time to spend with the actors. Al Pacino was constantly trying to get his attention to talk about his character and the motivation of the scenes, to no avail. Once the rain stopped, we started to move at a reasonable pace in spite of Al Pacino's coming down with a bad cold that turned into pneumonia. Al, to his credit, looked almost at the point of collapse but kept working. Bad luck followed us as we changed locations. Setting up a difficult shot, the crane driver parked the massive piece of equipment overnight on a steep hill, only to find the crane in a nearby river the next morning after a massive sudden rainstorm. Not only did it cost us time (and money) to rescue the crane, but quite a bit of acid had flowed from the equipment into the river. That was an ecological problem that didn't please the local officials.

Goldcrest kept pouring money into the production, and at that point I offered (they accepted) to contribute my entire fee to the production. Margo and I rented a house outside of King's Lynn and were able to have groceries from Harrods picked up when the driver went to London to deliver the film to the lab.

Dealing with a group of actors on a distant location is difficult at best. In King's Lynn there were no good restaurants, bars, or first-class hotels to escape to at the end of a long day. Usually on a location like this there is quite a lot of flirting and some passionate love affairs (and some drunken fights). We had the heavy drinking and a couple of fights but not much love. Nastassja Kinski had a boyfriend in Paris and was always asking us to change the schedule so she could get away for a long weekend. I accommodated her once, and she returned to the set two days late and threw the whole production into a last-minute change in shooting (at heavy expense). Sid Owen, the young actor playing Al's son, was a real trouper, but we had to adapt our shooting for his work hours, and that too became a problem. When Donald Sutherland arrived, it was a burst of fresh air—he was prepared, ready to work, and only complained when one of the Goldcrest executives showed up and blew cigar smoke in his face.

We finally finished shooting and headed back to London for editing. Margo and I rented a flat in the center of London, and every day I went off to the editing room to sit with Hudson. We tried to make sense out of some action scenes and good performances, but the story that had worked in script form certainly wasn't working on the film we were viewing. It was tiring and frustrating, especially since I kept reminding myself how much everyone had "loved" the script. What had happened?

Warner Bros. happily announced that *Revolution* would be released stateside for the Christmas holiday. That shortened our editing time considerably (and, believe me, we needed more time). While editing, I received David Rayfiel's draft of *Round Midnight*, the movie about an expatriate American jazz musician living in Paris in the 1950s that grew out of *New York, New York*. I was ready for Paris and a nice quiet musical after all the sounds of rifles and cannons on the set and in the editing room.

We opened at Christmas to no business and terrible reviews. Warner Bros. quickly pulled the picture from release, and Goldcrest took a big financial hit and took a hiatus from film financing for a time. Margo and I went off to Paris and *Round Midnight*.

Over time, Hugh Hudson and Al Pacino reedited *Revolution* and added Al's voice-over, but it didn't help or change much. No one seemed to care except the folks who handed out the Stinker Award for Worst Picture.

ROCKY IV (1985)

I've often thought that the political and social climate could affect the response to a work of art, and a work of art could affect the social and political climate as well.

Since the first *Rocky* we had continued Rocky's story, his triumphs and failures (occasionally).

By the mid-1980s the Cold War was raging, and President Ronald Reagan was facing down the Russian Communist regime, demanding that they bring down the Berlin Wall. We decided to symbolize the conflict with Rocky fighting a Russian opponent. The Russian fighter Ivan Drago, trained on high-tech equipment, is as heartless as the politicians in Moscow. Rocky's original nemesis, Apollo Creed, avoids training and commitment, preferring instead to wear an Uncle Sam hat and dance to James Brown's "Coming to America" when he faces down Ivan Drago. The result is dramatic and tragic.

After Sylvester Stallone, who was directing his own script, saw at least a hundred actors, fighters, and stuntmen, he asked me to meet Dolph Lundgren for the Drago role. Lundgren was a Swedish, highly educated (a Fulbright scholar at MIT), six-foot-five karate master. I met Dolph at a gym on West Forty-Seventh Street in Manhattan. He towered over me and certainly looked Russian (and dangerous). I agreed with Sly that we had a worthy opponent. Drago the Russian, who is controlled and manipulated by his comrade superiors, and Apollo, the freewheeling, confident, successful businessman and fighter, were well matched.

Both Carl Weathers (again playing Apollo Creed) and Dolph Lundgren had to do quite a bit of preparation for the filmed fights. So that the actors don't end up actually hitting each other (after all, we still had the dramatic scenes to shoot), every move in the ring had to be carefully choreographed: the opponent's head had to fall back at the split second the glove is about to hit his face, or he's to protect his stomach when a fist heads toward him. Dolph and Carl ended up as combative as the fictional characters they were portraying. At one point Dolph actually picked Carl up and threw him across the ring. Carl was furious, walked out of the ring, and said he wasn't coming back. Dolph apologized, and Carl came back but never really forgave his fellow actor. The continuing animosity, however, paid off in the ring when Drago actually kills Apollo viciously and Rocky must redeem his friend by fighting Drago. In the preparation for that fight, on location in Vancouver, Sly took a punch from a stand-in fighter and ended up in the emergency room with his blood pressure dangerously high. We had him flown to Saint John's hospital in Santa Monica, where he spent four days in the intensive care unit.

The fight between Drago and Rocky represented the underdog Rocky versus the high-tech Russian Drago. The training sequences were a contrast in styles. Starting with the everyman approach, Rocky trained in the snow with farm tools and natural obstacles, while Drago was coached by scientists with the most modern equipment. The Russian Communist versus the American is played out not only in the difference in the training sequences but in the depiction of the members of the Russian politburo (one looking very much like Mikhail Gorbachev, the Russian president) in attendance and the few familiar trainers and friends in Rocky's corner as the fight took place in Russia on Christmas day.

The *New York Times* in a 1986 editorial said it very well:

The New York Times

War-nography
January 8, 1986

Yevgeny Yevtushenko, the poet, and other Russians decry a wave of recent American movies as crude Soviet-bashing propaganda, even "war-nography." They have in mind movies like "Rocky IV," in which Sylvester Stallone, the prizefight champion, travels to the Soviet Union to battle a huge, merciless boxing machine named Ivan Drago.

The Soviet critics are right that some recent American films do portray Russians as villainous caricatures. But "Rambo" and, even more, "Rocky IV" also bear a somewhat different moral, one that has less to do with nationalism than populism.

A generation ago, at least until Sputnik, it was Americans who thought of themselves as the pioneers of science, Americans who tooled around in the latest cars, Americans whose laboratories conquered dread diseases or produced the latest weapons. To us the Russians were impostors, pathetically claiming credit for the airplane, telephone, television. We knew they were backward peasants who, if they rode at all, did so in droshkys; Soviet industry couldn't mass-produce inexpensive cars.

The iconography of "Rocky IV" is very different. The movie cedes science to the Russians. It is the dreaded Drago who trains on Nautilus-like machines, whose vital signs pulse brightly on computer screens, whose performance is monitored by sophisticated sports doctors. It is Rocky, meanwhile, who becomes the peasant underdog, training in the rural snows, pulling sleds, pushing boulders and climbing icy ridges.

His ultimate victory in the ring symbolizes more than the triumph of U.S.A. over U.S.S.R., more than simplistic chauvinism. The deeper message that Mr. Yevtushenko and his colleagues miss is even more simplistic: The losers are the educated, the elite, the high-tech intelligentsia of any society. The winner is the peasant, the child of nature, the little guy, the common man.

That's not American war-nography; that's universal box office.

In 2018, as we were in production on *Creed II*, once again America was at a standoff with Russia. The FBI and Congress were investigating Russia's efforts to influence the presidential election between Donald Trump and Hillary Clinton. Although the Russians deny any interference, Congress was considering sanctions against Russia, and the Justice Department has appointed a Special Counsel to investigate. In 2018 we seemed to be back to the Cold War.

The political influence of *Rocky* couldn't be more apparent than the American State Department's statement on the Ukraine a couple of years earlier, when Secretary of State John Kerry said, "We don't believe this should be an East, Russia–United States—this is not *Rocky IV*."

DESSA ROSE (1988)

When you pick up the phone and the voice at the other end says, "I feel terrible; this is the toughest phone call I've ever made," you know you're going to feel a lot worse than the caller, and it will probably be the toughest phone call you've ever received. That's the call I got from my friend Tony Thomopoulos, the president of United Artists, on July 22, 1988.

What was I doing in Charleston, South Carolina? I thought I was directing a film based on Sherley Anne Williams's novel set in the pre–Civil War South, examining the relationship between a runaway slave, Dessa Rose, and her white savior, the owner of a broken-down plantation. Dessa, based on a true character, led a revolt against a slave trader, killed an abusive white man, and was saved by Miss Rufel, who harbored runaway slaves on her isolated farm. Sherley Anne had written the book in response to William Styron's *The Confessions of Nat Turner*; she was "outraged by a certain, critically acclaimed novel of the early seventies that travestied the as-told-to memoir of slave revolt leader Nat Turner."

I had read a glowing review of the novel in the *New York Times*, took an option on the book, and had Sherley write her first screenplay. The premise I wanted for the movie was that even amid the darkest horrors of slavery, two seemingly helpless women could find strength in themselves and each other and persevere against the evils of the time. Several studios were after me for the project, and I decided I would produce it with my friend Tony Thomopoulos at United Artists. Sherley Anne and I enjoyed a close relationship as we worked on the screenplay. She was an accomplished poet but had never read a screenplay (or seen many films) and was inexperienced in the form and process. She was, however, very talented and enthusiastic. As we worked, Sherley Anne asked if I was directing the film. I had been thinking about directing a film ever since *Revolution*; seeing that really good script fail made me want to have more control over the the physical transfer from script to film. I told Sherley Anne I'd think about it. I went back through the book, worked through the details of the screenplay, and realized that my knowledge of slavery and the Civil War was largely (and falsely) based on my history courses in high school, some cursory reading, and a few movies (*The Red Badge of Courage*, *The Horse Soldiers*, *Gone With the Wind*). Time to correct that.

I talked to Tony Thomopoulus, and he assured me United Artists would back me with the necessary resources (crew, cast, and money).

We set the production in Charleston with Natasha Richardson and Angela Bassett playing the two brave women. Dessa, abused, beaten and pregnant, and Miss Rufel, clear-skinned, now poor and deserted with a slave-owning background, came together in sisterhood more familiar to 1985 than 1865. I had some problems casting the bad guy; several actors passed, and as we got closer to production, I was convinced that rehearsals would suffer if we didn't get the actor soon. When I called talent agent Ron Meyer, he had an idea (he always does): why not his client Donald Sutherland? Great idea, but he was busy, and Ron needed a few days to see if he could adjust Sutherland's schedule. Cicely Tyson and Laurence Fishburne, both just starting out, were excellent in rehearsal (no surprise they went on to outstanding careers). All the locations were pretty well set and built.

One evening two weeks before we were to start shooting, my friend Jerry Perenchio called and asked if Margo and I would join him in New York for dinner that Saturday. When I told him we were in Charleston, he replied that he would send his plane (a big DC-9) to pick us up. The plane took us to the private airport at Teterboro in New Jersey, where his helicopter took us to Manhattan and a waiting limousine that drove us to our hotel, waited for us while we dressed, and then took us on to dinner with Jerry and his friend the singer Andy Williams. Dinner was lavish, and Jerry complemented it with rare and very expensive wines. After dinner we ended up at Jerry's apartment to admire the new Picasso he had just bought. At the end of the evening Jerry asked a favor: could he put his luggage on the plane taking us back to Charleston? Confused, I asked why in the world he wanted us to take his luggage to Charleston, South Carolina (and it was his plane, after all). Jerry responded very sensibly: he was going to take the Concorde to Paris, and he didn't want to go to the carousel to wait for his luggage, so he'd have his plane fly on from Charleston to Paris with his luggage, have it delivered to his hotel, and have it unpacked by the time he arrived. Makes sense, I guess.

Back in the reality of the unreal movie world, Donald Sutherland called to say he was able to rearrange his schedule and could do *Dessa Rose*. It was good news to get, with just three days before shooting (and a key role now cast with a fine, fine actor). Ron Meyer closed the deal at $600,000 with Tony Thomopoulos that morning.

That was the evening, just a few hours later, that Tony Thomopoulos called to say that he was making "the toughest call of his life" and that *Dessa Rose* was to be shut down. Kirk Kerkorian, owner of United Artists, was cancelling all movies in preproduction. He didn't want to incur any costs that might affect the balance sheet, as he was planning to sell the company. The studio was going to write off about $5 million in costs, including the $600,000 to Donald Sutherland that they had committed to only a couple of hours earlier. They would also pay all the salaries that were due as if the movie was made. Nobody had warned the president, Tony Thomopoulos, that the studio was being sold out from under him, and he suggested I call Kirk Kerkorian, who was on a boat someplace in the Mediterranean and wasn't reachable. I flew to LA and met with Steve Silbert, Tony's boss, and got nowhere. *Dessa Rose* was not to be a movie. I returned to the location in Charleston and told a shocked and terribly disappointed cast and crew what had happened. Margo and I packed up and headed back to Los Angeles. It was my first attempt at directing a film, and it ended sadly. I've recently reread the script, and it seems to me that Sherley Anne Williams's story of these two heroic women would be inspirational to so many women in our society who are still being mistreated and not granted the rights and privileges they deserve.

CHAPTER TWELVE
A trip to Paris pays off

ROUND MIDNIGHT (1986)

WHAT WOULD JIMMY DOYLE, the character played by Bob De Niro in *New York, New York*, do after the film ended? That was the topic of a lunch in Paris in 1984 with Marty Scorsese, myself, and the director Bertrand Tavernier. Tavernier casually asked if we were happy with the ending of *New York, New York*, and we told him we had shot several different endings and were never completely satisfied. Tavernier, who was both a film and a jazz buff, suggested that the talented but unappreciated saxophone player would probably end up as an expatriate musician in Paris, just like Lester Young and "Bud" Powell in the 1950s.

On the plane back to New York, I thought quite a lot about our conversation, called Tavernier, and told him I was interested in making a film about the Jimmy Doyle character. He was enthusiastic and thought we could base the film on the relationship of the pianist "Bud" Powell and Francis Paudras, a Parisian lover of American jazz. Bertrand also had worked on a previous film with the screenwriter David Rayfiel (whom I knew as a frequent collaborator with Sydney Pollack) and arranged for Rayfiel and me to meet. Rayfiel, as it turned out, was very familiar with the Parisian jazz scene, knew the players, and agreed to collaborate with Tavernier on the screenplay. Rayfiel's move to Paris made sure I'd come to Paris frequently, as Tavernier had never made an English language film (Margo and I ended up with an apartment on the Left Bank, which we kept for seventeen years).

With a good final script, I went to CEO Terry Semel at Warner Bros. (who had paid for the script and my trips to Paris) armed with a tight budget and got a very quick turndown. Semel was convinced there was very little (actually he said "no") audience for a jazz movie. I decided to contact the Warner Bros. division heads in France, Germany, Japan, the UK, and Italy and posed the question: "What would the revenue be in their market for an average jazz movie with no stars?" With those very conservative estimates, excluding the United States, we were more than covered for the cost of the film. Semel double-checked with those local managers and reluctantly gave the go-ahead.

We decided we would get musicians, not actors, for the leading roles. It would be difficult and expensive to have actors learn to play as well as the jazz legends we were going to portray (we did it with Bob De Niro learning the saxophone for *New York, New York*, but that took time, and Bob is one of a kind).

Bertrand knew the saxophonist Dexter Gordon, who had a long career playing with some of the great American bands in the 1940s and '50s. When Gordon wasn't playing with Lionel Hampton or Louis Armstrong, he was on the road in Europe, where he was well received in spite of bouts of alcoholism and drug abuse. We then put together a group of top musicians led by Herbie Hancock (piano), Bobby Hutcherson (vibraphone), Billy Higgins (drums), Ron Carter (bass), Freddie Hubbard (trumpet), and one of the great American vocalist/trumpeters Chet Baker. We hired Baker, who was living in Amsterdam, paid him $1,000 (he insisted on cash, no check) for one song, off camera. It had to be off camera, as Baker looked awful. The few teeth he had were black and rotted, he was very thin, and he looked (and was) strung out on drugs. It was sad to see, especially remembering the young, handsome Baker of the 1950s *West Coast Sound*. Three years after he worked on *Round Midnight*, Baker was found dead in the street outside his apartment in Amsterdam. It is believed he was murdered, then tossed out of a window in a drug dispute.

Gordon, with his six-foot-six frame, commanded the screen, and his casting was so perfect, he really didn't have to act and take on a fictional character. He *was* the character Dale Turner. His dialogue was not from the script; it was improvised, like the notes on his saxophone, delivered in a voice damaged by years of cigarette smoke and drugs—too unique for an actor to imitate. He had not only played jazz, he talked jazz. He not only played drunk, he was drunk.

Opposite Dale Turner was his French savior, Francis Paudras, played by François Cluzet, who had worked with some of the finest French directors (Claude Chabrol, Diane Kurys). Cluzet was short and slight, and Bertrand shot him so that he was always looking up to his idol. The bandstand was crowded with all the great musicians having a great time doing what they loved, going into live riffs and drifting into improvised solos rather than the standard prerecorded tracks that would have inhibited them. Dexter's presence and size crowded the stage except when Wayne Shorter joined the band. Recognizing that he no longer could compete with the much younger, vital, and talented fellow saxophone player, Dexter did what Dale would have done: got drunk. Also on the set of The Blue Note, meticulously recreated from

Irwin Winkler and French Minister of Culture Jack Lang
Presentation of Commandeur de l'Ordre des Arts et des Lettres

the original by production designer Alex Trauner, Marty Scorsese, who was at the birth of the idea two years earlier, played a tough nightclub owner and, like the the jazz musicians, improvised his slick dialogue.

Early in the shoot, I was asked to wear a jacket and tie on the set, as there would be a surprise special guest. At lunch, which was very French, involving several courses, including wine (white and red) and cheese (a full selection of the finest), the French Minister of Culture Jack Lang arrived. He kissed me on both cheeks, spoke rapidly in French, and to my great surprise awarded me with a medal proclaiming me Commandeur de l'Ordre des Arts et des Lettres. After shaking hands all around and giving a similar medal to Herbie and Dexter, the minister left with his aides, and we went back to moviemaking. It was unreal.

Also unreal was the house we rented for weekends on the beach in St. Tropez. The house was owned by the American psychiatrist Arthur Janov (primal scream therapy), and after arriving at night and awakening in the morning, we found we were on a nude beach when an older gentleman walked past our beachfront wearing nothing but a hat. Not a pretty sight. I was hoping to see Brigette Bardot on my first visit to St. Tropez. No such luck; it was, instead, the old man in the hat.

For *Round Midnight* the nightclub owner of The Blue Note was played by the blacklisted American director John Berry (*Claudine; East Side, West Side*). Between takes Berry gave birth to *Guilty by Suspicion*. I had very little knowledge of the Hollywood blacklist, and John, recalling his escape from a visit to his home by the FBI and his involvement with left-wing groups in the 1950s causing him to flee to Europe, intrigued me. It led to my writing and directing *Guilty by Suspicion* starring Bob De Niro, the very same actor who was the subject of the ending of *New York, New York* that brought us to *Round Midnight*. To quote the song Kander and Ebb wrote for *New York, New York*: the world goes 'round and 'round and 'round. It certainly does.

The critical response to *Round Midnight* was terrific. At the New York Film Festival all the showings were sold out (standing room only). The *New York Times* review was excellent, but the next day, when the film played in a commercial theater down the street from Lincoln Center, no one showed up. I could never understand why people fight to get into a screening at the festival and skip going the next day. The New York Film Festival was special in another way: my son Adam, who was a student at New York University, took Melissa Bomes, a classmate, to the screening of *Night and the City* on a date. They have been together ever since and gave Margo and me a beautiful granddaughter, Dani, now fourteen.

Bertrand Tavernier, Herbie Hancock, Irwin Winkler
Round Midnight

At the Venice Film Festival *Round Midnight* played to a sold out screening and standing ovation for Dexter and Bertrand. The official who called the cast up to the stage didn't consider the producer part of the filmmaking team and ignored me. Bertrand, however, insisted I join the applause, only for me to be embarrassed when one of the hundred or so photographers asked me to step out of the group when, I guess, he didn't want the producer to spoil his picture. So easy to be embarrassed by some unknown thoughtless photographer.

Dexter Gordon had an incredible life: from playing at the New York bebop nightclub the Royal Roost in 1947 to recording with some of the big bands in the 1950s, from prison terms at Chino and Folsom to a long stint as an American expatriate musical star in Europe, then nominated for an Academy Award for Best Actor for *Round Midnight*.

CHAPTER THIRTEEN

Two political films and a couple of Goodfellas

BETRAYED (1988)

EXCEPT FOR THE TITLE *Betrayed*, a description of the film might sound like a traditional romance. The pert, pretty newcomer to the wholesome Midwestern town meets a handsome, virile, widowed rancher living with his two small children and his mother. The pretty girl and the handsome man are attracted to each other and fall in love, and she also falls for his cute children and moves in with the family. The couple have the usual problems of adapting to each other: she from the big city isn't used to small-town ways, and he isn't very happy with her big-city ways. They fight, break up, are miserable, separate, and the children bring them back together. The movie *Betrayed* has lots of these same elements, except the pert, pretty girl is played by Debra Winger (nominated for an Academy Award for *An Officer and a Gentleman* and *Terms of Endearment*) and the rancher by Tom Berenger (Academy Award–nominated for *Platoon*). We soon find out she's an undercover.FBI agent, and he's a secret militant racist. So, no, *Betrayed* is not a romantic movie at all. The film opens with an ambush and murder, by a neo-Nazi right wing group, of Sam Kraus (played by Richard Libertini), a Jewish political talk show host. It was based on the suspected murder of Alan Berg in Denver, Colorado, in 1984 by Robert Mathews and his racist gang the Order. In our script the FBI sends an undercover agent, Katie Phillips (Debra Winger), to a small farming community in Idaho to investigate suspect Gary Simmons (Tom Berenger). The two meet in the local hangout, and before you know it they do the Western two-step and fall in love.

Gary, one of the most respected men in the community, is a decorated Vietnam veteran who wants to have no secrets from the woman he loves; he wants her to see what he sees, look at America the way he

Debra Winger, Tom Berenger, Irwin Winkler
Betrayed

does, and experience "his" America. Katie, who lost her family at a very young age, sees Gary's family as the one she never had and is eager to be part of it. What Katie finds out, however, is that Gary's world is full of hate, violence, and disappointment in America as he sees it taken over by blacks, Jews, and foreigners. That is the world Gary wants to share with Katie. It is one of family cookouts, country fairs, and hunting, but the cookouts feature cross burnings, the fairs boast racist songs, and the hunting is not of deer or elk but of a kidnapped African American who is killed as sport, just like an animal. Katie has to stand by and watch this part of sick America so as to maintain her FBI cover, and her love turns to revulsion. But the FBI, anxious to uncover the next ambitious terrorist plot, orders Katie to stay and sleep with the man she despises. Her burden is now to expose her lover and his family (now hers) for the crimes they have committed.

As I wrote this in 2018, I realized that thirty years ago in *Betrayed* we pictured some Americans who hated immigrants, Muslims, Jews, and homosexuals and plotted against the American government through violence and fringe political actions.

Are we seeing the same ugly scenes today?

MUSIC BOX (1989)

Little did I know when I read a newspaper story about a grandfather living in Cleveland, Ohio, who was accused by the United States Justice Department of falsifying his citizenship application, that not only would I make a movie about the man, but I would also uncover a remarkable coincidence.

The accused, John Demjanjuk, was a guard known as Ivan the Terrible in the Sobibor concentration camp in Nazi-occupied Poland during World War II. He changed his name when he became a naturalized U.S. citizen, worked in an automobile plant, and lived quietly with his wife and four children until his past was uncovered.

Intrigued by the characters and how the accusation must have affected Demjanjuk's family, I called Joe Eszterhas, whom I had been in touch with socially since he wrote *Betrayed*, and asked him to read the newspaper article. Joe was interested, and we spent several weeks working on a way into a movie. We decided to tell the story through the eyes of the man's daughter rather than the accused. To keep her intimately involved in the investigation, we made her a lawyer who takes on the defense of her father. The father, played by the East German actor Armin Mueller-Stahl, was a sad-eyed, soft-spoken, likeable man perfect for a doting, loving father and grandfather (just like John Demanjuk).

Eszterhas completed a very good first draft of a script, and I gave it to the director Costa-Gavras, even though we had taken a critical beating on our previous collaboration, *Betrayed*. I was curious when Costa-Gavras said he wanted to direct *Music Box*. He had directed so many political films—the renowned *Z* about the overthrow of a democratic government in Greece, *Missing* about a coup d'état in Chile, *The Confession* set in 1950s Czechoslovakia, and *State of Siege* in a South American dictatorship. I asked Costa why, after *Betrayed*, he wanted to do another political film, not a thriller or a romance. Costa laughed. He told me of his growing up in a small impoverished village in Greece after World War II. Every Saturday a man came trudging up the the hill to the town square, put up a large white sheet, and showed a Technicolor MGM musical, sometimes with Esther Williams, other times with Judy Garland or some other glamorous star, and of course with fabulous costumes and great big orchestras. That, Costa said, was a political film, seeing America in luxury, wealth, and full color.

We saw a bit of the kind of political influence films can have while shooting several weeks of *Music Box* in Budapest, which at the time was still behind the Iron Curtain. Margo and I went to a concert at Liszt Hall and were stunned when the Hungarian Symphony Orchestra played John Philip Sousa. Walking home later, we passed a movie theater with a big crowd of young people eager to get in to see *Rain Man* with Tom Cruise driving around America (especially Las Vegas) in a shiny Ferrari and beautiful clothes. Margo and I shook our heads; there was no way Communism could survive. And not long after that the Iron Curtain came tumbling down. Who would have thought *Rain Man* or John Philip Sousa were political? But they were.

With Costa aboard to direct, our first thoughts were to star Jane Fonda. Jane showed some interest and had some good ideas but decided against accepting the role. Ron Meyer, Jane's agent, liked the script a lot, and immediately after Jane passed, he suggested another client, Jessica Lange (that's a good agent). Jessica was a bit young for the part, but she had done some wonderful work and had an Oscar for Best Supporting Actress (for *Tootsie*) and had been nominated for *Sweet Dreams, Country,* and *Francis.* Before we cast Armin Mueller-Stahl we spent some time with Marlon Brando, who by this time was very heavy, out of shape, hard of hearing, and mumbling all his words. We gave up and realized we'd be a lot better off with a relatively unknown European actor.

Jessica liked the *Music Box* script and asked Costa-Gavras and me to meet her at her farm in Charlottesville, Virginia. The farm was set against beautiful rolling hills, and Jessica, dressed in blue jeans and

Costa-Gavras, Irwin Winkler, Jessica Lange
Music Box

a western shirt, made a perfect picture out of *Town & Country.* She had the part on sight, although she had some concerns about Ann Talbot (her character) being too glamorous. Looking at Jessica, I assured her we could unglamorize her, but it wouldn't be easy. Her partner, Sam Shepard, wasn't around, and I had looked forward to seeing him, since we hadn't gotten together since *The Right Stuff.* I never asked him if it was true that the character of the film producer Saul Kimmer was fashioned after me or Bob Chartoff (as was rumored) in his Pulitzer Prize–winning play *True West.* I did ask Sam some years later, and he smiled and wouldn't answer.

With a tough script and Jessica Lange playing Ann, I was pleased when we had quite a bit of interest from United Artists, Columbia, Paramount, and Universal Studios. Tom Pollock, the CEO of Universal, would finance *Music Box* on one condition: we had to make the accused innocent at the end. I explained, with no success, that showing the U.S. Justice Department falsely accusing Mike Laszlo defeated the point of the film and set back the prosecution of suspected World War II criminals (including the case against John Demjanjuk, which was still pending). But Pollock wanted a happy ending even at the cost of betraying Holocaust survivors. At that point I thought it best to go with Carolco, an independent financier that would ensure our creative freedom. As it turned out, one of the partners, Andy Vajna, was from Hungary, had some business investments there, and was very helpful in arranging the production when we shot in Budapest.

We were tempted to shoot the American part of the film in Cleveland but felt it was too close to the Demjanjuk story and decided on Chicago. The shooting went well, and the casting paid off. Jessica, Armin Mueller-Stahl, and the young actor Lukas Haas playing Jessica's son were giving honest, emotional performances. The courtroom scenes were sad and even more emotional, with the elderly actors relaying the actual stories of the terrible acts of brutality, atrocities, and murder committed by the Hungarian Arrow Cross Party.

I found time during the shooting to write a draft of a script about the Hollywood blacklist that took place in the 1940s and '50s (then called *Fear No Evil*) and was deciding if I wanted to direct that story. One morning as I was leaving my room to go to the hotel gym for my workout, I passed Costa going to the set. He had a terrible cold, was exhausted, and told me he hadn't slept in four days, worrying about his shots, the actors, the cameraman, the sets, everything. I asked myself, do you really want to direct a film? I did.

We traveled to Budapest for the climax of the film and had a fine local crew and an authentic location, but spending time shooting in a hospital there, I was sure I'd be better off sick in a hotel room. The place was dirty, with cockroaches crawling all over walls that hadn't been painted or washed in years; it looked more like a prison than a hospital.

Costa edited *Music Box* in Paris, and that gave Margo and me a chance to have some long walks, some great meals, and to see *Music Box* completed as a compelling, passionate, emotional film with great performances by Jessica Lange and Armin Mueller-Stahl.

The preview audiences were great. The film scored 90 percent excellent and very good, which was a fine response for a drama.

TriStar, the studio releasing and marketing *Music Box*, enthusiastically agreed to a December New York and Los Angeles date in time for the Academy Awards. It worked. Jessica got nominated for Best Actress (she didn't win), but *Music Box* won the top prize, the Golden Bear, at the Berlin Film Festival, where the Germans were very sensitive to the subject matter.

The story of *Music Box* in human terms rests with the sad, terrible coincidence of Joe Eszterhas's father being accused by the Justice Department of the exact same crimes as John Demjanjuk. Joe Eszterhas knew nothing of his father's activities in Hungary when I asked him to research Demjanjuk for a movie.

Art imitating life?

Life imitating art?

In 2004, in his book *Hollywood Animal*, Joe wrote about the Justice Department accusing his father of some of the very same crimes Ivan the Terrible committed, and a year after *Music Box* opened, I received the following letter from Joe Eszterhas:

JOE ESZTERHAS
570 FAIRHILLS DRIVE
SAN RAFAEL. CA 94901

Dec. 21, 1990

Dear Irwin,

I can't bring myself to talk to you but I love you and feel
a need to and I'll just put the facts down.

The day that I left L.A., my father got a summons from the
Justice Department's OSI section telling him he was the
subject of an investigation for his activities in Hungary.

I've spent the last two weeks in Cleveland with an attorney,
Gerry Messerman, grilling him about what he did.

Last Wednesday we received a copy of a book from the OSI
which my father wrote in 1936. It was published in 700
copies. He never had a copy in this country and made several
attempts to get it from Hungary through the years.

A translator and I translated it. It refers to Jews as a
wandering, selfish people going from house to house "in
search of gold, going from country to country, exploiting,
sucking out strength." It refers to Jews as "parasites."
It talks about "the anti-semitism which we respect to this
day, which we served and always will serve." It
talks about "raising the iron fist of power" against Jews.

It's the worst kind of filth. It makes anyone dirty just
reading it. It makes me feel like I'm covered in shit.

I don't understand how a man who raised me the way he did
could have written it. I suddenly don't understand a great
many things and will spent the rest of my life trying to sort
them out. The person that I thought I knew and loved is dead.

I can't concentrate on anything. I can't sleep and even when
I do bits and pieces of the previous two weeks come back to
me. Something's been torn out from inside me that I never
thought could.

I need time and I need to be around Stevie and Suzi.

GOODFELLAS (1990)

Living in Paris in 1986 while producing *Round Midnight*, my ritual was
to visit the English-language bookstore WHSmith on the rue de Rivoli
every Monday afternoon. There I could get the Sunday *New York Times*,

the *New Yorker,* and *New York* magazine. One week when I picked up *New York* magazine I devoured the excerpt from Nick Pileggi's book *Wiseguy* while standing in the aisle. I knew Nick from the 1960s, and when I called him in New York, he said his book hadn't been sold and that the agent handling the film rights was Bob Bookman at CAA in Los Angeles. When I reached Bookman, he said he had several interested buyers and was preparing to auction the book. I called Bookman's boss, Michael Ovitz, then the most powerful man in Hollywood (according to the cover story of *Time* magazine). Ovitz told Bookman to sell *Wiseguy* to me and then quietly asked me to help him sign Marty Scorsese as a client.

When I had a celebratory call with Pileggi, he told me he'd heard that Marty Scorsese was interested in the book. I hadn't worked with Marty since *The Last Temptation of Christ,* and when we connected, he told me that, yes, he wanted not only to direct the film but also to write the script with Pileggi. Scorsese and Nick Pileggi started working up an outline for the film, and I gave them my notes as they moved toward a script. Marty, however, got the go-ahead on the long-delayed *The Last Temptation of Christ,* so we put aside *Wiseguy* for a year and a half until he finished that film.

Nick Pileggi's book (we changed the title to *Goodfellas,* as there was a television series *Wiseguy*) was based on interviews he had done with Henry Hill, who as a teen went to work for the mobsters in the Lucchese family. His story is one of a criminal who moved from petty crime to major robberies to murder but also found himself part of a very back-slapping, warm, protective Mafia family. It was a compelling story that ends with Hill caught up in drugs, turning on his "family" and sending them to jail, and ending up "a schnook" in the witness protection program.

After Marty finished *The Last Temptation of Christ,* we set up *Goodfellas* at Warner Bros. Terry Semel called with casting suggestions, which were worse than I'd imagined. Tom Cruise for Henry Hill and Madonna for Karen. I called Mike Ovitz, who was Cruise's agent, and asked him if Cruise had even read the script, since he was so wrong for the part (and Cruise is an actor who has a very good sense about what roles he should play). Did Cruise want to be a cokehead? And Madonna we wouldn't discuss. Semel didn't pursue Madonna but insisted that

Martin Scorsese, Nick Pileggi, Irwin Winkler
Goodfellas

Marty and Cruise meet. They did, and that ended Semel's casting suggestions. Marty wanted the virtually unknown Ray Liotta to play Hill. I told Marty I didn't think he had the charm to capture the audience after all the drugs, stealing, and womanizing that Henry practiced, but Marty kept insisting, and I kept putting it off, and one night Margo and I were having dinner at a restaurant in Santa Monica with my friend Dick Zanuck when Ray Liotta came over to our table and asked to speak to me. In a ten-minute conversation he (with charm and confidence) sold me on why he should play Henry Hill. Marty was right.

I was in Chicago on location for *Music Box* when Barbara De Fina, our executive producer (and Marty's wife at the time), told me Marty was getting impatient with the studio delays in giving us a green light. Marty then called and reiterated his commitment to *Goodfellas*, but there was another film that he was interested in, and if Warner Bros. was not giving us an OK, he would take the other film and would do Goodfellas after. I knew that kind of delay could easily kill our film. I went to work on Semel, who told me that with our casting of Ray Liotta and Joe Pesci and our budget of $16 million he couldn't OK the film unless we had a major star for the other lead. After a lot of arguing, Semel said that if I gave him my word that we would get a major star for the third role, he would give Goodfellas the OK. I promised but really had no idea who would play Jimmy Conway. Marty had an idea. He called me the next day and had spoken to Bob De Niro, and we had our star.

Marty spent the rehearsal period encouraging the actors to improvise. By doing so, he gave the actors the freedom to bring some of their own experiences to the film. In rehearsal Joe Pesci told Marty the story of a mobster who beat up a guy who'd questioned his sense of humor. Marty embraced the idea, rehearsed it quite a few times, and then wrote the scene where Joe's Tommy tells Ray's Henry about being beaten by a cop, and when Henry laughs, Tommy says, "So you think I'm funny?" It turns into a violent, threatening scene, a classic. Terry Semel of Warner Bros. visited the set that day and complained that we were doing a scene that wasn't in the script. We were over budget, he was quite upset at our shooting an unauthorized scene, and he insisted that he wouldn't OK the company going to Florida to shoot a scene at the Tampa Zoo. We spent some extra money on plants, built the small zoo in Queens, shot mostly closeups, and put up a sign TAMPA ZOO. It was worth it to get the classic "So you think I'm funny?" scene into the film, and the Tampa Bay Zoo scene turned out quite good.

In another classic scene, Marty found a way to have Henry Hill not only impress his date, Karen, but to show the audience why the world of Goodfellas was so attractive and glamorous. Henry and Karen drive up to the Copacabana nightclub, where Henry ignores the line of people waiting to get in, walks right into the basement, is greeted by all sorts of tough characters, slips money to everyone he passes, and goes through the kitchen and into the nightclub, where the head waiter ignores the people behind the rope, greets Henry, and has a front-row table set up, and another tough-looking guy sends over champagne. It was a six-minute, continuous shot. It took us all day to set the actors, hide the lights, time entrances and exits, and have the Steadicam hit the focus marks. By six that evening we were shooting and had six or seven takes that were off just a bit either mechanically or dramatically. Finally, we did a perfect take, at the end of which the camera leaves Henry and Karen at their table and moves to the headliner at the Copa, Henny Youngman, whose classic line was "Take my wife—please." Youngman, a borscht belt comic, had been doing that joke for forty years and was fine in rehearsal. Now, at this moment where everything went off perfectly, when the camera hit him, Youngman actually forgot his line. Marty's meticulous rehearsal was ruined over a missed joke. An hour later, after five more takes, we got it perfectly, and the crew applauded Henny Youngman.

The glamour of the Copacabana moves very quickly to the ugly violence of a simple card game with a couple of friends. It's all fun and congenial until Tommy, always out to show how tough he can be, shoots the card game attendant, Spider, in the foot when he doesn't show him enough deference. A second card game with Spider in a foot cast ends up with Tommy shooting and killing Spider when Spider disrespects him with a "fuck you." There's not a moment of guilt or conscience among the "guys" as they witness poor Spider lying dead on the floor before them. What's the big deal about "whacking" a nobody? However, when you kill a "somebody," you can pay with your life. When Tommy again feels disrespected, he attacks "made man" Billy Batts (played by Frank Vincent), beats him to a pulp, and pays for it with a promise of being "made" by the bosses but instead is shot in the face— the ultimate "disrespect," since his family can't mourn him properly with a closed casket.

The life of crime offers Henry a beautiful, sexy, Jewish wife (played by Lorraine Bracco), a fancy suburban home, lots of cash, a beautiful mistress, lots and lots of drugs, and when he's in prison, he's supplied with the best food, liquor, and, yes, drugs too. In a brilliant,

twenty-minute, cocaine-fueled sequence Scorsese brings all the popular myths of the mob life to a screeching halt. Henry, snorting cocaine,
tries to sell guns to Jimmy, takes a load of drugs from his mistress,
picks up his wheelchair-bound brother, cooks dinner, watches out for
a police helicopter that he thinks is following him, and tries to get his
drug runner on a plane to Pittsburgh to deliver cocaine. Scorsese shot
it in quick, short takes, the actors constantly moving and the music
and sound effects constantly pushing the action forward. The viewer is
almost in a cocaine-fueled state when the sequence ends. Marty's vir-
tuoso filmmaking, aided by Thelma Schoonmaker's editing, inevitably
brought Henry Hill to his downfall. He has been brought down not
by the police, whom he has no respect for or fear of, but by the "mob,"
who he is sure will "whack" him for his drug dealing. They don't get
a chance; instead, Hill turns in his mob buddies and sees them sen-
tenced to long prison sentences, some to die in jail. He saves himself
and enters the safety of the witness protection program, where he complains, "I'm a nobody. I get to live the rest of my life as a schnook."
That's the last we see and hear from Henry Hill, who two and a half

Robert De Niro and Irwin Winkler
Goodfellas

hours earlier told the audience, "As far back as I remember, I always
wanted to be a gangster."

The first scene in *Goodfellas* was one of the most violent in a
violent film. After the "made man" Billy Batts makes a couple of snide

remarks to Tommy, he beats, stomps, and kills Batts. Henry, Jimmy (played by De Niro), and Tommy go off to Tommy's mother's for a late snack and some mother-and-son wisecracks, and Tommy borrows his mother's kitchen knife. The three men drive to a country road to bury Billy Batts. When they hear thumping from the trunk, they stop and relentlessly stab and shoot the still (barely) alive Batts. It's as bloody a scene as is imaginable, and it opens the film.

After we finished our editing and sound mixing, we were ready for our public preview. It was in the very conservative Orange County, California. Marty and I and all the Warner Bros. brass sat down in our reserved seats. The film started, the titles came on, and the projection machine ground to a halt. We were then told it would take thirty minutes to repair the projector equipment, so we all went next door for a drink at a bowling alley (not very calming for a nervous producer and director). When we returned to the theater, the film started (again), and this time someone in the audience yelled, "Get Marty Scorsese." When a chorus joined the chant, we got out of the theater real fast and found a more comfortable place for our next preview. Nobody called "Get Marty Scorsese" at the Encino screening, but when in that very first scene Henry opens the trunk of the car and the audience sees the blood-splattered Billy Batts, they start streaming out of the theater. I counted forty-two walkouts in the first few minutes of *Goodfellas* and two-thirds of the theater gone by the end of the film. When we left the theater, Marty wanted to avoid the Warner Bros. executives, whispering that the two of us should meet at the Beverly Wilshire Hotel to decide what to do about the next day's certain postmortem onslaught from Warner Bros. Sure enough, the Warner Bros. executives wanted a great deal of the language and violence cut. They went through scene after scene, and we stayed with the strategy of the night before, agreeing to try everything they suggested. It's hard to really blame them for their nervousness, given the audience reaction. Some films just need the media, critics, and word of mouth to let the audience know a film is special. That was the case with *Goodfellas*, and ultimately we barely changed much from the terrible preview screenings.

Henry Hill died in Los Angeles in 2012 at the age of seventy-two of natural causes. He was expelled from the witness protection program for narcotics trafficking (he never could accept being "just a nobody"). As an FBI informant he had fifty members of the Lucchese family arrested. Henry's boyhood idol, Paul Vario (played by Paul Sorvino), died in a federal prison in 1988. Jimmy Burke died in a New York State prison while serving twenty years to life for murder. Tommy DeSimone (played by Joe Pesci) was murdered by the Lucchese mob in 1979 at the age of twenty-nine.

Goodfellas was nominated for six Academy Awards, with Joe Pesci winning Best Supporting Actor; received plaudits from the Directors Guild, LA Film Critics, Venice Film Festival, Cesar Award, and Golden Globes; and was included in AFI's 100 Greatest Movies of All Time and selected for preservation in the National Film Registry by the United States Library of Congress. Not bad for a film that the audience fled the theater from as if they were being chased by a bunch of Goodfellas back in Costa Mesa (no, not Cosa Nostra, Costa Mesa, California). After our screening of *Goodfellas* at the Venice Film Festival, we sat down to a gala dinner at one of the city's most famous restaurants. In the middle of our pasta course we were surprised when the crew of the Warner Bros. private jet walked in with a load of Nathan's hot dogs from Coney Island. Steve Ross, the Warner Bros. honcho, had sent his plane all the way from New York to Venice just to surprise us with good old-fashioned American hot dogs. We were all feeling like "Goodfellas" that starry night in Venice.

CHAPTER FOURTEEN

A career change from producer to director,
back to producer (almost)

GUILTY BY SUSPICION (1991)

WOULD YOU BETRAY A friend to save your livelihood, or would
you stand by your principles and face the loss of your income, reputation, and possibly your freedom? We all believe we'd never betray
our friends and put them at risk. But do we really know what we
would do? That's the dilemma faced by David Merrill, the Hollywood film director played by Robert De Niro in *Guilty by Suspicion*. I
asked that question of myself many times as I wrote and directed the
1991 film.

David Merrill, on his return from a film assignment in Paris, is
greeted by his best friend and a pervasive atmosphere of fear and suspicion around him. Even as his friends greet him with a welcome-home
party, the FBI is secretively listing the license plates of the guests. The
House Un-American Activities Committee (HUAC) has been hunting
down members of the Hollywood community who are suspected of
being Communists or sympathetic to left-wing causes, even though it's
perfectly legal to belong to any political party you choose. Merrill was
never a Communist; his worst transgression was that he attended some
meetings and a ban-the-bomb rally years earlier. He is (politely at first)
asked to name friends or acquaintances he thought might be Communists or who had associated with Communists. No proof required. Just
give the names, knowing that those people would be blacklisted from
working in Hollywood. Oh, yes . . . they had the names already, so this

was a test of your patriotism too. If you didn't "name names," then you're not cooperating with the United States Congress, and you could be in contempt of Congress and imprisoned. Once you were branded as uncooperative, the Hollywood studios would blacklist you, and you became unemployable.

I wanted to tell this harrowing story after spending time in Paris with the expatriate blacklisted director John Berry. I worked on the script with the French director Bertrand Tavernier and the formerly blacklisted writer Abe Polonsky. As I worked on the script, I felt more and more committed to exploring the story of a man who stood up for what he believed in. I decided that directing the film myself would offer me that unique opportunity. I knew that by doing so, I would be giving up opportunities to produce other films, but once determined, I wanted to see it through. After many months of research and draft after draft, Polonsky wanted David Merrill to be much like himself, a Communist. I disagreed and was more interested in all of the innocents who were caught up in the undemocratic, divisive, life-threatening process. I decided to write my own screenplay and, with the encouragement of Tavernier and my friend Marty Scorsese, I decided to direct the film myself.

On and off for the past thirty years I've kept a diary of my workdays, phone calls, meetings, lunches, and dinners. I guess, somewhere in the back of my mind, I thought my experience in the actual moment-to-moment, day-to-day process of getting a film made would be of value someday. The process of casting and getting the financing for *Guilty by Suspicion* (*Fear No Evil*) is relayed below.

1988
September 12
Doing a lot of writing on blacklist script. While doing research found a funny story. The producer Milton Sperling was married to the daughter of Harry Warner. Sperling had some success (*Battle of the Bulge, Marjorie Morningstar*) and during the blacklist was called to his father-in-law's

office, where Warner told Sperling how upset he was with Milton's association with Communist groups. Milton, surprised, said, "Harry I belong to the Young *Anti*-Communist League. Warner angrily replied, "I don't care what kind of Communist you are—just get out."

Sadly, the blacklist didn't end with a laugh. It ended with disrupted lives, friends betraying friends, broken families, loss of work, imprisonment, and, in some cases, suicide. I am working on a serious mark on American democracy, the Hollywood blacklist.

September 23
I made a deal to give Abe Polonsky $50,000 to work on the screenplay. I don't think he will give me anything special, but I keep hoping.

September 27
Bertrand Tavernier called, and we had an extensive conversation on the writing I'm doing on blacklist script. He is full of ideas that he is eager to share.

October 21–23
I have a new draft of *Fear No Evil*, and the plot is good. The character himself is a bit of a problem, and it's one of writing. I will try to put some clothes on the principal character.

November 1
Went through Victor Navasky's book *Naming Names* and really liked the way Arthur Miller handled himself before HUAC. Try to make David Merrill as honestly heroic as Miller was.

November 12—Budapest
Wrote a good scene in the Budapest airport lounge waiting to leave. I'll have a full script when I get to New York and see what's next. I wonder if a film can succeed if the climax is an accused man standing

up to a committee of the American Congress with a flag draped in the background.

November 20
I tried to stay away from *Fear* all day and just glanced at it toward the end of the day. I was reading a book and came across this quote: "The KGB wanted me to plead guilty, repent, and give false testimony against my friends." That's what HUAC expected the witnesses in the U.S. to do. How can I make a U.S. congressional committee the same as the KGB?

November 22
Abe Polonksy came to the house in the evening and laid out his version of the story. I didn't like it at all and told him the version of the story that I already wrote. He liked it except for the family relationship, and he didn't have great ideas about that.

November 24
Tony Thomopoulos, former head of United Artists, is the first to read my version of *Fear*. He liked it a lot. Had good comments: felt that he liked David a great deal and found the story compelling. I asked him if he thought it was a movie, and he wasn't sure anyone would be interested in seeing it.

December 27—Aspen
My script of *Fear* is in good enough shape to get a reading. Giving it to Ron Meyer for Michael Douglas. Right after I spoke to Ron, I ran into Michael Douglas at producer Jerry Bruckheimer's party. Told him a little about it—rather, I tried selling him without meaning to. Abe Polonsky kidded that he and Gersh spoke, and if they waited long enough, he would get credit for my writing.

December 29
Ron Meyer admired the script but warned me about the potential (or lack of) audience for *Guilty by Suspicion*.

MICHAEL POWELL PRODUCTIONS

PLEASE REPLY TO:-

c/o Sound One, 8th floor
1619 Broadway
New York, New York 10019

June 6, 1989

Irwin Winkler
c/o THE GOOD FELLAS PRODUCTION
1619 Broadway, 4th floor
New York, New York 10019   Re: FEAR NO EVIL

Dear Irwin,

It's a beautiful piece of script writing – realistic, and human,
and tragic, and I am sorry to tell you that it has had it's day.
There was a time when England was an important country, and now it is
an old curiousity shop. Likewise, there was a time when every
country had its witch-hunts, and every country had its scandalized
liberals, and martyrs, but now, when politics and governments are
seen for the shams that they are – now when the young people of every
country are on the march, this beautifully written, tantalizing,
expert dramatization of a minor artist's battle for self respect
will not receive the gratitude and attention that it deserves.

Are we still friends?

Yours sincerely,

Michael Powell

A note from the great director of *The Red Shoes*, Michael Powell, who said that no one would see *Fear*, but it was a beautiful piece of writing about "an artist's fight for self-respect."

1989
January 6

Had meeting with Ron Meyer. He convinced me to take a screen credit on *Fear*. Why not? He also felt my writing credit was good for the actors:

it would mean I have an insight into the script, and that would make them feel comfortable with me as a first-time director.

I'm still a bit cautious about directing. I want to get it right, and that goes for casting too. Ron Meyer spoke to Michael Douglas, and he won't read anything for a couple of months. I'm thinking of Robert De Niro, although I'm sure he can't look at me seriously as a director after my having produced four pictures with him.

January 8
Joe Eszterhas said he didn't like *Fear* script at all.

CAA [Creative Artists Agency] agent Amy Grossman loved *Fear*. Had a couple of good comments and wants me to give it to Robert Redford. I'm afraid he will eat me up.

January 18
The reactions I am getting on *Fear* force me to look further into the character. I can't rely on too many compliments. It's of course flattering to go to Morton's on Monday night and have [talent agent] Ed Limato sitting with Mel Gibson and go out of his way to tell me he heard I had a great script. We did talk later in the week, and he is pushing for Richard Gere. I don't have Gere high on my list, but I won't say no, just in case.

January 23
I felt strange about Dick Zanuck. I'm sure he won't like *Fear*'s portrayal of his father, 20th Century Fox head Darryl Zanuck, and I'll have to change it to Harry Cohen of Columbia Pictures probably.

January 25
Worked for last couple of days on rewriting *Fear*. I have changed virtually the whole script.

February 9
Lunch with agent Jeff Berg. He likes *Fear* a great deal. Suggested we give it to Richard Dreyfuss.

Dawn Steel, CEO of Columbia Pictures, said she heard about *Fear* and asked to see it. Told her would give her first look when I finished rewrite.

February 24—New York
Dinner with Tom and Sheila Wolfe. I told him about the blacklisting period and was surprised that he knew almost nothing about it.

February 27
The *Satanic Verses*/Khomeini threats make *Fear* more important to me. Must speak out against intimidation of free speech and thought. I also believe I've done it so far in an interesting story.

Margo liked this draft of *Fear* a lot. I was shaken by Mort Zuckerman. Although he said he'd never read a screenplay before, his reaction was that he and no one else probably cared about the area, about movies, about Hollywood, and, more important, he knew that the main character would turn out to be a hero. That really unnerved me. Have I changed it too much to a Hollywood kind of story? Have I listened to too many people?

Dinner Saturday night with Clay Felker, Kimba Wood, and columnist Mike Kramer. I talked to Mike and Kimba about blacklist period and was surprised that a very smart political reporter and a federal judge knew nothing about the blacklist. I thought about Tom Wolfe also not knowing, and throw that in with Mort Zuckerman's comments, and I'm nervous.

February 27—Chicago
On the way in from airport, got a call from Allan Rich, a blacklisted character actor. He thought *Fear* was "great" and that I should do

everything in my power to make the film. His wife read it and said it was the best script she had read in five years. He said he would dedicate himself and work on the picture for free in any capacity.

March 1

Nancy Geller, an agent at ICM (the talent and literary agency), was enthusiastic about *Fear*. She wanted to sign the writer (I used a pseudonym). For her, the script had it all. She will talk to her fellow agent Peter Rawley about Richard Dreyfuss.

March 5

Don Johnson's agent called. Loved *Fear* and wanted to give it to Don. I told him to hold off. I don't think I want him.

Right now my top choice after Bob De Niro is Gene Hackman. He is just a little old, but I can rewrite his character to fit his age. I was very pleased with our meeting on Thursday; we had good rapport. He listened attentively, and we both were easy with each other. He is available, and I'd be surprised if he doesn't want to commit.

March 6—Chicago

Dawn Steel called, told me she liked *Fear* very much, thought the writing great (said I could write a script for her anytime). She said she couldn't concentrate on making the movie because of her new TriStar responsibility and wanted the weekend to focus on it.

Michael Nathanson of Columbia liked *Fear* a lot. He will talk to Dawn Steel and push her. He talked about casting, start dates, etc. I told him I wasn't interested in a deal for just a script—it had to involve a list of stars that made the picture a go. He asked me to send him the list.

Dick Berger of MGM passed on *Fear*. Said that although MGM was making films, he didn't think that they wanted to make *Fear*.

March 12
Dawn Steel told me that Marty Scorsese loved the *Fear* script (I didn't know they even talked, and when they did, why did they talk about my script?). Dawn told me that Marty thought Paul Newman would be great. I told her I wasn't sure about Newman. She said she was very strong to make the movie but wanted the weekend to reread the script. She also told Ron Meyer that she wanted to make the picture but wanted to reread. That's strange and suspicious. My experience is, the studio head never has the time or inclination for a second read.

All this activity is moving me into the game of preparing to direct the film, and I'm convincing myself that it can work.

Tony Thomopoulos told me that the story editor at Columbia told him to check out the "young" writer who wrote *Fear*. They didn't know the name.

Marty Scorsese was very, very complimentary about *Fear*. Really liked it. Had no criticism.

Ron Meyer called on Saturday. Thought the rewrites on *Fear* were great and loved the writing.

March 13
Dawn Steel and Michael Nathanson called. Nathanson said Dawn would do *Fear* with anyone. Dawn said only with a star. Apparently the change came after she spoke to her boss, Victor Kaufman.

March 14
Surprise: Gene Hackman passed on *Fear*. I thought for sure he would commit. Is the character too bland?

March 15
I don't know why I have to start every day by having to defeat the world. Is that the track I follow, à la Joseph Campbell? Is that how I get off?

March 16
Ron Meyer and I talked about Michael Keaton for *Fear*. He will set up lunch. Is he too young? Ron said that Gene Hackman timing was wrong and that three weeks later (after he loses Academy Award to Dustin Hoffman) he will be more approachable.

I'm good at keeping the balls in the air, but will they fall on my head? Arthur Miller's line "I could not imagine a theater worthy of my time that did not want to change the world." Good words.

Phil Gersh got up at 6:00 A.M. this morning to read *Fear* and liked it a great deal. He thought that Abe Polonsky would be very unhappy in that I told him I would work with him on the script and then wrote it myself. I reminded Phil that I'd worked with Abe on four or five drafts over two years and had nothing to show for it but a lot of cashed checks (by Abe). I said I wanted Abe to work as executive producer.

March 17
Meeting with Michael Nathanson and Dawn Steel on *Fear*. They said all the right things, and so did I. We agreed on a list of actors that protected me if the big stars passed. She will call Richard Dreyfuss herself.

Phil Gersh thought he would call Abe Polonsky and tell him it was great news that I wrote the terrific script. He was going to be executive producer.

March 19
Based on the initial proposal from Columbia, they say *Fear* is a "go" picture, but they are putting up no money and are getting a free option.

March 22

Gersh told me that Abe Polonsky was very upset that I wrote the screenplay. Actually he didn't really believe I wrote it, it was so good. He didn't complain about the quality but that he thought he was my friend and was hurt and upset (again) that I would change every word of his. Gersh said I handled it wrong, and I did. I listened to Gersh. I've known all along that somewhere I'd have a problem with Polonsky. Either now or when the picture comes out. I'm secretly very pleased and surprised that Abe actually liked my script. Now it's about Abe's considerable ego.

March 27

Dustin Hoffman passed on *Fear*.

March 30

Lunch with Ron Meyer and Fred Spector. Talked about Gene Hackman. I hope the Oscar win of Kevin Kline doesn't put him out of *Fear*. The loss by Gene Hackman probably helps. But who knows? It's all up in the air.

April 4

Michael Nathanson told me that Richard Dreyfuss passed on *Fear*, but his agent, Peter Rawley, suggested I meet with Dreyfuss. I don't know if he thinks I can change his mind.

April 22

A lunch yesterday with CAA agent Rick Nicita. I'll have to decide who we go with: Michael Keaton, who Ron Meyer spoke to, or Kevin Kline, who Rick Nicita spoke to. I prefer Kevin Kline. It's tricky to handle.

April 25

Some little remark UA president Lee Rich made about the ending of *Fear* made me re-examine the entire ending. Worked on that for the last few days. I keep getting disgusted with the script, saying and feeling that I never want to look at it again. When I become aware of some point that needs to be fixed, I start again.

After lunch with Rick Nicita, I called Debra Winger just to say hello. I hope she might want to play Dorothy in *Fear*.

May 5

Last night dinner with my casting director Cis Corman. She liked *Fear* a great deal and liked Kevin Kline and Richard Gere.

May 16

Nathanson called to say that Dawn Steel OK'd Kevin Kline and wanted to think about Richard Gere on approved list.

May 17

Lunch with Fred Specktor and talked about Robert De Niro. He is shooting a Columbia picture and won't be available until January. That would suit me fine. Of course Bob would be my number one choice, but I've put it out of my mind, as I don't think I'll get him.

May 19

Nice lunch with Michael Keaton. He was intelligent and very charming. I felt a real actor behind the nice-guy attitude. He wanted to know why I wanted to direct this script after all these years. I told Keaton I felt it was an important story to tell and that personally I wanted the challenge of directing a film.

May 30–June 8

Ron Meyer said Michael Keaton loved his meeting with me and was rereading *Fear*. He read half, liked it a lot, but thought it was a little melodramatic in spots.

I spent some time thinking about *Fear* casting and decided to send the script to Richard Gere.

I wonder if it's worth it all (directing). I've gone from the position as a producer, where I'm in control, to a hat-in-hand director, waiting for an actor, listening to the studio, and suffering rejection. I never felt rejection when someone turned me down as producer. Why am I feeling it now? I didn't really want Keaton, then talked myself into him, and ended up getting rejected by him! Can't believe it.

Saw *Miles from Home* and liked Richard Gere. Did I like him, or am I starting to talk myself into him? CAA suggested Sally Fields for Ruth. A really good idea. No trouble talking myself into that.

June 8–14—Los Angeles
Ran a short festival of Richard Gere films. He was pretty good in most of them. Or did he just look pretty good because I'm not doing too well in the casting department of *Fear*? Ran *Dead Poets Society*, and Robin Williams looked good, but I really don't think he's right.

June 14–23
Last night's call from Rick Nicita was disturbing. I didn't mind losing Michael Keaton and Richard Dreyfuss and some of the other actors, but I really wanted Kevin Kline, and I'm a little shocked that he's passing. Now I'll wait for Richard Gere. At one point I thought I'd rather not make the picture with Gere, and now I'm hoping he'll agree to it.

Richard Gere likes *Fear* a lot. Lunch with him on Thursday. Talked to Michael Nathanson, who will try to position Dawn Steel. It will be a fight, but Gere is the only one left, so it's probably him or no one.

John Burnham called and said his client Diane Keaton wanted to play Ruth in *Fear*.

June 23
Enjoyed lunch with Richard Gere. He loved the script and wants to do the film. I felt very comfortable with him. I don't know if I just grabbed for good impressions because there isn't anyone else.

John Candy's people are high on his playing Bunny, friend of David Merrill. So now I've got a cast but no go-ahead. I've been here before.

June 28
Patrick Wachsberger called and said he and another independent financier, Arnon Milchan, are going to make an offer for foreign on *Fear*. Dawn Steel called, and I told her it was a mistake to sell foreign, since if Wachsberger and Milchan can make money on it, why can't she? Her attitude was that through foreign sales and ancillary she was covered on the picture and therefore at no risk.

July 11–14
Everything Dawn Steel asked for, she got. Wachsberger came up with $4.5 million for foreign (they would put up $5 million), and she is still not willing to OK the film.

July 14
Today I'm peddling again. I now have to pitch *Fear* to RCA Columbia Pictures Home Video. One of the reasons I wrote it and want to direct it is to get away from all that hustling, and here I am.

July 16—East Hampton
Bob De Niro came over for lunch on Saturday. I told him about *Fear*. On Sunday I went to Bob's in Montauk and had quite a lengthy discussion on the subject of the blacklist and Elia Kazan, whom Bob likes a lot (they did *The Last Tycoon* together). I carefully didn't say anything about Richard Gere, because if Bob likes it . . . Well!

July 20
Word came down that Columbia won't make the deal because they didn't want to use up one of their HBO cable spots. A reason not to make a picture. The corporate mentality is ruling supreme. It's all

about HBO spots, home video adverts, foreign sales. It has nothing to do with liking the script. Alan Ladd, who liked it a lot, didn't want to do *Fear* as his first film as head of MGM. Orion liked it a lot but was afraid the marketing cost would be too high.

Arnon Milchan says HBO will make video offer. He called John Candy, and I reluctantly agreed to meet, although I'm not in the mood with the deal up in the air.

August 7
A terrific response from Warner Bros., who loved it but would only do the film with Bob De Niro, Dustin Hoffman, or Michael Douglas—not Richard Gere. Bob De Niro read the script and called yesterday (Sunday) and likes the script a lot. I'm going to fly to the Caribbean on the WB jet and get his feelings, but it looks good. I'll tell Richard Gere the facts: I just couldn't set the film up with him.

August 10
Flew into New York instead of the Caribbean on the corporate Warner Bros. jet. Met with Bob De Niro. He had some specific ideas about the script. After spending time with him, I decided not to make the film with Richard Gere, even if Bob doesn't work out. No one would be as perfect as Bob. That was it.

August 14
On Friday I met with De Niro's agent Fred Specktor and talked to Mike Ovitz (also De Niro's agent) and Warner Bros. VP of production Mark Canton. Everyone ready to make the deal for Bob De Niro. Bob told Arnon Milchan that even his girlfriend, Toukie Smith, liked my script. He told Arnon he would call me today. Secretly, I'm hoping he'll say no, and that will be the end of it. Really caught between ambition and satisfaction. Ambition to do something new and different and satisfaction at continuing producing, which is easy.

Bob De Niro called and said he'll do *Fear*. So now it's really special. I'm thrilled and a little nervous. I was dreaming of reading *War and Peace* in St. Tropez . . .

Robert De Niro, Irwin Winkler, Annette Bening
Guilty by Suspicion

Dalton Trumbo, the screenwriter, who went to jail for refusing to name names, wrote: "The blacklist was a time of evil . . . no one on either side who survived it came through untouched by evil . . . [Looking] back on this time . . . it will do no good to search for villains or heroes or saints or devils because there were none; there were only victims." Those who named names worked in Hollywood for a while but never lived down the betrayal.

At the core of *Guilty by Suspicion* were individuals who were affected by the blacklist. They were the director David Merrill (Bob De Niro), his wife, Ruth (Annette Bening), his son, Paulie (Luke Edwards), his best friend, screenwriter Bunny Baxter (George Wendt), his lawyer,

Felix Graff (Sam Wanamaker), his friends the Nolans (Patricia Wettig and Chris Cooper), the director Joe Lesser (Martin Scorsese), and the studio head Darryl Zanuck (Ben Piazza). The script, although it's about one man being blacklisted, exposes how so many people around that singled-out person are affected.

Elia Kazan was perhaps the most famous of the witnesses. After he testified, he took out an advertisement in the *New York Times* explaining his actions and spent his very productive life defending his actions. When I was casting *Guilty by Suspicion* at Bob De Niro's request, an actor named Craig Smith came to see me. I asked Smith what his connection was to Bob. Smith said Elia Kazan had asked Bob to set the interview with me. When I asked him what his relationship with Kazan was, he said Kazan had "named" his father. I then asked Smith where his father was now, thinking I would give his father a part in the film; he said his father was dead. He had committed suicide because he couldn't get any work. I cast Craig Smith in the part of a cinematographer on the re-creation of a scene from *High Noon*. Gary Cooper starred in that 1952 film as a small-town marshal who stands alone when surrounded by evil forces. Cooper, who was a conservative Republican, very much wanted to make a statement about the blacklist. *High Noon* was one of the few films the studios "dared" to make that even could be interpreted as "democratic." Cooper's performance, in spite of the fear in Hollywood, won an Academy Award. At a birthday party for Bob De Niro, Kazan, one of the guests, walked toward me, shook my hand, complimented me on *Guilty by Suspicion*, and said De Niro gave a great performance. I agreed and added that Bob was playing John Huston to some extent. No, Kazan answered, "He was playing me." Even though David Merrill stands up against naming names.

Since I wanted to portray Darryl Zanuck, as he was an important studio head and ran 20th Century Fox during the blacklist period, I wanted to set the film at Fox and needed their cooperation. The lawyers at Fox turned me down flat. I not only could not use their facilities, but if we tried to duplicate them anywhere else, we would be sued. Frustrated, I mentioned it to my friend David Geffen. David suggested I call

Barry Diller, who was running Fox. Diller asked to read the script, called me the next day, and gave me access to all of Fox's facilities in spite of his lawyer's refusal. I asked Diller if he was sure, since the owner of Fox studios was the right-wing Rupert Murdoch and Diller's boss. Diller replied that forty years ago Fox had participated in the blacklist, and it was part of American political history and should be told. Diller, unlike the studio heads of the past, stood up for what was right.

What do you do in Hollywood when you're in trouble? You call your friends, right? From his house overlooking Los Angeles David Merrill spends his days (and nights) in a fruitless attempt to get a job. That's all he wants, a job, and at the end of his countless attempts, he realizes the result of his inherent decency. His promising career has come to a sudden halt. De Niro in that one scene went from a Hollywood star to a nobody in a fine piece of acting.

In playing Monroe Stahr in F. Scott Fitzgerald's *The Last Tycoon*, Bob De Niro was Irving Thalberg, the legendary, autocratic producer. In *Guilty by Suspicion* Bob showed a very different side of a Hollywood artist. His David Merrill was a decent, gifted, ambitious artist. He certainly was no martyr. Although his ambition destroyed his marriage, in times of trouble he goes to and is welcomed by his ex-wife, Ruth, and their son. The family will always stand together in times of trouble. It was something I felt deeply about when I wrote the screenplay. To create the atmosphere of a Hollywood under siege, I used several screen devices. We showed film clips of the real Ethel and Julius Rosenberg, who were executed for committing espionage for Russia, on the television sets in the background of scenes of Merrill's home life. We staged a scene from *Peter Pan* where David and Ruth watch their son's school performance when Peter asks the audience for a "miracle of faith," as there is nothing Peter cannot do. We used songs such as "Bye Bye Birdie," "It Never Entered My Mind," "Straighten Up and Fly Right," "They Can't Take That Away from Me," "I'm Just a Lucky So and So," and "Easy Come, Easy Go" that commented on the character of David Merrill and what he was going through. Sam Wanamaker, who was one of the first actors blacklisted and who fled to England (where he ran the Globe Theatre), turned the tables on the blacklist, playing a smooth, fast-talking lawyer the studio hires to try to convince Merrill to cooperate with HUAC and get on with making movies. He tells Merrill that everything can be handled behind closed doors and in ten years no one would really care about the blacklist. We also played the HUAC members much the same as they themselves appeared and how they shamed and humiliated the witnesses before them. I used some of the testimony of the actor Larry Parks (*The Jolson Story*) who pleaded "not to be dragged through the mud" and forced to testify. Parks finally named names and ended up in tears, and even then was dropped by his studio, Columbia Pictures. Parks never regained his stardom. He was sixty years old when he died of a heart attack, not having worked as an actor in almost a decade. If there was any consolation (and there really is none), the bully chairman of HUAC, J. Parnell Thomas, when charged with fraud by the U.S. government, refused to answer questions based on his constitutional rights. The Hollywood Ten (ten directors, producers, and screenwriters who appeared before HUAC) were imprisoned for taking the same stance. Chairman Thomas was sent to federal prison in Danbury, Connecticut, where he joined the writers Lester Cole and Ring Lardner Jr., who were serving time for their refusal to answer questions before Thomas's committee.

Marty Scorsese played a director (Joe Lesser), based on Joe Losey, who is flying to Europe to avoid the blacklist. The scene takes place in an editing room where the film editor is working on *The Boy with Green Hair*, a film directed by Losey about a young boy whose hair turns green and people's reactions to someone who's different. Lesser asks his friend Merrill to finish the film for him, even as he's fleeing his homeland, more concerned about his film than his own safety. The commitment to the work is as important as the politics.

Every filmmaker makes mistakes; some are major and costly. I made a whopper. I cast Margo Winkler, who had done excellent work for Marty Scorsese in *Goodfellas* and *The King of Comedy*, in the role of a theater agent based on the agent Sue Mengers. David Merrill, blacklisted, can't find work and in desperation goes to see his former agent.

She's bitter and angry that he fired her once he became a hot director, and she excoriates him for his lack of loyalty, noting that only now that no one will hire him, he comes running to her. Margo, who knew Sue

Martin Scorsese, Robert De Niro, Irwin Winkler
Guilty by Suspicion

Mengers well, was great. It was a terrific scene. But when I edited that scene, I felt it took too much sympathy away from Merrill, and I cut it from the film. That night I very hesitantly told Margo. She took it fine. Just arranged for us to go to Van Cleef & Arpels the next day. (The edit was costly. The scene is in the director's cut on the DVD.)

The climax of the film was set in the HUAC hearing room where Merrill testified. The circus atmosphere and the unnecessary bullying ignites Merrill's conscience, as he had agreed to cooperate. I wanted to catch every nuance of De Niro's performance and set up four different cameras at different angles, and Bob, using dialogue I had researched from the HUAC testimony of Arthur Miller and Lillian Hellman, brought courage to the character. The shallowness of the real HUAC members was clear when Arthur Miller was told by the chairman that he would be excused if Miller's wife at the time, Marilyn Monroe, took a publicity photo with him. Miller chose to testify, and his words were in large part responsible for the termination of HUAC by Congress.

My experience directing *Guilty by Suspicion* was life changing. The concentration level was such that if I picked up a *New Yorker* magazine, I felt guilty that I was not studying a scene. Margo would come to the set in the late afternoon, hang around until I was finished shooting, and watch dailies with me. We'd stop off and have a bite to eat on the way home, talk to no one except our family, and remain completely immersed in the film.

Guilty by Suspicion was nominated for the Palme d'Or at the Cannes Film Festival in 1991. The red carpet was laid out for our arrival, and the film received a standing ovation. Warner Bros. hosted a lavish dinner for the cast and me. I missed John Berry, who had started me thinking about the Hollywood blacklist in Paris five years before, while we were making *Round Midnight*. John Berry was working on a film at the time, he outlived the blacklist, and Margo wore her Van Cleef & Arpels earrings.

BASIC INSTINCT (1992)

Margo and I were in Paris on the way to the South of France for a holiday when I got a call from the writer Joe Eszterhas, who told me he had just written a script he thought was quite good and wanted me to read. We had done two movies together, *Betrayed* and *Music Box*, and I was very proud of both films, although they were not commercially successful.

I had a friend who was flying from Los Angeles to meet me in Nice and had Joe give him the script (no FedEx yet). My friend, who was not in the entertainment business, having nothing else to do on the plane, read the script and thought it was good. I really wasn't interested in reading anything, as I was still very involved emotionally with *Guilty by Suspicion*. On the way to St. Tropez from Nice, Margo read the script and said I should read it, that it was a good, sexy thriller. I put it off for a couple of days, and when I read it, to my surprise, I liked it a lot. I called Eszterhas and said I'd produce it. I wasn't yet sure how much time I would give to producing in the future, but I thought, why not? It will be like a vacation after directing *Guilty by Suspicion*. Joe told me he was going to put it up for auction and would have his agent, Guy McElwaine, call me. McElwaine promptly said he already had an offer to sell the script for $1 million. I told him it sounded great and that he should grab it. He disagreed and said he was sure he could do a lot better. Sure enough, the next day he had an offer of two million dollars, but to my continued surprise, he was sure he could get more. I didn't hear from McElwaine for a couple of days and called Joe to see how it was going. He told me the script sold for three million dollars. Probably the highest price for a spec script since William Goldman sold *Butch Cassidy and the Sundance Kid* for the then-unheard-of price of one million dollars. The buyer was Carolco Pictures, an independent production company that sold off the foreign rights and used the major studios to distribute their films domestically. When I got back to LA, I met with Andy Vajna and Mario Kassar, the owners of Carolco, and Joe Eszterhas at Kassar's home, and we started working out a plan to cast the lead role and hire a director. They informed me that the script had been given to a couple of directors and actors and had been turned down. Suddenly this hot script that they had paid a lot of money for was looking shaky.

When I got back to my office, Ron Meyer called and said he knew Carolco was getting quite a few turndowns and Vajna and Kassar were scared that they might have blown a lot of money on a script that they couldn't cast. Ron said Michael Douglas liked the script and, if Carolco was ready to pay his price, he would be available to do the film. Kassar immediately agreed. Now to get a director! I started to check availabilities when Kassar told me they had interest from a director they were high on and were sure Douglas and I would approve.

The next day I met with Paul Verhoeven, and I sensed he was quite uncomfortable not about the script or Michael Douglas, but about me producing. I felt he hated the idea that this director (me) was going to produce the film, and he was afraid of being second-guessed. I was uncomfortable myself and reluctantly set up a meeting a couple of days later with Michael Douglas, Verhoeven, and Joe Eszterhas. In my living room Verhoeven started to explain to Michael, Joe, and me how he was going to expand the horizons of sexual perversity in this film. Michael and Joe looked very, very uncomfortable, and I immediately thought he was kidding until he said that we were going to show male frontal nudity and described a couple of proposed scenes that were demeaning to the female characters as well as Michael. He went on an almost nonstop diatribe about sexual tools and positions he imagined. Finally I said to him, "You know, I don't think I want to hear this. I'll tell you what I'm going to do. I'm going to go up to my bathroom, and I'm going to take a shower, because I really feel dirty, and when I come down, I want you, Mr. Verhoeven, to be gone." I'm not sure whether Verhoeven's performance was to get me to walk away from "his" movie, but it worked. I called Vajna and bowed out that evening.

Basic Instinct was a big commercial hit and made a star out of Sharon Stone by keeping her legs apart when she's questioned about a murder by the detective played by Michael Douglas. More surprising, it was a nominee for Best Picture at the Cannes Film Festival, nominated for two Academy Awards and two Golden Globes, and even led to *Basic Instinct 2*.

Happily, when I saw the film, my name was not included in the list of producers.

The experience of producing and then not producing *Basic Instinct* pushed me more toward directing and writing my films. Truth be told, I really liked being the man on the set, dealing with the actors, the cameramen, the camera operator, the prop man, wardrobe, makeup, the art director, the location manager, the storyboard artists, the editors—all the details that go into a scene and then into a movie. There were periods, however, over the next ten to fifteen years when I coproduced films with Rob Cowan while I was directing others that were unique in some way to me, but only some are written about here. They are the ones that stand out in my mind, but there are others—*Enough* (2002), *Trespass* (2011), *The Mechanic* (2011), and *Survivor* (2015)—that took less of my effort and fewer of my thoughts.

NIGHT AND THE CITY (1992)

In May of 1991 I had a great time at the Cannes Film Festival. The limousines with the police escort, the red carpet with hundreds of paparazzi snapping away, the black-tie screening, the standing ovation at the end of *Guilty by Suspicion*, the glamorous after-parties, the luncheon the next day on the sun-drenched terrace of the Hotel du Cap—all heady stuff. I had worked on *Guilty by Suspicion* for the last two years, and the climax was the film being a nominee for the Palme d'Or, the grand prize at the festival.

On the flight from Nice, France, to New York, I kept thinking, "Well, that was fun. Let's take the next couple of months off." That didn't happen. Waiting for me in New York was a script, *Night and the City* by Richard Price. Price had written the screenplay for Marty Scorsese's *Color of Money* (Paul Newman and Tom Cruise), *Sea of Love* (Al Pacino), and *New York Stories* (Marty Scorsese). I had been an admirer of Price for a long time. His novel *The Wanderers* was adapted for the screen and directed by Phil Kaufman, and I liked it so much that when Bob Chartoff and I were looking for a writer/director for *The Right Stuff*, *The Wanderers* was part of our decision to engage Kaufman. So here it was: a script I liked—no book to buy, no writer to find, no financing to find, and no disappointment when the screenplay wasn't up to snuff.

I recalled some time ago that Bertrand Tavernier had mentioned to me, when we were talking about the Hollywood blacklist, that Darryl Zanuck, then the head of 20th Century Fox, had saved the director

Jules Dassin from the HUAC purge by assigning him to direct Richard Widmark in *Night and the City* in London. Zanuck, apparently wanting to sweeten the pot, also sent one of Fox's biggest stars, Gene Tierney, to costar. Bertrand also told me that he always thought the 1950s London-set film would make a fine remake in 1990s New York. Well, here it was!

Robert De Niro and Margo Winkler
Night and the City

Bob De Niro wasn't far from my thinking. In Cannes everyone was talking about what a great performance he'd brought to *Guilty by Suspicion*. The Harry Fabian character in Richard Price's script was the polar opposite. While David Merrill was talented, honest, sincere, and moralistic, Harry Fabian was a liar, a cheat, a hustler (and a dreamer). I thought that Bob might be interested in yet another different character, as he had played several in the films we had done together: a bike-riding fake priest in *The Gang That Couldn't Shoot Straight*, a talented jazz saxophonist in *New York, New York*, the raging Jake LaMotta in *Raging Bull*, an ambitious Los Angeles priest in *True Confessions*, and a murderer in *Goodfellas*. Coincidentally, when we were leaving Cannes after the awards ceremony, Bob mentioned that he might be free to do a film in the fall and wanted to be in New York if possible. After a second reading of the script and after viewing the original film, I called De Niro and told him how much I liked *Night and the City*, and, to my surprise, he had read it recently and was enthusiastic for us to do it together. Immediately after he was told of my and Bob's interest, Joe Roth, who was running 20th Century Fox at the time, said he was ready to finance the film. Jane Rosenthal (De Niro's partner in Tribeca Films) set up a reading in New York with some very good New York actors, including Eli Wallach, Barry Primus, and Mercedes Ruehl (who had won a Tony Award the night before). The script played a lot funnier than it read, and Bob, always questioning, asked if I knew any Harry Fabians. Gene Kirkwood, who had introduced me to Sylvester Stallone back in 1975 and had been a friend of both of us, was a classy version of Harry (without a law degree). Bob smiled, said he got it, and we never had to discuss his character again.

When I called Joe Roth and his right-hand man, Roger Birnbaum, to tell them how well the reading went and that we were all set to go, they had decided they would only finance half of the budget and they/we should find a foreign distributor for the rest of the money. From June to August 1991 we looked for partners without success, and I was pretty sure *Night and the City* would be just another "almost" film. To my great surprise, on August 1, the same Gene Kirkwood that De Niro would be playing as Harry Fabian called me from Milan, where he had arranged the foreign financing with a company owned by Silvio Berlusconi, the Italian billionaire who was to be the fiftieth prime minister of Italy. The other partner with Berlusconi was Vittorio Cecchi Gori, who owned the rights to *Silence*, but that's another part of this tale. I hadn't known that Kirkwood was trying to arrange the financing but happily accepted it, and Fox closed the deal without incident until, at the last minute, Fox, never satisfied, demanded that I put up completion money (any amount spent over the approved budget). I reluctantly (of course) agreed, and to my delight, when Bob De Niro heard about it, he volunteered to share any overages with me. Not many actors would offer that kind of support.

The casting of Jessica Lange was special. When I met with her to discuss the part of Helen, who is the wife of the owner (Cliff Gorman) of the local bar where Fabian hung out, she stopped me short. Jessica had worked as a waitress in Greenwich Village in the 1970s, when she was starting out as an actress. She recognized Helen as the owner's wife of the Waffle House all those years before. The rest of the cast were the best of New York, and each had special moments: Eli Wallach as the loan shark telling Harry, "You're like Murphy's Law, anything that can go wrong will go wrong," Margo Winkler as a judge who has seen Harry too many times before she throws him out with, "Fabian, get the fuck out of my courtroom," Jack Warden talking about old times with, "When I was a kid, it was a different time, I had a gun, it was an honest robbery, not like today," Alan King as the crooked fight promoter humiliating Harry by putting his hands around Harry's face, and Jessica Lange just glancing over at Harry, who she hopes will get her out of her unhappy marriage to Phil.

Shooting in New York in mid-winter was no fun. I wonder why I was surprised—after all, it's called *Night and the City*—but at three in the morning when it's eight degrees below, the cast has been sent home, and you're shooting the feet of the stuntman on a deserted street, you have to wonder about the glamour of the job. We finished the film with Gene Kirkwood playing a sleazy nightclub owner. As close as I was to the crew for four months, I'd felt the same way when I was in the army during the Korean War; once you leave the group and there is no longer a shared singular goal, your differences become more apparent.

Fox was very high on *Night and the City*, so much so that when Tom Sherak, Fox's head of marketing, wanted to show the film at News Corporation's (the owner of Fox Studios) seminar in Aspen, I agreed. Joe Roth reported that the screening was a disaster. The right-wing conservative News Corporation executives, including (especially) Rupert Murdoch, hated the New York street language and the hustlers, conivers, and lowlifes. (Those are the very same people who publish *The Sun* in London with a picture of a half-nude woman on page 3, and their tabloids give credence to three-headed infants.)

In spite of Murdoch's comments, the Fox marketing group embraced the New York Film Festival when they invited us to screen *Night and the City* as their prestigious closing-night attraction.

CHAPTER FIFTEEN

Working with some special ladies—Sandra Bullock and Demi
Moore—and a special doctor, Oliver Sacks

THE NET (1995)

WHAT HAPPENS WHEN YOU'RE suddenly without an identity? The computer has gotten into the DMV and your driver's license is altered, your house has been sold, your bank and medical records have been tampered with, even the medication you take has been changed at the pharmacy. On top of that, the airline computers have failed, traffic lights have been manipulated, there is chaos in the stock market, as Wall Street's computers have crashed, and the national defense has been compromised by a cyber attack. All this and more takes place in *The Net*, a cyber thriller I directed in 1995. At the time, some of the power of the computer was just hinted at, but as I wrote this in 2018, the computer has changed the lives of all of us, even to the extent of cyber attacks on the most sacred political process in America, the election of the president of the United States.

As I worked on the script with screenwriting duo Mike Ferris and John Brancato (*The Game*), I got more and more intrigued with the world of cyberspace. After *Guilty by Suspicion* and *Night and the City*, I thought, why not make a thriller like some of my favorite Alfred Hitchcock films, *Notorious* and *North by Northwest*, but instead of a big male star like Cary Grant or James Stewart, have a woman on the run instead? Instead of Cary Grant chased by an airplane in an open field, we'd have our heroine chased by the mystery of cyberspace. Columbia Pictures was eager for me to commit to directing the script, but I put them off. I had been working on a media-mogul idea based on the takeover of *New York* magazine some years ago by Rupert Murdoch. Clay Felker, who was knowledgeable about everyone and everything in the art world, the media, and high (and low) society, had been introduced to Murdoch by the owner of the *Washington Post*, Katharine Graham. Felker and Murdoch became fast friends, went on vacation together, and spent many dinners discussing Murdoch's ambition to get into the newspaper business in America and how Felker could help his friend. Felker knew that Dorothy Schiff wanted to sell the *New York Post* and arranged for Schiff and Murdoch to meet. Murdoch bought his first important American media platform. Felker then arranged a celebration at the chic New York restaurant Elaine's, and as the two friends left the party, Felker told Murdoch how he envied his ability to write a check to buy the *Post* without having to get an approval from a board of directors. Felker went on to tell his friend of the trouble he was having with his board at *New York* magazine. Murdoch then secretly bought up *New York* magazine shares from the unhappy board members and fired his great friend. Felker told me that when he confronted Murdoch, the new owner said, "It's just business. Let's still be friends, dear boy." I had been working on the story for a couple of years, and I hated to give it up, but it still seemed a ways off. I liked the idea of the new experience of the world of cyberspace and told Columbia I would direct *The Net* if I could get the perfect actress for it. I met quite a few but none that I wanted (or wanted me) until an agent called and said Sandra Bullock had read the script and was interested. Sandra had done a couple of films, one hit being the action thriller *Speed* and another the charming *While You Were Sleeping*. After one meeting I decided that I would direct *The Net* if Bullock agreed to star in it. After meeting a second time, we both decided to do the film, and I put the media-mogul idea aside (I've yet to do it).

Sandra was a joy to work with, prepared, professional, extremely talented, and always had a smile for her fellow actors and crew. As a matter of fact, at one time Margo, even after thirty years of a very happy marriage, asked me if I had a crush on Sandy. I told my wife I did, and didn't she? She did.

The world of the computer was still new when our casting director contacted Bill Gates about playing one of the cyber company executives (the bad guy). I was all set to meet him, when I was told he'd

Sandy Bullock and Irwin Winkler
The Net

thought better of it. Still, Apple was so eager for recognition, we were
invited to shoot at a Mac convention in San Francisco, where they not
only gave us free rein over the space, they asked us which of their prod-
ucts we'd like to take home—anything to help Apple get noticed.

My shooting was interrupted by Oliver Stone. I had dinner with
Stone at Rob Reiner's a couple of weeks before I started shooting *The
Net*, and he was quite pleasant and rather deferential. We had worked
some years before on another project that never got made and talked
about what each of us was up to. While I was shooting in a water tank
on the Paramount lot, directing the crash of a speedboat, Stone came
by and asked if I would help him out. I didn't pay much attention to
what he was saying, but he kept after me, and I figured the only way to
get rid of him was to hear him out. He had a script in which Anthony

Hopkins was to play Richard Nixon, and he asked if I would produce it. I told Stone that I was directing my picture and didn't have time to figure out what the next day's shooting would be, much less read his script. With boyish charm he claimed his script would be the defining historical examination of the disgraced president. That interested me.

I liked a lot of Stone's controversial, passionate films—*JFK*, *Born on the Fourth of July*, and *Platoon*—so that weekend I put aside *The Net* script and read the *Nixon* script. I told Stone that I would help in setting up *Nixon* now and that when I finished shooting *The Net* I'd have much more time to work with him on his film. He hugged me and repeated several times how happy he was that I would produce the film. I gave the script to Columbia, and they liked it. I set up a meeting for Stone. Obviously I couldn't attend the meeting, but both Stone and Columbia reported that they wanted to make the film. Stone came to *The Net* set unannounced the next night and during a break in the shooting asked if I would talk to Terry Semel at Warner Bros., although Semel had already passed on the script. I was surprised, as Stone had been so enthusiastic after the Columbia meeting, but he thought maybe we could get a better deal at Warner Bros. I told him I doubted we could, and Stone said, whatever happens, "Let's not lose the Columbia deal; it's a good one, and they're very enthusiastic." The next afternoon Stone's agent (not Stone himself) called to tell me that he had made a deal with 20th Century Fox and I wouldn't be needed. I didn't care that much, but Stone's unwanted badgering on my set, calling me at all hours for advice, telling me the night before not to lose the Columbia deal because they were so enthusiastic and he was so looking forward to our working together, all annoyed me. He didn't even have the guts to call me himself. The best part of the whole affair was, I never had to speak to Oliver Stone again.

As we shot scene after scene, we found more and more ways to strip Angela Bennett (Bullock) of not only her identity but every part of her existence. Every innovation we conceived was plausible (and scary). Here once again art and life interchange.

Columbia, that August after I finished editing, asked me to show the film to a gentleman (he never gave his name) from the U.S. Justice Department Computer Crime Division, who after the screening murmured something under his breath and left. November 25, 2014, twenty-one years later, Columbia (Sony Pictures) suffered a massive hack into their computer system by GOP, the "Guardians of Peace." Sony's network was taken down, and the personal information of many employees was leaked as well as thousands of pieces of highly sensitive corporate private correspondence. The Guardians of Peace were not much different from the Praetorians who attacked Sandra Bullock's character in *The Net*. The FBI Cyber Division blamed the break-in on North Korea, but do we really know? Could it be Russia? Could it be some sweet seventeen-year old sitting in the basement of his parents' home in Des Moines, Iowa?

THE JUROR (1996)

The process of making a movie usually starts with a producer reading a book, seeing a play, reading a newspaper article, hearing an idea or a pitch, developing that basic material into a story, then finding the money to buy that play/book/article, and then hiring a screenwriter to adapt that source. When that's done (if successfully), the producer will attach a director and ultimately cast the film. The last part, casting the film, is often the most difficult. Difficult because there are not that many actors who can guarantee you get the financing you need, and they are usually overwhelmed with scripts and offers, and, if they're working, they won't be able to set aside the time to read scripts.

The Juror went an untraditional route. The novel, written by George Dawes Green, was a very hot book that a literary agent at CAA had offered to several studios. I was quite busy finishing *The Net* and didn't give it that much thought until Rob Cowan, who joined me as an assistant director years earlier and now was my producing partner, read it, and his enthusiasm was matched by the executives at Columbia

Pictures, who bought it for $1.5 million and wanted me to produce the film. I closed my office door, ordered dinner in, and finished the novel that night. I thought *The Juror* would make a good movie with the right stars. The plot was intriguing: a single mother is called for jury duty, and the defendant is a Mafia boss who sends a professional killer to persuade her to vote not guilty. If she doesn't, she and her son will be murdered. There are plenty of surprises after that.

Ted Tally, who won an Oscar for his screenplay of *The Silence of the Lambs*, delivered his adaptation of the novel in a quick three months. We all thought it was in good enough shape to interest a director. Then a strange thing happened. Ron Meyer read the script and gave it to his client Demi Moore, who was eager to play the starring role of Annie Laird. Demi Moore at the time was just about the hottest box office star in movies. Since *Ghost* in 1990, she'd had big commercial and critical hits with *Indecent Proposal* with Robert Redford, *Disclosure* with Michael Douglas, and *A Few Good Men* with Tom Cruise and Jack Nicholson. She was also getting top fees, comparable to those of her male costars. I met with her, and she was smart, direct, beautiful, and wary. I was sure she could turn her natural vulnerability to a Rambo-like violence as she fights the Mafia hit man to the death, just like an animal in the jungle, to protect her child.

The process of getting a top director with a hot commercial book, script by a recent Oscar-winning screenwriter, a major studio willing to pay top dollar, and a perfect star proved to be difficult. The directors who wanted to sign on (and there were quite a few) either had their own choice of actresses to play Annie or didn't want to "audition" for Demi, since she had director approval. I spoke to (or met with) Adrian Lyne, Jonathan Demme, Ridley Scott, Mike Newell, Tony Scott, and even Francis Ford Coppola, and all blanched at *not* being the one who hired the star or developed the script (none wanted to be the last creative force to sign up). At that point we were glad that Brian Gibson (*What's Love Got to Do with It?*) agreed to meet with Demi, who was shooting *Now and Then* in Savannah, Georgia. Gibson called to tell me he and Demi had a four-hour dinner and a three-hour breakfast, and he wanted very much to do the film with her. We happily cast Alec Baldwin as "The Teacher" who threatens and then becomes psychologically involved with his victim. We hired Gordon Willis (*The Godfather*) as cameraman.

After some wrangling with Columbia about locations, we set the picture for production in New York, with Rob Cowan capably running the set. Rob told me that Demi was into everything. She told Gibson that she looked better and had to be shot on the left side and sets should be built accordingly. Demi also called the hair and makeup people who worked with Gordon Willis to check on his "specialties." It was good that she cared so much, but I was surprised by her lack of trust.

Irwin Winkler and Demi Moore
The Juror

I was editing *The Net* in Los Angeles when Rob Cowan alerted me to troubles on *The Juror* set. It seemed that from the start, Gibson was not getting along with Alec Baldwin, Demi Moore, or Gordon

Willis. Reluctantly, I moved *The Net* editing crew and equipment from Los Angeles to New York and spent part of every day on *The Juror* set trying to keep the actors acting, the director directing, and the cameraman shooting. I wasn't able to keep Gordon Willis. He apologized to me but said he just couldn't work with Brian Gibson, as Gibson never could make up his mind and was not respectful of Willis or his talent. For me it was personal. Gordon Willis and I had worked together in 1971 when he shot *Up the Sandbox* in New York and Africa. While in Africa we spent many a night comparing our New York upbringings— Gordon's in Queens, mine in Coney Island—and even discovered we were born on the same day. Willis and I also worked on the Western *Comes a Horseman* in 1978 that starred Jane Fonda and James Caan. Sadly, Willis just about gave up his craft after *The Juror*. That certainly was an unhappy end to the career of one of the all-time great cinematographers. Just imagine *The Godfather, The Godfather Part II, All the President's Men, Annie Hall, Zelig, Klute,* and the unforgettable scene of Woody Allen and Diane Keaton sitting on the bench near the Fifty-Ninth Street Bridge as the dawn comes up in *Manhattan.*

Demi Moore and Alec Baldwin, with excellent support from the young Joseph Gordon-Levitt and James Gandolfini (just before he shot to stardom with *The Sopranos* television series), delivered really fine performances and finally found common ground with Gibson. Demi Moore was particularly committed, maybe because she was the first one in or maybe that's just who she is. I'm not sure. She certainly worked on every moment of every scene and never complained about hours or time off, though she did get upset at our travel agent when her private jet was smaller than she expected.

With the release of *The Juror*, word in the media was that Demi Moore was one of the highest-paid stars in Hollywood. Shouldn't that have been celebrated? An actress finally being compensated at the same level as actors? No, Demi was criticized for being too strong, too ambitious, and overpaid. As far as I was concerned, she deserved her salary and more (but not a bigger jet).

AT FIRST SIGHT (1999)

Come to think of it, I never did a romantic—a real romantic—movie. I've done tough love stories: *New York, New York* with Bob De Niro and Liza Minnelli fighting it out over their musical careers, Bob De Niro and Cathy Moriarty jealously raging in *Raging Bull*, Ray Liotta and Lorraine Bracco hardly a happy couple in *Goodfellas*, Jane Fonda asking Michael Sarrazin to put a bullet in her head in *They Shoot Horses, Don't They?* Well, maybe Rocky and Adrian had a beautiful relationship, but *Rocky* was a lot more about the fighter believing in himself and her coming to believe in him and herself. The one film I tried as an out-and-out romance, *At First Sight*, didn't quite do it, in spite of a compelling story by Dr. Oliver Sacks, the renowned neurologist and author. As in most of Oliver Sacks's writings, the story was unusual. Shirl Jennings, who lost his sight as a child, has adapted to his blindness and works as a masseur. He meets a woman, Barbara, makes her "feel" his world, they fall in love, and she convinces him to try cutting-edge, experimental surgery. He regains his sight but is troubled by what he sees. Their challenge is to keep their love in a "new world" for Shirl and Barbara. Fate steps in, and Shirl's blindness returns.

Columbia Pictures had paid for the script but had little enthusiasm to pay for the movie. MGM, now run by Michael Nathanson, was high on the script but would finance it only if I directed it. I hadn't thought about directing it, as I had another script, *Jack America*, about a Ted Turner type of character, that I wanted to direct. I had flown down to New Orleans to meet with Alec Baldwin, who was interested, but I was having trouble raising the financing. MGM was firm about my directing *At First Sight*, and, considering I had spent a great deal of time on the script, admired Dr. Sacks, liked working with him, and was fascinated by Shirl Jennings's story, I agreed to direct the film. It took me a while to realize I was more interested in Shirl (Virgil in the script) and his plight than the romance he had with the woman who changed his life. I got a cautious note from Nathanson's boss at MGM: "Whatever you do, don't make it an art film." God forbid.

The New York crew put together by Rob Cowan, who did quite a bit of writing on the screenplay with me, was headed by cameraman John Seale (Oscar winner for *The English Patient* in 1996). I wanted

Irwin Winkler and Dr. Oliver Sacks
At First Sight

Seale's artistry to help me bring Virgil's "seeing" world into a visual context. In New York we had all the wonders, from the city streets, the cars, buses, taxis, the subway, the crowds, the theaters, the skyscrapers, museums, slums, and even Madison Square Garden, where we could shoot a hockey game.

The emotional roller coaster of the everyday life of an unseeing person was important to portray in simple terms. Virgil's home is comfortable, he knows where everything is, his travels to and from his job are familiar, as are his family and friends, and he even skates and can play hockey. Amy (the real-life Barbara), on the other hand, dislikes her job, her boyfriend, has few friends, and, when comforted by a massage, just sobs. Yes, she can see, but she doesn't like or appreciate what she sees.

Who to play Virgil? My first thoughts always go to Bob De Niro. Bob had starred in *Awakenings*, also adapted from an Oliver Sacks story,

where he played a catatonic patient. For that performance he was nominated for an Oscar (1991). As it turned out, Margo and I were guests
over a July weekend in 1997 at Nick Pileggi and Nora Ephron's home
in East Hampton, Long Island. Nora was a hostess who made your
weekend magical. She was the best cook, the house was comfortable
without being fancy, and when you looked out the window, you treated
your eyes to the most beautiful, flower-filled garden imaginable. There
were lunches and dinners with great guests. Jane Rosenthal came by
for lunch, and I told her about *At First Sight*. Jane said Bob De Niro
was leaving for Russia, and she would give him the script to read on
the plane. The rest of the weekend at Nora and Nick's, when friends
came by, they inevitably (just like Jane) asked what I was doing next. I
honed my storytelling skills and waited for reactions. They went from
blank stares to enthusiasm as I described the plot of *At First Sight*. Most
of the listeners thought the story would end with Virgil regaining his
sight and he and Amy going off into the sunset together. The surprise
was Virgil regaining and then losing his sight and no happy Hollywood ending.

On July 31, Bob De Niro called from Moscow to tell me he didn't
feel comfortable with the love story. He liked the Virgil character but
not the relationship with Amy. When Bob got off the phone, I suddenly
felt abandoned. For the first two films I'd directed, *Guilty by Suspicion*
and *Night and the City*, Bob had signed on quickly. Was I making a mistake going forward without him? Before I had a chance to think about
it, one of my agents at CAA, Rick Nicita, called to say that his client
Val Kilmer wanted to play Virgil. Kilmer, at that time, had given some
excellent portrayals in *Tombstone* (playing Doc Holliday), *The Doors*
(playing Jim Morrison), Michael Mann's *Heat* (playing a criminal), and
the crowd-pleasing *Batman Forever*. Kilmer also had a very mixed reputation; some said he was a "whole lot of trouble," while others (Michael
Mann) adored him. I told Nicita that I would meet Kilmer but I would
make no promise of an offer. MGM, aware of Kilmer's interest, called
to remind me that they were making *At First Sight* because I was directing. The decision to use Kilmer was mine, although they were very

high on him. On August 29 I had a three-hour lunch with Val Kilmer. I came away thinking he was either a great actor or a split personality, as he thoroughly charmed me, and I felt he would charm the audience as

Irwin Winkler and Nathan Lane
At First Sight

Virgil as well. He was knowledgeable, had notes and questions, and was quite articulate. On September 2 Val and I had another couple of hours together. I was looking for the cracks in his façade that had given him such a dicey reputation. I couldn't find any. I told MGM to go ahead and lock him up, with some feelings of loss. I would have much preferred my first choice, Bob De Niro, but I knew he couldn't be in every movie I was involved with. Actually, we didn't work together again until *The Irishman* in 2017, twenty years later.

The casting of Amy proved to be a long and difficult affair. We had to get an actress who was a romantic match with Val but tough, as I was fearful of too much sentiment. We met lots and lots of talented actresses; some were too young, some too old, some not available for our time frame, and some just turned us down or vice versa. Robin Wright, Jeanne Tripplehorn, Kyra Sedgwick, Julianna Margulies, Embeth Davidtz, Uma Thurman, Janet McTeer, Kim Bassinger, Rene

Russo, Debra Winger, and Ashley Judd all were considered (or considered us). No luck until Mira Sorvino's people called to tell us she was interested in the role. To me, that helped with my worry about too much sentiment. In her first film role she had won an Academy Award in Woody Allen's *Mighty Aphrodite* (1996), playing a tough hooker with a sense of fun, reminding me of Judy Holliday in *Born Yesterday*. The rest of the major casting went well. Nathan Lane played the part of a therapist, and he was a joy, brilliant and funny on and off the screen. The then little-known Diana Krall played and sang in a nightclub scene. Kelly McGillis, who costarred with Kilmer in *Top Gun*, played his sister in a part that could have been shrill but never was.

When I rehearsed with Mira and Val, I felt slightly uncomfortable, not with Val or Mira individually, but together. Mira seemed to want Amy to be sympathetic, as Virgil's blindness almost automatically makes *his* character sympathetic. That was a lot more more sympathy than I thought necessary, but Mira worked on it and found a way to make her character likeable and understandable without being mushy.

Val Kilmer, Mira Sorvino, Margo Winkler
At First Sight

How all the characters, including Virgil, react to Virgil's blindness and his regaining his sight was what the movie was really about. Also, what does "seeing" mean to him? He can't tell the difference between a smile or a frown; day and night are the same. What does the naked body of a woman he loves mean to him? He knows how people respond to a blind person, but not to a seeing person. Virgil and Amy's reaction to his regaining his sight was worth exploring. The romance, less so.

The shooting went well, and we finished the sixty-day schedule on April 2, 1998. The first screening after a couple of months was for Dr. Sacks and Shirl and Barbara Jennings. They were very congratulatory and felt their story was authentic and moving. MGM was high on the film, but we received "mixed" reviews. "Mixed" means "not great." The audience seemed unsure if *At First Sight* was the romance they expected to see. Had my fear of sentiment taken away from the romance?

My record is intact: I still haven't made a romance. *At First Sight* is about overcoming obstacles and never giving up.

Sound familiar?

In writing about *Life as a House*, I'm struck by the strange coincidence on the third anniversary of Bob Chartoff's death from pancreatic cancer of the character of George Monroe that Kevin Kline played. Kevin portrayed a character who wanted to accomplish something worthwhile before the inevitability of his death from cancer. Bob Chartoff accomplished many worthwhile goals long before his death. Bob's professional instincts mirrored his personal ones. When unknown, down-on-his-luck actor Sylvester Stallone walked into our office in 1975 and talked about a story of a broken-down, down-on-his-luck fighter, Bob and I instinctually responded and wanted to give Stallone the opportunity to make something special of himself. Stallone did, and *Rocky* was born.

Bob Chartoff's life was one of charity and discovery. When he felt that filmmaking didn't offer him the personal challenges he needed, he found them in human form. On a trip to India he was approached by a man who offered to sell his two sons to Bob. Bob didn't shrug that off as many tourists might have. In the village of Bodh Gaya, Bob convinced the man that there was a life that the two young boys could have by Bob paying for their education. Shortly thereafter Bob returned to Bodh Gaya and opened a school, the Jennifer Chartoff School,

Irwin Winkler and Robert Chartoff

named after his oldest daughter, for "untouchable" children, which he supported for decades.

The fictional character played by Kevin Kline saved his son; Bob Chartoff saved many sons and daughters.

CHAPTER SIXTEEN

Life with Kevin Kline is De-Lovely; *a director gets bullied
into not making a film*

LIFE AS A HOUSE (2001)

HOW DO YOU TURN a tragic story into one that is life affirming?
Life as a House, the film I directed in 2001, stars Kevin Kline as an
emotionally cold, disconnected, angry father with an equally angry,
disconnected son. I had seen the great Japanese director Akira Kurosawa's (*Rashomon*) film *Ikiru* and was fascinated by his picture of a
middle-aged bureaucrat who had achieved very little in his life, but
after discovering he has less than a year to live wants to leave something meaningful to his family and community.

I liked the writer Mark Andrus's *As Good as It Gets* for its humor
and crankiness (a great Jack Nicholson performance) and worked with
him to find a way to translate Kurosawa's movie to a contemporary
Los Angeles story. We came up with George Monroe (Kevin Kline),
a divorced father of a sixteen-year old, self-destructive son. George,
plagued with cancer and having only a short time to live, wants to
build a house as a way for him and his son to connect. I hadn't thought
about directing *Life as a House*, as I was a bit tired after the long New
York winter shoot of *At First Sight*, but as I met with several directors, I
was strangely uncomfortable. The directors were telling me what they
would do with *Life as a House*, and I frankly didn't like what they had
in mind. Was it them or was it me? As I was thinking about meeting
another group of directors, Michael Douglas called (Ron Meyer had
given him the script) and said it was one of the best scripts he had ever
read. Kevin Kline's agent also called and said Kevin had read the script

and wanted to play George. Both actors assumed I was directing the film. With two Academy Award–winning actors wanting to star in *Life as a House* and no director I had reacted well to, I decided to direct the film myself. After a drink with Kevin Kline, I was taken with his intelligence and understanding of George. He was available, and although he was known as an actor who often declines, he enthusiastically committed. Thankfully, I didn't have to make a choice between Michael Douglas and Kevin Kline. Douglas wanted to put the picture off until the next year, as his wife was about to give birth.

Columbia Pictures had paid Mark Andrus $850,000 for the script, and even though one of the finest actors had signed on and I was onboard as director, they wanted a rewrite, which I didn't think necessary (nor did Kline or Mark Andrus). At that point Columbia put the script in turnaround (an opportunity to submit it to other studios). A couple of studios were interested. Universal would go ahead only with Michael Douglas, Warner Bros. would only make it with George making a miraculous recovery from his fatal disease (missing the whole point of the story), and Paramount asked why he was building a house. The usual!

Playing golf one Saturday afternoon, my son Adam brought along a college friend, Eric Reid, who was a lawyer at an independent production company, Lakeshore Pictures. Reed asked if I had any scripts available, as Lakeshore was looking for projects. I told him to stop by my house and pick up a copy of *Life as a House*. First thing Monday morning, Reed called and said that Lakeshore was prepared to make an offer to finance the film at $17 million, subject to their approving a costar for the role of George's ex-wife. The next day New Line Cinema (a mini-major) made an offer of $18 million and no costar requirement. Although I was sure Lakeshore was sincere and wanted to make *Life as a House*, the costar approval would have taken time, and if we didn't agree, Lakeshore could cancel the film. We closed the deal with New Line, and Tom Rosenberg, the owner of Lakeshore, filed a lawsuit. This was the first time I had ever had two studios wanting to make a picture of mine; I had always felt lucky if I had one, especially for a drama about a man dying of cancer. Lakeshore, however, settled quickly by buying the distribution rights to *Life as a House* in Italy and Spain (at a good price) from New Line. Tom Rosenberg, showing no hard feelings, wrote me a very complimentary note after he saw *Life as a House* and some years later asked me to direct Philip Roth's *Elegy* with Kevin Kline. Kevin declined, and I did too.

Sometimes casting can be embarrassing. When we were casting George's wife, I met with Rita Wilson, who is a friend. She gave a great reading but was just too young for the part. That's when you wish you were making a special-effects film with *no* actors. Kristin Scott Thomas (an Oscar nominee for *The English Patient*) was the perfect age opposite Kline to play Robin, his wife. Sam, George's son, was a lot tougher. I had seen about fifty young actors before Hayden Christensen showed up. He read with Kline, and I hired him on the spot.

At our first read-through I kept thinking of Bob Fosse's *All That Jazz*, when the director has a heart attack at *his* first read-through. Fosse, always inventive, shot the scene with no sound, the camera panning across the actors at the table, full of confidence, then down the back of the director, who is holding a pencil. The pencil breaks. That's the only sound, and quickly the director is off to the emergency room. The *Life as a House* script read with laughs and tears, and I smiled all the way through it. I couldn't wait to start. No heart attack.

We shot the film pretty much in sequence, which is rare, as a film's locations often determine the schedule (if you're on one location, you don't leave it and come back later for a different scene; it's too expensive to go back and forth and hold the location while you're shooting somewhere else). Shooting an early scene in a hospital after George collapses and is diagnosed with terminal cancer, I had a thought. He is attended by a nurse played by Sandra Nelson. Her acting was low-key, warm, and caring. It struck me that George had died in the hospital, the nurse was a vision of eternity, and the rest of the film was George fulfilling his dream—the dream of him and Sam finding their love for each other and leaving something that they both built (the house). Maybe the notion was fanciful on my part, but it stayed with me through the shooting, into the editing, and even through the scoring.

I dipped into my own past when I looked into music for a romantic sunset dance between George and Robin. I thought I'd use Joni Mitchell's "Both Sides Now," and when I asked for a price quote, I was told that Joni would give us the use of the song for free, instead of the usual several hundred thousand dollars. Joni remembered that Bob Chartoff and I had worked with her in the 1960s and managed her very early career. At David Geffen's seventieth birthday party, Joni, I, and Mo Ostin, who was formerly the head of Warner Bros. Records, were chatting, when Joni said she was celebrating fifty years with Warner. She asked how she had originally signed up with Warner Records. I told her that Bob Chartoff, who was was in New York at the time, had called me and asked me to try to find a record company that would be interested in Joni. I knew Mo, called him, and he immediately made a deal for three albums. I asked Mo how come he'd agreed to sign her when she was virtually unknown. Mo smiled, remembering that he had heard about Joni, then couldn't find her, and then, out of the blue, I called.

Going from winter in New York on *At First Sight* to the sun-drenched Palos Verdes location on the Pacific coast was a pleasure. Our cameraman, Vilmos Zsigmond (Oscar winner for *Close Encounters of the Third Kind*), was the artist who captured the sunsets and the waves of the ocean as if they were on cue.

Some notes I made after the first week of *Life as a House*:

December 2000
Finished first week of shooting on Life. Very tired after last night's shoot. Got home at 3:00 A.M. and couldn't sleep. The days are long but fruitful. The casting has paid off. Every actor is really good, from Kevin to Jena Malone to Hayden and even to Jon, who plays the small role of Josh. Most of my directing went into my preparations. I know my shots (at least my first setup). Vilmos Zsigmond is very fast and an artist. I've gotten him committed, and it's a good collaboration. Very often he fights me; I like that (he cares).

Kevin Kline is a real pro and a wonderful actor. He tries things and gives me options. He doesn't need a conference after each take and doesn't go off into space like some actors. The crew is very good, fast and cheerful, and I try hard to be one of the guys. It makes for a nice feeling and good cooperation, though I'm not sure it makes the picture any better.

The dailies were excellent. So much so that Kevin came to me outside the projection room and was positively bubbly. He also told Rob Cowan how much he liked the work. I do too! So one week is gone. I love the directing and seeing the creation. The breaks are short because the set-ups are mostly outside with little lighting changes, so I'm not getting much rest during the day. I kid Vilmos that he should slow down, but the fact is, if I had more time during the day, I'd just shoot more. Never understood directors who stop for the day when they can get a couple more setups in.

Kristin came for makeup tests, and after she and Kevin went off to rehearse. I felt slightly, only slightly, sorry I didn't participate, but the actors are so good, I don't have the need to coach them, just guide them. I got lucky late in the afternoon—staged a scene against the late-afternoon sky, and the low sun broke through! Beautiful!

Lucky in not only the weather. Kevin Kline led the way. On Christmas holiday he shot a video of his real son Owen splashing in the surf, which we used in a scene later in the film to star Owen as a younger version of Sam. Kevin lost thirty pounds to play the cancer-ridden George, and Hayden, who started thin (the effects of his character's drug use), gained ten pounds as he got healthier in spirit and body. Kevin and Hayden spent all their spare time using hammers, buzz saws, and all kinds of equipment needed to build a house. When the camera was on them, it looked real, because, in fact, it was real. They were building a house.

We finished shooting *Life as a House* on February 22, 2001, and I returned to real life. Directing a movie is a great escape; you can put your life on hold and just live in the fantasy world of filming, where you can order it to rain or snow (special effects), make it day or night (lights), and have people in love or hate! Directing is the easiest and toughest thing I ever did.

Irwin Winkler and Kevin Kline
Life as a House

On April 4 I ran the rough-cut film in our small editing room for the CEO of New Line, Bob Shaye. Shaye insisted on wearing sunglasses and fell asleep halfway through the screening. I was told later never to show a film to Shaye after he's had his lunch (and wine). When the film ended, he woke up and told me it wasn't his kind of film. So why did he put up the money to make it if it wasn't his kind of film?

In spite of Shaye's reaction, his head of production, Toby Emmerich, was a fan, as was the entire staff of New Line. A series of very good research screenings and industry reactions set up *Life as a House* for a Christmas release, but first it would go to the Toronto Film Festival for our world premiere.

On Sunday September 9, *Life as a House* had a sold-out screening at the Toronto Film Festival. New Line executives, on a high from the reception, started planning for an Academy Award campaign. A bit of a damper were the not very good reviews in the Hollywood trade papers, but then came an excellent "think" piece in the Sunday *New York Times* by Janet Maslin. On Monday, September 10, Margo and I flew to New York for some press events on the way to Boston the next day for a screening at the Boston Film Festival. September 11, Tuesday, started bright and clear. I got into a car to pick up Margo at the hairdresser on the way to LaGuardia airport. Margo was getting her hair combed out, and there was a small television set at the hair salon that I glanced at as I waited. What I and the television announcer assumed was a small plane had accidentally flown into the north tower of the World Trade Center, but it didn't prevent Margo and me from heading up Park Avenue to the airport in the car. We heard a noise and turned around to see billowing black smoke from downtown New York. Our driver turned on the car radio, and we heard the news that all the airports had closed and the World Trade Center was on fire and about to collapse with thousands of people trapped inside. We quickly drove to our hotel on Sixty-First Street. Glued to the television set for the next few hours, we called our family in Los Angeles to assure them we were OK and left the hotel for some fresh air. We weren't greeted by much fresh air; instead the air was thick with ash and the sounds of air force jets flying overhead and sirens from fire engines and ambulances screeching continuously. Then came the strange sight of hundreds of mostly well-dressed men and women walking uptown on the deserted streets. The women had taken off their high heels, the men carrying their jackets in the heat—the ragtag group were office workers from downtown trying to get home with no cars, subways, or buses to take them. Margo and I found a restaurant that was open and had a tasteless meal. No surprise.

Anxious to get back to California, I kept calling American Airlines Special Services to see if any flights would be scheduled soon. I was told there would be seats for Margo and me on Thursday at noon. Pleased that we'd get home, we had a car drive us to JFK, and I told the driver not to leave the airport for the next hour, in case we didn't take off. JFK was very quiet, and security, when entering the airport, two days after the worst terrorist attack in U.S. history, was almost non-existent. After boarding our plane, while waiting to take off, we saw a SWAT team suddenly show up and board the plane and take (in shackles) a passenger from the plane parked next to ours. Our flight was then cancelled, and our driver was waiting to take us back to the hotel. I opened the newspapers the next day and found no mention of a man being taken off a plane at JFK. I wonder who that person was and where in the world he might be.

As the details of the attack on the World Trade Center were reported, we realized that we were to leave Boston on Wednesday, September 12, on the same American Airlines flight that left on September 11 and crashed into the south tower. One day earlier and . . .

Unbelievably, the Boston Film Festival ran *Life as a House* on the evening of September 11. I never asked how it played.

THE SHIPPING NEWS (2001)

On April 7, 2001, I flew from London to Nova Scotia and visited the set of *The Shipping News*, the film based on Annie Proulx's Pulitzer Prize–winning novel. It was a script in development that Columbia Pictures had asked me to produce about a year before. When I agreed to produce the film, I had not committed to directing *Life as a House*, and once that film commenced, I spent very little time on *The Shipping News*. But while it was in development we got a good script from Ron Bass (*Rain Man*) and very quickly were in negotiations with Billy Bob Thornton to star and direct, then just to star, then just to direct, and finally neither. Lasse Hallström (*What's Eating Gilbert Grape*) came aboard to direct and threw out Bass's script and brought in Robert Jacobs (*Chocolat*). In short order Kevin Spacey agreed to play Quoyle, an emotional cripple who moves from New York with his young daughter to his family home in Newfoundland to rebuild his life.

With Kevin Spacey, Cate Blanchett, Julianne Moore, and Judi Dench, *Shipping News* had as strong a cast as imaginable. After all the time and effort, however, Amy Pascal at Columbia Pictures decided she would only do the film if she had a financial partner. The partner she chose was Harvey Weinstein. The deals were done on the cast, the director, writer, key crew—except for our star, Kevin Spacey. Spacey's agent, after we agreed on a fee of $3 million, said he was sure Spacey would win the Academy Award for Best Actor for his role in *American Beauty* and demanded $4 million, because the Oscar enhanced his value. We agreed, and Kevin Spacey won the Oscar and the extra million. To my great surprise, the day after the Academy Awards, Kevin Spacey called me and turned down the extra million dollars. He said he didn't want the award to be about money; the recognition of excellence was enough.

With the cast in place, Columbia now decided to turn over *Shipping News* to Harvey Weinstein in its entirety. Now Weinstein was responsible for the film, and he reimbursed the studio for all the costs they had incurred. Meanwhile I was directing *Life as a House* and paid little attention to *The Shipping News*. It was very well cast, on schedule, and there were no complaints from the set. That is, until a couple of weeks later, when I finished *Life as a House* and flew to *The Shipping News* set in Nova Scotia. When I greeted Lasse Hallström, he asked if we could talk privately. Hallström had an offer to direct *Catch Me If You Can* starring Leonardo DiCaprio (whom Hallström had directed in *What's Eating Gilbert Grape*). He liked the script, but the film was being produced by Dreamworks, and Harvey Weinstein would only allow Hallström to accept if Weinstein got the rights from Dreamworks for the U.S. distribution. I asked Hallström if he had some kind of contract with Weinstein that allowed him to do (or not do) the film. Hallström said he didn't, but Weinstein threatened to ruin him in the movie business if he disobeyed him. Lasse was sure that Weinstein had the power to make sure he never worked again. Since he had no contract with Weinstein and he was a multi-nominated Academy Award director, I assured him Weinstein's threats were meaningless and urged him to do what was best for him. If he wanted to do *Catch Me If You Can*, he should.

A few weeks later Margo and I were invited by our friend Nora Ephron to a clambake at the beach in East Hampton. Steven Spielberg was there, and as we were chewing on our lobster, he asked me what I thought of Lasse Hallström. I told Steven I liked Lasse, he was a fine director, and I heard he might be directing *Catch Me If You Can* for his company, Dreamworks. Spielberg told me that he and DiCaprio had gotten word that Lasse would not be directing *Catch Me If You Can*, and he decided to direct it himself. He said he never knew why Hallström decided not to do the film.

Lasse Hallström made one more picture with Harvey Weinstein but never got bullied again. He moved on and made some very fine films with studios that treated him with the respect he deserves.

DE-LOVELY (2004)

To me, George and Ira Gershwin, Irving Berlin, Rodgers and Hammerstein, and Cole Porter were the iconic masters of American theater music in the early twentieth century (and Stephen Sondheim joined that illustrious group in the 1960s).

Marty Scorsese and I had worked on a Gershwin movie since 1983 but were never able to come up with a dramatic story that satisfied us or the Gershwin family. That was in spite of scripts by John Guare (*Atlantic City*) and Paul Schrader (*Taxi Driver*). George Gershwin seemed to find success in everything he tried. As a young man he wrote the hit song "Swanee," for Broadway; he wrote "Oh, Kay!" and "Lady Be Good" and then symphonic music like "An American

In Paris" and the great American opera *Porgy and Bess*. The only real drama in George Gershwin's life was his sad and sudden death in 1937 at the young age of thirty-eight.

Working on the Gershwin movie, I met Robert Kimball, who was the artistic advisor to not only the Gershwin family but the Cole Porter Trust as well. Kimball suggested that I consider a film based on Porter's life, and he would arrange for me to meet Robert Montgomery, the attorney who represented the trust. I knew a little about Porter, that he was an openly gay man when homosexuality was considered an aberration (in England a gay act could result in jail as late as 1967). In spite of his homosexuality, Porter was in love with and married Linda Lee Thomas, an American divorcée (who was called the most beautiful woman in all of Paris), and lived with her as husband and wife until she died in 1954. I was familiar with the 1946 movie *Night and Day*, which purported to be about Cole Porter, and although it was directed by Michael Curtiz (*Casablanca*), it was laughable, as it never dealt with Porter's sexuality, a very important part of his life and his work. Porter, after seeing the film, remarked, "If I could survive that, I can survive anything."

I was surprised when Montgomery had only one restriction: I could not portray a particular "friend" of Porter. Montgomery told me that the "friend" was a longtime lover of Porter and inherited, upon Porter's death, half of his large estate and half of the royalties earned from his music. That was all well and good, except the friend's family never knew he was gay. When he died, his survivors found themselves rich and ashamed. They instructed Montgomery to only contact them (send the checks) through a bank and never use the Porter Trust name on stationery; it had to be anonymous. Montgomery insinuated that the family, living off Porter's money, never worked again, succumbing to idleness and suffering from alcoholism.

Montgomery also agreed that we could have rights to the entire Porter catalogue of eight hundred-plus songs. Ordinarily the licensing of one of Porter's songs would cost approximately $200,000. That opened the door for us to use as many songs as we needed to tell the Porter story musically as well as dramatically.

I asked my longtime friend Jay Cocks (*The Age of Innocence*), who was formerly the film and music critic at *Time* magazine, to write the original screenplay. That screenplay had two goals: we didn't want the structure to be in the tradition of standard Hollywood musical biopics (*Rhapsody in Blue*, George Gershwin; *Three Little Words*, Harry Ruby and Bert Kalmar; *Words and Music*, Rodgers and Hart), and we wanted (and had the opportunity) to use Porter's songs to portray the characters and advance the plot. We also decided, since Porter's life was in theater, to show his life through the theater and his reflections on it as he's dying. Songs to portray his character were all in the library. We used "Experiment," a little-known Porter song, when he's trying to tell Linda he intends to continue pursuing an active gay life in Hollywood. Similarly, "Let's Fall in Love," "Anything Goes," "Easy to Love," "Let's Misbehave," "True Love," "Get Out of Town," and "Blow, Gabriel, Blow" all are used to enhance particular dramatic events in Porter's life.

MGM, with some nostalgia for the glory days of the studio when they made musicals like *An American in Paris*, *Meet Me in St. Louis*, *Ziegfeld Follies*, and *Gigi*, came aboard to finance *De-Lovely* in spite of its sad ending with Porter an old, crippled, bitter man singing "In the Still of the Night" with its touching lyrics of dreams fading out of sight.

Natalie Cole singing "Ev'ry Time We Say Goodbye" as Linda, suffering from emphysema, dies in Cole's arms again mirrored the sadness of Porter's later life.

Kevin Kline, after *Life as a House*, was my first and only choice to play Cole Porter. Not only did we have a warm friendship, but he was a two-time Tony Award–winner in musical comedy (*On the Twentieth Century* and *Pirates of Penzance*), an accomplished piano player, and had an excellent singing voice. At one point in rehearsals, however, Kevin was not sure he could sing some of Porter's intricate lyrics and melodies as well as he wanted to. I played Porter's own actual recordings, and Kevin and I agreed that, although he wrote great, he sang pretty poorly (although I still used Porter singing "Anything Goes" over the end credits).

Casting Linda Lee Thomas was not as easy. Linda was a beauti-ful, worldly, rich, sexually abused woman. She not only had to be a fine actress, she also had to look great, be a clothes horse, and be indepen-dent and strong in her relationship with Porter and his open sexual adventures. We went through all the usual casting possibilities. When Ashley Judd's agent called and told me Judd had read the script and would definitely want to play Linda, I invited her to come to New York to meet with Kevin and me. Ashley Judd came in like a whirlwind. She was sure of herself, looked smart and sophisticated, and had all her notes. She wasn't auditioning; she took over the part, just as Linda Porter would take over Cole's life. After she left, I was thrilled, but the executives at MGM were hesitant until Judd cut her salary in half.

The British government, in order to support their film indus-try, offered a very favorable tax rebate (approximately 25 percent of the

Kevin Kline, Ashley Judd, Irwin Winkler
De-Lovely

money spent on a film in England is refunded). Since we were pressed on the budget (not unusual at all) to reproduce Porter's lavish lifestyle on screen—custom-made clothes, antiques, hard-to-find period cars, and the like—we needed the financial help. The problem was to find locations in England that could stand in for Paris, Manhattan, Hollywood, Connecticut, Long Island, Arizona, and Venice. As we started out in a heatless van in a cold London winter to look for these locations, Rick Yorn, Marty Scorsese's manager, called. Marty had committed to direct Leonardo DiCaprio in a big-budget picture, *The Aviator*, about the eccentric billionaire Howard Hughes. Rick asked if I would produce the movie, which was scheduled to start shortly in Los Angeles. I could get a handsome producing fee, sleep in my own bed, and play golf on the weekends instead of riding around in a cramped, cold van trying to find Arizona in London. But I liked the challenge, liked Kevin Kline, liked the Cole Porter story, and stayed with it and had to put off working with my old friend Marty Scorsese. We did find a gravel pit in London, put up some cactus plants, and had Arizona. We found a movie set in Luxembourg, of all places, that became Venice (we did import the gondolas).

Through Jay Cocks's friendship, Giorgio Armani (Jay wrote the Armani cover story for *Time* magazine years before) agreed to supply the wardrobe in exchange for promotional credits. Kevin and I flew to Milan and met with Armani at his studio. He had a group of designers surrounding him but, to my amazement, got down on the floor with pins in his mouth and chalk in his hands and fitted Kevin's clothes himself. When I remarked that we needed a wedding gown for Linda Porter, Armani sat down and in ten minutes sketched one himself. I had thought that, with all his business interests, Giorgio Armani would be in a boardroom somewhere, not fitting clothes. But maybe that's why he's so successful.

With our principal cast in place, we received an extra bonus. Elvis Costello had heard about the film and asked if there was a song he could perform. When we met, he surprised me with his knowledge of the Porter catalogue, and he agreed to sing "Let's Misbehave." Costello volunteered that his wife, Diana Krall (who played a nightclub pianist in *At First Sight*), wanted to sing "I Get a Kick Out of You." From there, we cast Sheryl Crow ("Begin the Beguine"), Alanis Morissette ("Let's

Fall in Love"), Natalie Cole ("Every Time We Say Goodbye"), Robbie Williams ("It's De-Lovely"), and Mick Hucknall ("I Love You"). Because of our limited budget, we flew each performer to London for two days only. The day they arrived, they rehearsed their song, had costumes fitted, and pre-recorded the music that night (I would come directly from the set to supervise). The next day was for the performance in front of the camera, and then they were gone. Each performer got one fare to London and received minimum scale for their three days of singing and acting. They did it just so they could perform a Cole Porter song.

After the first week of shooting I had the editor in Los Angeles send me the edited film so I could see the musical number "Let's Fall in Love" that Alanis Morissette sang (and danced). I was appalled. I thought it was terrible and wanted to fire the choreographer, the dancers, the cinematographer, and the director (me). I sent the producer, my son Charles, to Los Angeles, where he met with our editor but felt he was in over his head and couldn't make out what I had shot. I asked Charles to hire our editor from *Life as a House*, Julie Monroe. A week later Julie had re-edited the footage, and it was great. The same raw material, just an editor who knew how to assemble the scene.

I set our sights high and felt we wouldn't need an editor when I had Vivian Green sing "Love for Sale." I set the performance in a gay men's club that Cole frequented. "Love for Sale," originally written for a prostitute to sing in the show *The New Yorkers*, was called "Sex for Sale" by the press at the time and was banned from radio play. My idea was to show Cole's promiscuity, and I wanted to do it with one continuous shot showing the passage of time. While Vivian Green sings, Cole enters the club, chats, dances, and leaves the club with a male companion, then returns to the club in different wardrobe as Vivian continues singing. The camera moves off Cole to the now newly costumed Vivian, Cole leaves again, and the camera goes back to Vivian and catches Cole entering again with a costume change. The camera acted like a time machine, picking up entrances and exits, people chatting and drinking, all while Vivian is singing "Love for Sale" with the illusion that it's over time because of the multiple wardrobe changes. The wardrobe and makeup people would re-dress Vivian or Kevin when the camera was on the other performer and then become background characters in the scene. The crew, so pleased with successfully getting this very tough day's work accomplished, insisted on buying me a drink at the pub next door.

How do you do a sex scene between a gay man and a woman who has been sexually abused? Jay Cocks wrote a scene in which Linda, at the piano, plays "True Love," and sitting next to her, singing along, is the daughter of Porter's friend Sarah Murphy. Cole realizes that Linda loves the little girl and wants a child of her own. In the next scene Cole enters Linda's bedroom with champagne and says, "How do you want to play this? Comedy? Tragedy? Musical comedy? Farce?" and Linda answers, "Why don't we just . . . play?". It was a scene with two wonderful actors and a director smart enough to sit back and let them do their thing.

In June 2003 the weather was the hottest London had endured in a long time. The production also endured, but barely. After three hours of having makeup applied, Kevin and the other actors found their makeup melting (air conditioning made too much noise). My job turned out to be having the actors get their lines out before their makeup ran down their faces. Some scenes were tough, for example Cole having his leg amputated after a horse fell on him in a riding accident. Cole was at that point in his life terribly bitter, nasty, and unhappy, and I really believe that the oppressive heat and melting makeup helped make the scene feel real.

The shooting ended on July 26, 2003, in Luxembourg (for Venice). So, after years of preparation and shooting, the film moves to the editing room, where there are no schedules (for a while), no worries about getting all the shots in, no waiting for the actors, the makeup crew, the lighting of the set, the prop man who's not prepared, the actors who won't light their own cigarettes, pianos that aren't tuned, sets designed with no sense of the camera position, furniture that's rented but too heavy to move, clothes that don't fit the actor and have to be refitted just as you're about to shoot, actors who don't like each other, dancers who are out of step, singers who are out of tune, and never enough time. But with it all you can't wait to get the next good script and start filmmaking all over again.

Julie Monroe asked me to come to the editing room on a Sunday. She had been coming to work on Saturdays and Sundays without getting paid; she gets neither wide recognition nor thanks for that. She's quite a lady. People like Julie, who just care about the film and their work, who are unheralded and hardly appreciated, are truly the ones who make the movies.

After ten weeks *De-Lovely* was ready to be seen. A group of friends were invited to see the rough cut. But would they be critical enough? Margo, my best and most honest critic, was smiling.

On November 13, 2003, all the work, all the hours and hours, all the man power, woman power, resources, money, talent, imagination, and risk came together in a two-hundred-seat theater in Westlake, Cali-

Front: Rob Cowan, Kevin Kline, Ashley Judd, Sheryl Crow, Irwin Winkler, Alanis Morissette, Lara Fabian
Back: Natalie Cole, Mario Frangoulis, Lemar Obika, Charles Winkler, Sandra Nelson Winkler
De-Lovely premiere at the Cannes Film Festival, May 22, 2004

fornia. The audience was suburban, not a jacket or tie in sight. Could this audience relate to the black-tie tuxedos and shimmering silk gowns of a highly sophisticated couple with a very unusual relationship? If they didn't respond, the studio would run for cover, try to recut the movie, and cut down their marketing budget. But the response was wonderful. A few people walked out at the gay love scenes, but that was to be expected. The audience loved the music, how it was performed, and how it went with the unconventional love story. The preview cards were excellent, and MGM was thrilled, as were Kevin Kline, Ashley Judd, Jay Cocks, and me.

The Cannes Film Festival screened *De-Lovely* and offered us the closing-night gala screening. That honor, we hoped, would help with the film's European release. *They Shoot Horses, Don't They?* was in that same prestigious spot at Cannes in 1970. It was May 28, my birthday, and it couldn't have been better. We got a standing ovation after showing *De-Lovely*, and then all of us took our bows and headed into the night in our tuxedos and evening gowns, just like the Cole Porter crowd in the Jazz Age of the 1920s.

CHAPTER SEVENTEEN

From Camp Polk, Louisiana, to the Iraq War

HOME OF THE BRAVE (2006)

THE AMERICAN INVASION OF Iraq in 2003 was one of the most unpopular armed conflicts the country participated in. Few in America knew or cared about the returning veterans after the violent occupation. Over 150,000 men and women served, with over 3,000 soldiers killed, 25,000 injured, and thousands more suffering from post traumatic stress disorder.

As a nineteen-year old enlistee I had served for two years in the U.S. infantry during the Korean War and, luckily, had never been assigned to combat. I had, however, been posted at a discharge center at Camp Polk, Louisiana, and spent months dealing with the soldiers returning from that battleground on the other side of the world. Those men (and some women) knew the tragedy of war with its many injuries and great loss of life. Although it was many years before the Iraq War of 2003, the trauma of the veterans never left me. I felt I had to tell the story of those who came back.

While I was in production in London on *De-Lovely*, the British press following the Iraq War was highly critical (as I was) of George Bush and the group of neocons who had encouraged the conflict. I started making notes based on news reports of the conflict, and after we finished shooting *De-Lovely*, I sketched out a story of a group of men and women war veterans very different from the classic film of the returning soldiers of World War II, *The Best Years of Our Lives*. In that movie (and that era) the veterans we knew of were all white males, as the army was racially segregated and the women who served had a separate division, the Women's Army Corps (WAC). Although *The*

Best Years of Our Lives is one of my favorite films, a story about the Iraq War had to deal with an unpopular conflict very different from World War II, when our soldiers were thought to be saving the world from the great evils of fascism. With the screenwriter Mark Friedman, we set up a racially, generationally, and gender-wise mix of soldiers. A black combat surgeon (Samuel Jackson), a pert gym instructor (Jessica Biel), and three boyhood friends (Brian Presley, Chad Michael Murray, and Curtis "50 Cent" Jackson), all who had enlisted in the National Guard in their hometown of Spokane, Washington, now found themselves not on a weekend retreat in the countryside of Spokane but in a hot and shabby barracks outside Baghdad.

Usually the lead part, the one that gets the movie green-lighted, is the hardest to cast. Actors you want are unavailable, too expensive, don't like the script, don't like the director, don't like the location, don't like their costar, don't like the studio, don't like the wardrobe, or they do like their wife and kids and have just completed two location movies in a row and promised their family they'd stay home for a while. Lots and lots of reason to say no. Sam Jackson was just the opposite. His agent, Toni Howard, gave him the script, he read it immediately, we had lunch, he said he liked it and understood it was a film that would not be a big payday, but he felt great sympathy for the character. Casting Vanessa, the gym teacher, was a lot more difficult than I thought it would be. We had written the part as a single mother who loses an arm when the armored car she is in is hit by a mortar. We had interviewed many actresses, and most were leery of shooting under severe conditions for next to no money. Jessica Biel, however, embraced the notion. She was smart, gave a very good reading, and when I asked if she would cut her long blond hair, she never hesitated. The financier pushed for a name in every part and suggested Curtis "50 Cent" Jackson for Jamal. I didn't know what to expect when this famous rapper showed up. He came to meet me with no entourage, no attitude, and lots of enthusiasm. Brian Presley (Tommy) and Chad Michael Murray (Jordan) rounded out the cast. After we cast Presley we got a bit of help from an investment fund he was associated with. They agreed to put up a small amount of money toward the budget. Chad Michael Murray was starring in a television series and was able to rush from that location in Georgia to Morocco in time for a couple of days of rehearsal before we shot our first scene.

I had no illusion that we could get a major studio to finance *Home of the Brave*. It was to be a sober look at a very unpopular war fought by citizen soldiers. After a quick turndown by a couple of studios, I didn't hesitate when Rob Cowan informed me that a small distributor, Millennium Films, was interested in financing the film. With the major studios in a blockbuster mentality, spending hundreds of millions on comic book adaptations, *Home of the Brave* was only welcomed by the independent distributor that would sell off foreign rights and hopefully cover the cost of the film with those sales. Companies like Millennium would not develop their own projects; they would pick up scripts that were too different or too small for the major studios.

The budgets on independent films are, necessarily, tight. Hours and hours, days and weeks went into the budget negotiations with Millennium. They wanted us to shoot the Iraq scenes in Bulgaria (they backed down when we pointed out there was no desert nearby). Could we shoot Spokane, Washington, in Bulgaria? No, we couldn't. We could use digital cameras, but some of the older models were cheaper. Could the actors fly to locations business class, rather than first class? Would the crew fly tourist instead of business class? Have the actors take a cab rather than a town car to and from the airport? Ask the leading lady to use a local (Bulgarian) hair and makeup person rather than the one she's had for years? Can you buy the wardrobe at a local shop rather than manufacturing it? Every aspect of the budget went through a very, very thorough vetting. When it came to the salaries of the producers and director, they had to be the absolute minimum. Millennium knew that by the time we came to them, we had nowhere else to go.

One of my agents at CAA, once we had a green light, blithely said, "I don't know why you're going to knock yourself out doing *Home of the Brave. Rocky Balboa* I can't wait to see. *Home of the Brave* I *can* wait to see." My own agent's send-off.

With a final budget approved, our location team reported that there was a town near the Atlas Mountains in Morocco that would substitute for Iraq and was cost effective. I was a bit apprehensive when we

Irwin Winkler, David Winkler, Sly Stallone
Rocky Balboa

arrived in Ouarzazate. After all, here was an American film about the war in Iraq with Americans shooting Muslims and Muslims shooting Americans, coming to shoot in a Muslim country with a Jewish director. I needn't have worried; as we checked in to our hotel, I heard familiar music. An Israeli tour group was dancing the hora in the lobby.

The whole town of Ouarzazate was very friendly. When we went scouting for locations, we were always invited to tea and cakes, which again surprised me, as I never imagined we as Americans would be so welcome. While being embraced by the Muslim citizens in Morocco I got word that we'd lost one of our locations in Spokane, Washington, as the owners of the house we'd rented wouldn't allow for a scene of premarital sex to be shot on their premises! As we worked from one section of Ouarzazate to another, our local assistant director stopped off at a tiny cave on a side street to buy fresh-baked bread, and we saw a hooded woman baking on stones over an open fire, just as I imagined her ancestors had been doing for centuries. That was in sharp contrast to the opulent, luxurious Governors Palace that we were invited to the next night for dinner, wine, and cigars.

The Moroccan army kept us on pins and needles until the night before our first day of shooting. They had promised us that the equipment we rented from them (at a fair price) for our combat scenes would be delivered a week ahead of time so it could be examined for safety, repaired if necessary, and painted to match the American military equipment. At 6:00 P.M. the armored cars, tanks, and props arrived, and Rob Cowan stayed up all night having the exteriors painted, American decals applied, and the vehicles checked for safety.

The first day of shooting went well with our cast and a mixture of local actors and anyone we could collar in and around Ouarzazate who looked good in a U.S. Army uniform. The action had us follow the unit's mission to deliver medical supplies to a hospital in a nearby town. Once the soldiers arrive, they are ambushed and attacked by mortars, rifles, and roadside bombs.

The ambush we re-created was just one incident out of hundreds in the history of the Iraq War; it was hardly even notable. These attacks, however, changed the lives of not only the soldiers fighting (and dying) but of their families, friends, and neighbors. That was the essence of *Home of the Brave*.

We spent twelve days shooting the soldiers ambushed and under fire, with Charles Winkler directing the second unit (action sequence without the principal actors). It was a strange experience. I had done movies about big bands, singers, gangsters, boxers, marathon dancers, voyeurs, student uprisings, blind people, sick people, blacklisted people, astronauts, composers, priests, cops, killers—just about every subject imaginable—but never mortars, tanks, and soldiers in battle. I found a great deal of it technical as to where a mortar lands, how an armored vehicle flips when it runs over a roadside bomb, and how big bullet holes should be and how red the "blood" should look when someone is shot.

The crew, a mixture of British, Italian, American, Spanish, and very congenial Moroccans, got along a lot better than our real American soldiers got along with the Iraqis they had come to "bring democracy to" (according to President Bush). With the crew so in tune with one another, we were able to move quickly and get the opening twenty minutes of the film shot in two days less than we anticipated. Leaving Morocco and scheduled to shoot in Spokane three days later, we chartered a plane to fly us to Paris, where we were scheduled to fly nonstop to Los Angeles, then on to Spokane. Our plane stopped at the private terminal in Orly Airport, and Margo, I, and Sam Jackson, who accompanied us, went to clear French customs. The officers escorted the three of us to a private lounge, glanced at Margo's and my passports, stamped them, and invited us to have snacks and coffee. Sam, on the other hand, was put through the mill. His luggage was carefully and slowly examined, he was asked a multitude of unnecessary questions, and it was obvious he was being subjected to a racist ordeal. I started to object but saw that Sam remained calm, never complained, and got through it with a lot more dignity than I would have shown. He is quite a man.

That sent us on to Spokane, Washington, where the consequences of the battle are dramatized. Will Marsh (Jackson) is haunted by his helplessness as a surgeon in the madness of combat, Vanessa Price (Biel) has to deal with the loss of an arm and the need to regain a semblance of her former life, Jamal (50 Cent) must try to live with his accidental killing of a civilian, and Tommy (Presley) must cope with the loss of his best friend, Jordan (Murray).

In Spokane, we expected a reception at least as welcoming as we got on arrival in Morocco, but that was not to be. Our financier, Millennium, was in a dispute with IATSI, the union that represented most of the Spokane crew. After two days of shooting, unable to make a deal with Millennium, the union called a strike. Millennium, instead of settling their differences, told us to move the shoot to Vancouver, Canada. Rob Cowan and I went for a quick look at Vancouver and found that it would be impossible to shoot without at least four weeks of preparation (finding and leasing locations, casting local actors, and hiring local crews if they were available). Faced with abandoning the film we'd shot in Morocco and shutting down the movie, I called the head of the union in New York and made a deal for Millennium, whom the head of the union refused to talk to. Millennium reduced our shooting schedule by the three days we lost because of the strike.

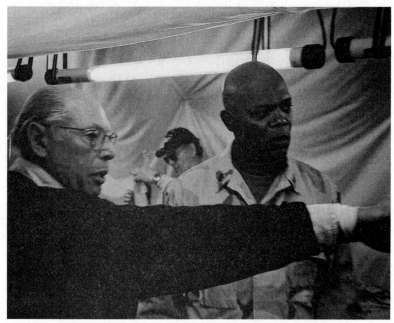

Irwin Winkler and Samuel L. Jackson
Home of the Brave

In the film, the tranquil atmosphere of the all-American town of Spokane is interrupted by the reception the returning soldiers receive from their family, friends, neighbors, and, surprisingly, the Veterans Administration. When the returning soldiers managed to get an appointment with the Veterans Administration, they found unending bureaucracy and overworked doctors, nurses, and psychiatrists. The veterans asked, "Is this what we fought for?" The veterans also felt hopeless to explain to family and friends what it was like to face death every day in combat, whether it was a civilian shooting at you from an apartment window or a dead animal stuffed with explosives on the road you were traveling on.

The bravery of the soldiers from the Iraq War was evident at the Veterans Administration facility. We filmed a basketball game with paraplegics. Their energy and talent was stirring. When it started to rain and we couldn't shoot, they continued to play in the rain. The crew, instead of finding shelter from the rain, stayed to watch the men play in their wheelchairs.

After our editing process, I was eager to show the film to the military, and we set up a preview showing at Camp Pendleton, California. The audience of military men was silent as Sheryl Crow's song "Try Not to Remember" (nominated for a Golden Globe) ended the film. Not a lot of words but lots of emotion from the combat veterans in attendance. Later, at the USA Film Festival in Dallas, Texas, at the closing-night event, the Q and A after the screening was just the opposite of the lack of interest we had received from the press and audiences up to then. An army captain just back from Iraq said he "had been very much for the war, but the film touched every aspect of my feelings" and made him now question the American involvement. Another returning soldier got up and said that we never should have been in Iraq and thanked me and said he was in tears watching the film. Yet another uniformed soldier said he hadn't been able to talk to his family about his experience and how it affected him, but when his wife and daughter saw the film, they would know what was troubling him. The audience of mostly servicemen and their families was emotional and very complimentary. It's hard to understand the harsh reaction of some critics versus the audience reaction, but the truth is, the film is tough. That's the good thing and the bad. The media may not have wanted to feel sympathy for anyone or anything about this unnecessary, terrible war and its aftermath. We wanted to tell about the almost forgotten soldiers who came back, and we did.

PART V

HOME OF THE BRAVE was certainly not the last small, independent, personal film ever made. But it was made against a background of Hollywood blockbuster, big-budget movies. Movies that got their financing from entertainment giants. The traditional movie studios have become a small part of the multimedia conglomerates. Universal Studios is now part of the NBC network, the theme parks in Florida, California, and China all owned by the cable giant Comcast. Twentieth Century Fox and its sister company, 21st Century Fox, are owned by News Corporation, which has major ownership of Fox News, Fox Sports, Sky Television, FX, Fox Network, newspapers in the United States, England, and Australia, and sports teams. The Walt Disney Company, in addition to its ownership of the studio and theme parks, owns ABC Television Network, ESPN, and cruise ships, and outbid Comcast for the ownership of 20th Century Fox from News Corp. Time Warner owns Warner Bros. Studios as well as Turner Broadcasting, CNN, HBO, and TNT and is in the process of being taken over by the corporate megagiant AT&T for $85 billion. These corporations are in the business of supplying big entertainment with worldwide appeal over multiple platforms—movies, theme parks, television, cable, Internet, toys, clothes, even Broadway blockbusters (Disney has grossed billions with *The Lion King* and *Beauty and the Beast*). The world of Marvel brings fun, entertainment, and sometimes an important cultural message with its films. When Ryan Coogler finished *Creed*, he was asked to direct the Marvel comic *Black Panther*. I told him I didn't think it was a good idea, suggesting he do something "more personal." Ryan told me that as a youngster growing up in Oakland, California, he went looking for a comic book that featured a black hero. He found *Black Panther* and wanted to bring that story to the screen. *Black Panther* has sold over one billion dollars in tickets and has brought an appreciation of African culture to a worldwide audience and given that audience an opportunity to understand and applaud the hero a young Ryan Coogler found inspiration in.

So the big blockbuster can not only entertain audiences, but teach them as well. I'm very pleased that Coogler didn't listen to Winkler.

CHAPTER EIGHTEEN

A wild ride to Wall Street, a gamble turning over a classic to a new generation, a sad loss, and a long-delayed Silence

THE WOLF OF WALL STREET (2013)

THE HISTORY OF MOVIE financing goes back a century to the nickelodeon—usually vaudeville houses that ran movies as a pause between singing, dancing, comics, and sometimes striptease acts. In the case of Carl Laemmle, the founder of Universal Studios, he had a dry goods store in Chicago in the early 1900s, and since his merchandise laid flat on his counters, he projected "flicks" at night over the cotton goods without any obstruction. Because customers flocked to the films, he gave up the dry goods and financed movies instead. The film industry moved from vaudeville theaters and dry goods stores to short silent films, longer complete stories, talking pictures, and animated stories, from black-and-white to Technicolor to widescreen, stereo sound, special visual effects, IMAX theaters, and very, very expensive comic book style "franchise" films. With these films starting to cost two hundred million to make and another hundred million to market, the major studios looked for financial partners to share their risks. *The Wolf of Wall Street* was financed not by a Hollywood studio, rich real estate mogul, or oil tycoon, but by a Malaysian investment fund. It was one more strange way to finance a movie.

Don't get me wrong: I'm very, very glad it got made. *The Wolf of Wall Street* is a fine film, and it was a lot of fun to make. It was nominated for five Academy Awards and was an enormous audience success, selling $450 million in worldwide ticket sales. It's remembered for "furious, yet exquisitely controlled, kinetic energy, complete with a plunging and soaring camera, mercurial and conspicuous special effects, counterfactual scenes, subjective fantasies, and swirling choreography on a grand scale" (Richard Brody, the *New Yorker*). It's also known for its financing from a "massive Malaysian fraud," according to *Fortune Magazine*: "It is once again a case of life imitating art. The Department of Justice has confirmed that it believes the ultimate bad boy financier movie *The Wolf of Wall Street* was financed through some pretty naughty financial maneuvers." The U.S. government asserted that the fund 1MDB, overseen by Malaysia Prime Minister Najib Razak, had stolen assets from the billion-dollar fund. The stepson of the prime minister, Riza Aziz, has been named as a "relevant individual." When I came aboard to executive produce *The Wolf of Wall Street*, I questioned Aziz and his partner, Joey McFarland, about where the financing was coming from and was told it was from Abu Dhabi government officials whose names they (or I) couldn't pronounce, but since Aziz was the prime minister's stepson, all seemed legitimate. In the end the film made a great deal of money for production company Red Granite Pictures and, I hope, the fund.

The process of making *The Wolf of Wall Street*, however, started with a phone call (don't most things in Hollywood start with a phone call?). The call was from Rick Yorn. He asked me to read the script written by Terence Winter based on the reminiscences of Jordan Belfort, who made a fortune on Wall Street through every shady deal imaginable, indulged in every excess imaginable, was sent to prison, and ended up holding motivational seminars all over the globe. Yorn said Leo DiCaprio was set to play Belfort and asked me to produce *The Wolf of Wall Street*. Leo had read the book in 2007, and Warner Bros., who purchased it, had passed on making it, as they felt it was too sexy, too raunchy, and too druggy. Leo found the screenplay audacious, funny, raunchy, risky, and very good and was committed to making it regardless. Yorn wanted me to give my thoughts to Marty Scorsese, as Leo believed he was the perfect director. We met, and Marty told me he had read the script and liked it a lot but first wanted an update on *Silence* (a script Marty had written with Jay Cocks about two Jesuit priests on a mission in Japan in 1650) before we got into *The Wolf of Wall Street*. I told Marty we had no immediate prospects for financing *Silence*, but I was very optimistic that we would eventually get the funding. Marty then reread the script, met with the writer, Terence Winter, met with Leo quite a few times, and decided to direct the film. Marty also liked the fact that Red Granite Pictures, who had picked up the rights from Warner Bros. on Leo's behalf, was funding *The Wolf of Wall Street*. With independent financing the film could stay true to Belfort's excesses. It was a unique opportunity. Studios by their nature are conservative, and the freedom we enjoyed ultimately made *The Wolf of Wall Street* the success it was.

Marty Scorsese strives for authenticity in his movies. The actors have to know their character better than know themselves, and he makes sure that he and the actors spend time with the characters they are playing. In *The Wolf of Wall Street* real stockbrokers worked in scenes with our actors and were encouraged to contribute lines of dialogue, the look of their wardrobe, their eating and drinking habits, even their after-hours activities. Marty rehearsed the actors in phone conversations that were as smooth as silk or agitated to the point of a slammed-down phone. The actors, of course, never took drugs or drank liquor that might affect their acting, but Jonah Hill snorted such a great amount of fake drugs that he got so sick, he couldn't work for days. We had to shoot an alternate scene to give his body time to recover. Leo got expert advice on how to react to quaaludes directly from the expert Jordan Belfort. Although I have no idea how Belfort really remembers his quaalude high! The reality went too far in one crazy scene where an actress had to be dismissed when she came on to Leo too enthusiastically in a supposedly "simulated" sex scene.

Other than DiCaprio the casting was mostly unknowns or up-and-coming actors. Jonah Hill was, I thought, a bit young for Leo's sidekick, but he put himself on tape and went toe to toe with Leo and had the cast and crew in stiches with his brilliant improvisation. Margot

Robbie, playing Leo's wife, impressed Marty with her understanding of her character. She told the press that she insisted on doing her seduction scene with Leo totally nude, as that was the only way her character could win Leo's very successful Jordan Belfort. Matthew McConaughey, already a pretty big star, worked for scale, and in preparing for his first scene with Leo, McConaughey pounded his chest and hummed. Marty thought it was right in the zone of what the film needed. Leo told me that after the film opened in France, while he was walking in Paris, he was greeted by crowds of young kids imitating him and Matthew McConaughey pounding on their chests and humming. Leo was able to show Belfort's character having just about every emotion. He went from serious to comic to drunk to drugged out, sometimes angry and anxious and sometimes sad. In a scene where he tries to open his car door while he's high on quaaludes, he opens the door with his feet, lying on his back. It was funny and reminded me of the great silent film actors Charlie Chaplin and Buster Keaton. Leo also had a backache for days. We cast an ex–James Bond girl, Joanna Lumley, to play Margot Robbie's aunt, and Leo, playing his Jordan Belfort character, got a lot more friendly than Lumley expected from her niece's husband. The shock showed in her face. Initially we wanted Julie Andrews for the role, as it would have been fun having Mary Poppins in an R-rated movie, but at the last minute she couldn't clear her schedule. Andrews did however bare her breasts in her husband Blake Edwards's movie *S.O.B.*, so maybe it wouldn't have been too much of a shock to have Mary Poppins get kissed rather passionately by Jordan Belfort.

While shooting outside Trump Tower on Fifth Avenue one night, we were greeted by the future president, who hinted that he wouldn't mind a part in *The Wolf of Wall Street*, but it couldn't be a walk-on. He also remembered calling me almost thirty years earlier, wanting me to shoot *Rocky IV* at his Atlantic City hotel, and said I'd made a big mistake by turning him down, because he would have made a "great deal."

The first cut of *Wolf* ran three hours and fifty-five minutes. An hour too long, and theaters wouldn't play it, as they would lose a showing and lose sales of not only box office receipts but popcorn and candy (where they make the big money). But what to cut? Marty had managed to shoot just about every scene as entertainment in its

Martin Scorsese, Leonardo DiCaprio, Jonah Hill, Irwin Winkler, Margot Robbie
The Wolf of Wall Street

own right. The story had a traditional line: poor ambitious guy gets a break, succeeds beyond his wildest dreams, gets himself (and others) in trouble, ends up in the slammer. But with *The Wolf of Wall Street* it's a helluva lot of fun to watch as Belfort goes from rags to riches. As played by Leo, you can't help but like him. The editing process was slow and measured, not cutting too much off a scene or cuting too little. Thelma Schoonmaker, our editor, labored with Marty for months, and every couple of weeks Margo and I would fly to New York to see the latest cut. Every trip was another screening, as we would bring in fifteen to twenty acquaintances to get reactions. By the time the film was down to three hours we were getting close to the release date and had a screening for an audience of about one hundred. The film played great—lots of laughs, lots of nervousness, and lots of applause. We celebrated that night at Mr. Chow's with champagne flowing—not quite up to Belfort partying but close.

The last-minute cuts pushed our release date to Christmas from Thanksgiving, and we had to deal with the ratings board before we could lock up the picture. Marty reminded me that on *Raging Bull* I'd met with the board, refused to make any cuts, and they'd backed down. He wanted me to do the same for *The Wolf of Wall Street*. It wasn't necessary, as they, surprisingly, asked for a few very minor cuts, and we obliged. On December 14 in Los Angeles I held a screening for friends, Academy members, and industry big hitters. The film played great, and after the showing we had a party at my house. The directors Francis Ford Coppola, Norman Jewison, Scott Cooper, and Rupert Wyatt couldn't get over Marty's energy, courage, and originality. On December 16 in New York my friend Mort Zuckerman hosted a screening for about seventy-five friends and got the same response. The strongest reaction was from Justice Stephen Breyer, who had a fine time, liked the film a lot, but couldn't believe our R-rating (I'm glad I didn't have to defend it to the Supreme Court). The film received excellent reviews. The *New York Times* ("One of the best films of the year"), *Rolling Stone*, and the *Los Angeles Times* raves all gave Paramount Pictures, who distributed the film domestically, a made-to-order marketing campaign on a film that needed the legitimacy of critics to get the audience into a hard-R-rated film, especially during the Christmas season.

The Wolf of Wall Street didn't win any of its five Academy Award nominations. I guess the Academy members were somewhat turned off by all the sex, booze, and drugs. Leo did win a Golden Globe for Best Actor, and the film did get wins from many other festivals.

The U.S. government has seized many of the Red Granite assets, and Red Granite says they are cooperating in the investigation of the 1MDB.

The film has been banned in Malaysia by Prime Minister Najib Razak, although the 1MDB, according to the U.S. Justice Department, financed the making of *The Wolf of Wall Street*.

THE GAMBLER (2014)
(AND THE ORIGINAL IN 1974)

April 25, 2010: the quickest deal I've ever made. Of course the deal was quick, but the movie took four years to make. On to the deal.

At lunch with Rick Yorn I mentioned that I thought *The Gambler*, a very good film Bob Chartoff and I made in 1974 starring James Caan, would be a good film to remake for a contemporary audience. Rick asked what I thought about Leo DiCaprio playing the Caan part and Marty Scorsese directing. Silly question. Rick texted Leo that I wanted Marty and him to be involved, and before we ordered our salads, Leo was in. Rick then texted Marty that Leo was in, and Marty joined us. Next was Adam Goodman, president of Paramount (they owned the rights). I was now halfway through my salad when Goodman confirmed that we had a deal with Paramount to develop *The Gambler*. All this done by the time coffee came.

Just as quickly as the development deal was made, Bill Monahan agreed to write the screenplay. Monahan was an Academy Award winner for his script of *The Departed*, which was directed by Scorsese and starred DiCaprio, Matt Damon, and Mark Wahlberg. It was a natural.

The casting of the charismatic James Caan for the original was also a natural. Caan had been nominated for an Oscar for his memorable performance as Sonny, the tempestuous son of Marlon Brando's godfather in Paramount's *The Godfather* in 1972. With our hiring of the British director Karel Reisz (*Morgan, Saturday Night and Sunday Morning*) and our budget approved, we were all set to go. I was surprised when Paramount's Robert Evans, head of production, asked me to come to his office for an urgent meeting and bring Reisz along. I told Evans that Reisz was in London, and he insisted that our meeting was urgent and Reisz should fly to Los Angeles immediately. Evans wouldn't tell me what the problem was, but we found out the minute Reisz and I walked into his office. The news was bad! Evans said even though he had green-lighted the film, he now realized there was a very

serious script problem. Evans pointed out that Axel (Caan's character) loses $77,000 to his bookmaker. According to Evans, that would
never happen; no bookmaker would lend that amount of money. Evans
was sorry, but the picture was now off. I told Evans that Reisz and I
needed to discuss the situation, and we'd be back in his office in half
an hour. Reisz was speechless as we walked around the Paramount
lot. I told him to just follow my lead, and when we returned to Evans's
office, I told Evans we had considered the problem, and we were sure
we could make it work with Axel losing $44,000. Evans beamed and
said, "If you guys make that work, go make the picture, and I'll see you
at the premiere."

James Caan, Irwin Winkler, Karel Reisz
The Gambler, 1973

No such problem in 2014. Bill Monahan and I met and decided
that we would stay with the characters and plot of the original. That
is, a college professor whose gambling addiction destroys his family,
his lover, his friends, and his self-respect. The downward plunge of an

addict is easy to predict; the challenge is to make that character inter-esting, and that's where the casting of Leo DiCaprio comes in.

Monahan started writing in June of 2010, and I didn't hear from him until January 2012, in spite of my many attempts to reach him. In the meantime, I had my hands full with James Toback, who wrote the original *Gambler* and wanted a payday, although he had no rights and was well paid all those years ago. *Deadline Hollywood*, a trade blog, ran a piece criticizing Paramount (and me) for not discussing the mak-ing of the film with him. Coincidently, the same night that the *Dead-line Hollywood* piece appeared, I ran into James Caan, who remarked, "What a full-of-shit" guy James Toback was. No argument there. The Paramount executive who was assigned to *The Gambler*, Liz Raposo, told me that they would deal with Toback and they knew him to be a troublemaker.

Although Monahan took over a year to write his first draft, he finished my notes in one week. Liz Raposo didn't take a week. Over-night she read *The Gambler* and said it was "near perfect." The rest of the executives at Paramount felt pretty much the same way. Now to get Leo DiCaprio to read it. As far as Marty Scorsese was concerned, I knew that *Silence* was singular and primary in his thinking, and we would have to find another director. We started the process of seeing who was available, who was interested in the subject, who would do a remake of a successful, well-thought-of original movie, and who might be acceptable to DiCaprio. Paramount had asked us to consider an interesting, not very obvious director, Todd Phillips. Phillips had directed the extremely successful, outlandish comedy *The Hangover*. I'd not ordinarily think Phillips would be interested in a serious drama, nor would I necessarily be interested in his directing *The Gambler*. But because *The Hangover* was so original, innovative, and risky, I arranged to meet Phillips. I also knew that Phillips was a gambler: he had turned down a $6 million fee on *The Hangover*, taking instead a profit partici-pation that earned him $60 million instead of $6 million. So Phillips certainly knew about risk taking. When Phillips and I met, I sensed his edginess and gambler instinct, and he liked our script.

Now that we had a movie that looked like it was a go, James Toback showed his teeth. Jeff Berg, Toback's agent, asked me if his client had any rights to a *Gambler* sequel or remake. I told him no. After that conversation Paramount then called me and said they didn't want to get into a fight with Toback, as they were planning their hundred-year anniversary and didn't want any bad press. They asked if I would give Toback an executive producer credit, a fee, and let him read the script. I reluctantly agreed. Shortly thereafter, Toback called from the Cannes Film Festival, where he was making a documentary about two hustlers (Toback and Alec Baldwin) trying to raise money for an independent film. Funny thing about the Cannes Film Festival: I miss it when I'm not there and hate it when I am. I find myself having a black-tie dinner with someone whose phone calls I would ordinarily hesitate to return. Toback was not very complimentary (no surprise) about Monahan's dialogue and offered to fix it for a price in addition to his executive producer fee. I told him we, Todd Phillips, and Paramount were happy with the script and didn't want to rewrite it. Toback then said he knew that DiCaprio would be reading the script, and he (I didn't know he knew Leo) would tell him how bad it was. It was a stupid, amateurish blackmail stunt, and I told him I was sure DiCaprio would make up his own mind. The saga continued in Los Angeles when Todd Phillips and I sat through another harangue from Toback about the script. The director Brett Ratner, a friend of Toback's, then called and asked if Todd Phillips and I would personally pay his friend to rewrite the script, as he understood Paramount wouldn't. Again we declined.

I shouldn't have been surprised that Toback was willing to subject himself to so much humiliation to get money from Paramount Pictures, Todd Phillips, and me. That humiliation didn't nearly compare with the humiliation and pain he allegedly caused dozens—no, hundreds—of women in predatory sexual encounters. But the many women who have come forward in the Me Too movement have encouraged many more women to speak out against men like James Toback.

After Leo DiCaprio read *The Gambler*, he felt that the Jim Bennett (formerly Axel) character was not tough enough, and he passed.

Before we could get into other casting, Warner Bros. insisted Phillips start *Hangover Part III* immediately, as the script was ready and the actors were available. We then went through a long list of directors and actors, and I remembered that my son David had had me see *Rise of the Planet of the Apes*, and I liked that director's work. Rupert Wyatt liked Monahan's script and signed up quickly to replace Todd Phillips. In short order Ari Emanuel, Mark Wahlberg's agent, called and said his client had read the script, was enthusiastic, and was free to start in January (and he knew it was a drama and not a big commercial film and would cut his fee dramatically).

There was a small but well-written part of the rich grandfather of Jim Bennett that Paramount thought would be good for Jack Nichol-

Mark Wahlberg, Rupert Wyatt, Irwin Winkler, John Goodman
The Gambler

son. I didn't think Nicholson would do it, and David Winkler suggested Kirk Douglas, who was ninety-seven years old. I called Douglas and went to his home for a drink and a close-up look. Kirk had suffered a stroke some years back, and it was hard to understand some of what he said, but I felt it worth pursuing to work with one of the greats. After we talked (he was also a bit hard of hearing and used a walker to get around), he smiled and said, "Do I get the part?" Two weeks later Mark Wahlberg, Rupert Wyatt, and I returned for another visit. Kirk said he thought his part had too much dialogue, and he was generally critical of the character. After about a half hour it was apparent he didn't have the energy he would need to actually go to the set, prepare, and act. Kirk, apparently realizing it too, said we could find lots of other actors to do the part, and he passed. A classy man.

Brie Larson (who in 2015 was an Academy Award winner for her performance in *Room*) agreed to play Wahlberg's love interest, Jessica Lange signed on as his mother, and George Kennedy, the grandfather. I'm glad Douglas decided against the part, since we ended up cutting the part to one brief scene.

The shooting of *The Gambler* went well. Mark Wahlberg was thoroughly professional; he knew his part and everyone else's too and gave a good, risky performance, as did John Goodman as a loan shark. The results of our previews went well, and we seemed to be ambitiously heading toward the awards season. We were turned down by the Telluride Film Festival, and the Paramount marketing group seemed to go from confidence to attrition and pulled the film from the Toronto Film Festival. That's all it took, one turndown by the folks in Telluride. There were to be no awards for *The Gambler*, but I wonder how it would have played with Kirk Douglas. He's still smiling at over one hundred years old.

CREED (2015)

I had thought that after the success of *Rocky Balboa* in 2006, we were through with *Rocky*. After all, it had been forty years since the original *Rocky* was an Academy Award Best Picture and a worldwide cultural phenomenon.

One sentence changed all that.

Sly Stallone's agent, Adam Venit at William Morris, called me many times in 2013, trying to get me to hear a pitch for a new "Rocky." The pitch was from a USC film school graduate who lived in Oakland, California. I told Venit I really wasn't interested in hearing from another young filmmaker with an idea. We get these pitch calls constantly, and sometimes a pitch is similar to an idea that we have worked on, and then we get a lawsuit for using *their* idea. The classic one was in 1976: after *Rocky*'s success we were sued by a young man who said we "stole" his idea for *Rocky*. He claimed he'd written a story exactly the same as *Rocky* and gave it to the cop at the entrance to MGM Studios, where we had our offices. He didn't make a copy of "his" story, didn't have the name of the officer he claimed he gave the story to, and no receipt, no proof at all. We questioned the entire MGM police force, and no one remembered receiving the story or meeting the young man. When I called his very well known entertainment lawyer and asked why he was pursuing the case, he told me he'd had to take the case, as the young man's father was a big-money client at the firm. In spite of my protests, the insurance company paid out $25,000 to settle the claim. Their response was, *Rocky* was such a big success, and who knew what a jury might say?

And, yes, we were sued on *Creed*. But not by Ryan Coogler, the young filmmaker from USC. A New Jersey man, Jarrett Alexander, claimed he tweeted Stallone in 2013 with his idea to do a "Rocky" about the orphan son of Apollo Creed. Though he never heard back from Stallone, he claimed Stallone used "his" story. He further claimed that Ryan Coogler, Stallone, and Chartoff-Winkler stole his idea, even though he had no proof that any of us received his tweet or ever made contact with him (never mind that he used our copyrighted characters and *Rocky* film clips to make a video that he put online). This time we made sure the insurance company didn't pay him off. Instead we went to court, and the judge threw out the case.

So I was reluctant!

Sly's agent wasn't. While I was fending him off, to his credit (and determination), he got Sly to agree to meet with Ryan Coogler. Coogler was four days from directing his first film, *Fruitvale Station*, in Oakland, California, when Venit told him Sly would see him. Unbelievably he left his set, flew down to LA, stopped off at a Best Buy store, got a DVD of *Rocky II* (his father's favorite), and thought if nothing else came of the meeting, he'd at least get Sly's autograph on the DVD box. To his surprise, Sly liked the idea, Coogler went back to Oakland, gave his father the autographed *Rocky II* DVD, and shot *Fruitvale Station*. I knew nothing of this!

Six months later, while looking for a director for another film, I ran *Fruitvale Station*. I admired it a lot and remembered that the director was the young man from USC who'd wanted to pitch me his new "Rocky" idea. Bob Chartoff ran *Fruitvale Station* and was similarly impressed.

Coogler's agent chuckled when I called and said I now wanted to hear Coogler's pitch. He then told me of Coogler and Sly's meeting all those months before. It turned out we were both in New York, so I invited Coogler to lunch at the Pierre Hotel. He arrived with his girlfriend, Zinzi, and sold me with one sentence: Adonis Creed, the illegitimate son of Rocky's adversary, Apollo Creed, wanted to be a fighter and wanted Rocky to train him. I realized we could get a "Rocky" film that would cover new characters in a different social and generational order and said yes to Coogler right then and there. It would be the first time, after six "Rocky" films, that Sylvester Stallone wouldn't write the script.

Coogler brought his *Fruitvale Station* star, Michael B. Jordan, to play Adonis Creed. It was perfect. Jordan, acting since he was fifteen years old, was not only a fine actor but also had the physicality for the part.

Coogler's process was deliberate. We were used to Sly's quick writing, usually eight weeks or so for a screenplay after we agreed on the concept. Coogler started writing on August 5, 2013, delivered the outline on October 30, and finished the draft (with Sly's and our notes) on September 1, 2014. Thirteen months. The script was 205 pages, too long by 85 to 90 pages, as one page of script usually means one minute of film, so we'd be dealing with a two-hour-and-forty-five-

David Winkler, Irwin Winkler, Charles Winkler
MGM Beverly Hills offices, 2018

minute film (the final film was two hours and thirteen minutes, the longest "Rocky" in the series). During that time, we went through many variations. Coogler wanted Rocky to have a fatal illness and die. We wouldn't go with that (nor would Sly). Then he wanted Rocky to be incapacitated, and we passed on that. Finally we came up with an illness, non-Hodgkin's lymphoma, a curable cancer that gave Adonis the opportunity to help Rocky in his illness and balance Rocky's support for Adonis in his quest. As we worked toward production, another major issue was discussed: whether Creed wins or loses the final fight. In the script we gave MGM, Creed wins. Once we started production, Ryan Coogler wanted him to lose. Bob Chartoff and I were on the fence. MGM was adamant that the film they green-lighted had him winning, and we had to shoot it that way. We had a reluctant Ryan Coogler shoot it both ways. When we screened it for our first preview audience, we had the film shown with the two different endings simultaneously in two theaters next to each other (to insure the same audience profile). The scores were very, very high (95 and 96 percent excellent and very good and 89 percent definitely recommend), a toss-up, but a win-win for the film either way. I felt that we should end with an African American, Creed, wearing the red, white, and blue boxing shorts representing America against the bad-boy Englishman Ricky Conlan. Coogler, Michael B. Jordan, and Sly convinced Bob and me (and MGM) that the losing ending (just like the original *Rocky*) was truer to the reality of the film, as Conlan was a champion, and Creed still had a ways to go. We finally agreed, and it worked fine. Gary Barber, CEO of MGM, felt we lost as much as $10 million at the box office with that ending. We'll never know. It certainly never hurt *Rocky*!

The production proceeded well. I was surprised by Coogler's self-confidence on the set. He got his performances and shots on budget and schedule. Sly and Michael got along as well as Rocky and Adonis got along. Rocky was "Unc" to Adonis on screen, and Sly was Unc to Michael (and Ryan). Michael bulked up, gaining twenty pounds of muscle through months of training and diet. Sly, playing to his illness, lost twenty pounds and also resisted wearing makeup as his weight loss already made him look sickly. He was able to do it through some very good acting. Ryan directed the scenes of Rocky's illness with a personal passion, as his father had suffered a debilitating illness when Ryan was growing up. Sly, now trading his boxing gloves for the role of Adonis's trainer, reminded me of how good Burgess Meredith was in the original *Rocky* (he was nominated for an Academy Award for Best Supporting Actor), and Sly, sure enough, got the same nomination forty years later.

I was surprised when Ryan asked for a director of photography with little major filmmaking experience. After all, Ryan was still a novice director, and I expected he would want a very experienced D.P. to work with, especially on the tough sequences in the ring. But when I

screened Maryse Alberti's work on *The Wrestler*, I knew we had someone who could get the fight scenes but also the grit of South Philadelphia. Can't help but admire Ryan Coogler's guts. He doesn't go for the
easy way out.

Charles Winkler, Michael B. Jordan, Tessa Thompson, Irwin Winkler
Creed II

On the set I found myself a lot less hands-on than I expected
to be with a young, rather inexperienced director. When he told me he
wanted to shoot one of the fights Adonis has early in the film in one
long Steadicam take, I was concerned. How was it going to cover all the
punches, the crowd reactions, the cornerman? He pulled it off, and it
was hailed by critics and fight aficionados and the crew, who are always
proud when they accomplish something difficult, especially with a
young director with only one small film under his belt.

Adonis and Bianca's relationship played very much to Michael
and Tessa Thompson's background. Tessa, cast as a singer, was
recruited from the electro soul band Caught a Ghost and, like Bianca

in the film, was just starting her career as a singer/songwriter. Her song in *Creed*, "Grip," won several critics awards.

After the shooting ended, we all felt the Adonis character needed more background. Ryan wrote a scene of a young Adonis in juvenile detention that opened the film. We shot the scene two months after we had finished principal photography, and it reminded me of the reshoot of the original ending of *Rocky* two months after we had "finished" that film.

Ludwig Göransson, Ryan Coogler, Irwin Winkler, Michael B. Jordan, Charles Winkler
Creed scoring session

Ryan put together a first cut and showed it to a few of us just five weeks after we wrapped. I was surprised how much I liked it. Margo once said (early on) that I never saw dailies I didn't like, and I never saw a first cut I did. Well, on *Creed* I liked both, but of course it's a long road from first cut to final.

When we had our scoring session, Ryan asked me to address the hundred-plus musicians (including the lead trumpeter of the Los Angeles Philharmonic). I was reminded of Bill Conti's half dozen musicians recording "Gonna Fly Now" for *Rocky* and the feeling of freedom and exhilaration when we combined it with the film of Rocky training and running up the steps of the Philadelphia Museum of Art and looking as if he was about to fly with joy.

Sly, having long been considered nothing more than an action star, in recent years was anything but! As I watched dailies, I was moved by his depth. And not only was his performance honest and true to the character he'd created so many years before, but all the actors around him were at their best; Coogler had cast them carefully and well.

Sly's performance in *Creed* and the film were treated much, much differently by the *New York Times* than *Rocky* was back in 1976. Critic A. O. Scott said of himself watching *Creed*: "This cynic, however, was too busy choking up and clapping" and wrote that *Rocky*, way back in 1976, was "a terrific boxing movie." The *New York Times* critic Vincent Canby had written of *Rocky* in 1976: "Be warned, the story is too foolish to go into." Canby went on to call *Rocky* "unconvincing" and "fraudulent." Quite a difference between Canby and Scott and the passage of forty years. Hard to believe, but the *New York Times* put a photo of Sly on the front page after he won a Golden Globe for Best Supporting Actor in *Creed*. I keep Canby's *New York Times* review framed right next to the Oscar statue. Two prizes.

Our initial press event in Philadelphia went well. Mayor Michael Nutter presented Sly, Michael, Tessa, Ryan, and me with a proclamation on the library steps. I noticed that celebrity culture outweighed the importance of the mayor of the city of Philadelphia; the press only wanted to talk to Sly, Michael B. Jordan, and Ryan Coogler, and the mayor, left standing by himself, obviously embarrassed at being ignored, quietly and quickly left.

The November 20 Los Angeles premiere of *Creed* was a triumph and reminded me of the first screening of *Rocky* at the Motion Picture Academy when Sly walked down the steps from the theater to the lobby, and the audience of academy members cheered and applauded him wildly. I knew then that we had a hit (and a chance for an Oscar). Only at this preview it wasn't about just *Rocky*; it was also very much about *Creed*—our young director out of USC Ryan Coogler and our new *Creed* hero, Michael B. Jordan.

Sly's performance was recognized by numerous film critics, and he was nominated for an Oscar for Best Supporting Actor. The film itself and Ryan Coogler, Michael B. Jordan, and Tessa Thompson

Steven Caple, Irwin Winkler, Michael B. Jordan
Creed II

crossed both racial and social barriers with awards from the African American Film Critics Association, NAACP Image Award, AARP Movies for Grownups, and the Teen Choice Awards.

Needless to say, Ryan's one sentence—"I'd like to do a 'Rocky' about Apollo Creed's illegitimate son"—has now brought us to *Creed II*, which started shooting March 14, 2018, in Philadelphia, the eighth in the series. We hired Steve Caple Jr., another young (twenty-nine-year-old) African American director out of USC, to direct *Creed II*. I promised Michael B. Jordan that he'd get his chance to direct *Creed III*.

Creed is dedicated to my partner, Bob Chartoff, who passed away in June of 2015, and who responded with great enthusiasm when he read Stallone's first script in 1976. He was a champion for the underdog all his life.

Irwin Winkler and Robert Chartoff
In their first office as producers at MGM

SILENCE (2016)

On a trip to London in 2010 I visited with Marty Scorsese, who was shooting *Hugo*, a 3-D film based on Brian Selznick's book *The Invention of Hugo Cabret*. Scorsese was deep into the film's technical challenges and had editor Thelma Schoonmaker screen some of the footage for me, and I was bowled over by Marty's use of 3-D. Afterward, we talked about the future. I told Marty I wasn't ready to direct another film just yet, and he said that after all the technical difficulties he had gone through on *Hugo*, he wanted to direct the much simpler *Silence*, a script he had written with Jay Cocks some twenty-five years before.

Silence is based on a novel by Shusaku Endo about two Jesuit priests who try to find their mentor who had gone missing years earlier in seventeenth-century Japan, where Catholicism was outlawed and any attempt to propagate religions other than Buddhism was dealt with harshly (burning at the stake, beheading, drowning, torture).

Marty reminded me of the history of the script and his attempts over the years to obtain funding for the film. It seemed that the Italian financier Vittorio Cecchi Gori had originally purchased the book for Marty and had financed the writing of a script. Over the decades the project had passed through several bankruptcies. Cecchi Gori had a strange history: he was also a senator in Italy's Parliament, and he had been imprisoned twice for nefarious financial dealings. The producer of *Hugo*, Graham King, also had claims on *Silence*, as he had financed prior location scouts to Japan and had advanced substantial funds over the years.

After rereading *Silence*, I found it moving and inspiring, and it touched a nerve. I don't know if there's a better way to describe my feelings. I welcomed the opportunity to work with my old friend, since Marty and I hadn't done a film together since *Goodfellas* in 1989, and *The Wolf of Wall Street* was yet to come.

As we slowly started to clear the rights with Cecchi Gori and Graham King's lawyers, we started a long negotiation with a French distribution company, MK2 Films, owned by Marin Karmitz. MK2 had been the French distributor of *Guilty by Suspicion* many years before and was very enthusiastic about *Silence*. Karmitz wanted to move into the international market, and *Silence* would be his calling card, but at a price. We assured him that we would only hire a cast that worked for scale and that Marty and I would take little more than expenses, that the money would go on the screen. MK2 tried to find interesting ways to keep the budget low, even attempting to shoot the Japanese landscape in Europe for the financial advantage (tax benefits). Ultimately the cost of acquiring the rights from Graham King and Cecchi Gori discouraged MK2, and they withdrew. It had been a two-year affair, with trips to Paris, dinners at Karmitz's art-filled town house facing Luxembourg Gardens, and even a soiree at the Élysée Palace, but no financing. We decided to do *The Wolf of Wall Street* while we looked for new financing.

A year and a half later, while we were editing *Wolf*, my cell phone rang, and Randall Emmett, an independent financier who had put up some equity in *Home of the Brave*, was calling. He had heard that we were looking for financing for *Silence* and asked if he could fly to New York and discuss it with Marty, Emma Koskoff (our coproducer), and me. By this time we were all pretty desperate, and I thought, what could we lose? I told Emmett to get on a plane. When we met, Emmett was very nervous, and he said all he wanted to do was produce a film with Marty Scorsese, and he had the money to finance a $35 million budget. He assured us that Ari Emanuel, the head of William Morris Endeavor (and Marty's agent), would vouch for his new financial resources. I called Emanuel, and he confirmed Emmett's resources.

We then went about clearing the COT (chain of title). On February 1, 2013, Ari Emanuel, Jake Bloom (Marty's and my lawyer), Rick Yorn, Randall Emmett, and his partner, George Furla, and I met in Emmett's lawyer's offices and started the rights clearance process. To make a point of all the difficulties we were about to face, a lawyer came into the conference room with a three-ring binder containing several hundred pages of documents. We started with Cecchi Gori's Italian costs and the Italian bankruptcy laws (very different from ours). The lawyer's binder produced some strange documents, even a contract Gori had made with Nicholas Kazan to write a script that neither Marty nor I nor anyone else knew about (giving Kazan executive producer credit and a generous fee). The rights that Graham King claimed were estimated in the neighborhood of $7 million, which put our budget way out of line. King brought that down to $2 million after we convinced him the film had a chance to get made with a limited budget and he was better off with $2 million than nothing. Sounds simple, but it wasn't. While this was going on, Emmett arranged a partial financing deal for the foreign rights with New York billionaire Len Blavatnik. The process, however, of clearing the rights continued; every time we thought we were clear, another claim came out of the woodwork and had to be dealt with. The Italians made new demands continually. Cecchi Gori even demanded producer credit, and we reluctantly said OK (we had no choice). His emissary, Niels Juul, then demanded a credit for himself as executive producer. We ended up with a list of almost forty executive producers and associate producers, an unheard number of useless people who just wanted to be associated with the film without making any significant contribution.

Next stop, the Cannes Film Festival. Although Blavatnik was guaranteeing the foreign financing, his salespeople wanted Marty and me to meet with potential territorial buyers who were attending the festival. In a large suite at the Majestic Hotel we did our best to charm, and we sold the film to buyers from just about every country that had a movie theater. Many of the buyers somehow thought Daniel Day-Lewis was set to play the lead role of Rodrigues (he wasn't), some didn't like our ending (too depressing), some had a girlfriend we had to meet (we didn't), but we were very polite and patient with all. We were told the film was creating a stir on Cannes's Boulevard de la Croisette and sold well according to IM Global, who handled the sales.

Mr. Blavatnik was a very good host for cocktails on his yacht, and then he took the entire group to a French restaurant, Tetou, on the beach, my favorite but not with that big of a crowd. After dinner Blavatnik asked if we would join him for drinks at his friend's house nearby. The friend was the Russian oligarch Roman Abramovich. The "house" was a mansion that the Duke of Windsor had lived in with his duchess after he abdicated the British throne in 1938. After an extensive and thorough search by the ex-Mossad security guards, we entered the long entrance hall lined with paintings by Modigliani, Picasso, Braque, and Francis Bacon (we were told our host had paid $86 million for the Bacon). Mr. Abramovich and his wife greeted us like old friends and brought us into their enormous dining room, where the cast of the The Great Gatsby, including Leonardo DiCaprio, were celebrating the screening of their film at the Cannes Film Festival. I was sure Abramovich could have paid for Silence just with the Rosenthal antique china that, I was told, was priced at $10,000 a plate. It was a very worldly crowd: the Australian Baz Luhrmann (the Gatsby director), DiCaprio the native Californian, Blavatnik the American billionaire, our multibillionaire Russian host Abramovich, Marty from the Lower East Side of New York, and me from Coney Island. We toasted one another with enormous champagne glasses and left dazzled by the wealth.

The next day Emmett received a cease-and-desist order from Graham King, who pointed out that he still owned the rights to Silence and that Emmett, IM Global, and Mr. Blavatnik had no right to sell them. Emmett, to his credit, somehow raised $1 million on the spot and satisfied King without getting any kind of written agreement but got reassurance from Ari Emanuel that it was kosher. With Graham King and Cecchi Gori and the Italian bankruptcy court all satisfied, it now seemed that we were on our way.

A few weeks later, on a flight from New York to Los Angeles with Paramount CEO Brad Grey, I convinced him that we were on the path to make Silence, and he agreed that Paramount would distribute the film but would make no financial commitment other than marketing costs. Emmett was now able to patch together the remaining financing against the Paramount domestic release. After several meetings with the producer David Lee, we were convinced that filming in Taipei could serve both our budget and artistic needs. Lee and his brother Ang Lee, the noted director, had lived in Taiwan and had vast experience making films there. We set a start date for principal photography in early 2015.

Now that we had dates, locations, and the funding, the cast came together quickly: Liam Neeson to play Ferreira, the Jesuit who has gone missing, and Andrew Garfield and Adam Driver, the young priests who must find their mentor and teacher. All three principals worked for union minimum. The cast of Japanese actors were committed to *Silence*, as the book is revered by the Japanese (and they also jumped at the chance to work with Marty). With Marty, Emma Koskoff, and I taking no fee, only expenses, we were able to meet the costs of building the sets, making the authentic Japanese costumes and props, and bringing key crew and actors from Japan and America to Taiwan.

Emma Koskoff, who was the first to move to Taipei and set up the production (I don't think she ever slept—she worked from early morning until late at night, seven days a week), dedicated both her talent and know-how to preparing the film when Emmett informed me that one of his equity investors had come down with a serious illness and wouldn't be able to fulfill his $6 million commitment (he still got credit as executive producer). We had gone through a series of crises the past couple of months with funding, but with sets being built, we would have been in real trouble if money hadn't come through quickly. Emmett was able to substitute the missing funds with a Mexican group led by Gastón Pavlovich. With the financial takeover of the entire production by Pavlovich, the financial crisis was over, and we were making *Silence*. At least on the first day of shooting I *thought* we were making *Silence*.

On January 22, 2015, I was swimming laps in the cold Taipei hotel rooftop pool when I got a tap on the back and was told there was an emergency and I was needed in the hotel conference room immediately. It seemed that there was an old set on the studio's back lot that our art department was considering using but felt it was unsafe. The studio was informed that the set had to be brought up to *our* safety standards before we would consider using it. While workers were securing the roof of a hut, the timbers cracked, and the roof fell. Two construction workers were injured, and one of them died on the way to the hospital. Koskoff and I met with the public safety and other Taipei government officials, who held the studio and the subcontractors responsible for the accident. We rechecked the safety of all the sets under construction by the studio to make sure, independently, that our cast and crew were safe.

During our week of safety inspections we were informed that our paperwork on the $2 million tax credit we were to get from the city of Taipei was incorrect, and we were denied the funds. We would have to find some more savings in the budget. We did, and shooting started (or resumed after the first day's accident).

All crew and cast were totally committed. Liam Neeson and Adam Driver each lost twenty pounds in preparation for their roles (Driver lost another ten pounds during production). Driver and Andrew Garfield spent a week at a Jesuit retreat without speaking (and you can

Back: Producer Emma Tillinger Koskoff and Irwin Winkler
Front: Editor Thelma Schoonmaker and Martin Scorsese

imagine how hard that would be for an actor). The Japanese actors also went well beyond expectations. They went from acting in freezing cold, rain, and heat to being hung upside down for torture scenes. Adam

Driver, in a climactic scene where his character saves a woman tied with straw from drowning, instead of using a stunt double jumped into the freezing ocean himself. Driver had to be wrapped in heated blankets to stop him from shivering but insisted he could do another, better take. Liam Neeson spent hours hanging upside down over a fire in another scene of Japanese torture. No stuntman for him either.

No one in the cast or crew, however, was more committed than Marty Scorsese, who was finally actually fulfilling his decades-long ambition. He climbed hills in the heat and rain, worked sixteen-hour days (and nights), never complained, and when on distant locations lived in second- (and third-) class accommodations.

The filming of *Silence* took seventy-three exhausting days, and on July 25, 2016, I saw a first cut. The commitment Marty and I had made in London on September 26, 2010, five years before, to make *Silence* was finally realized. Now, was it any good?

It was great!

Inspiring, ambitious, thought provoking, beautiful to look at, great performances, and at this stage of the editing, a bit long. My own last testing ground was Margo, who was in tears at the end of the film. At various stages of editing we screened the film for several Jesuit priests with very moving and positive responses. We had the world premiere at the Vatican and a private screening for Pope Francis.

The critical response was generally excellent with some carping about the length and violence. That might have hurt our holiday release. However, in my opinion (and most others') *Silence* is a great artistic success; I believe it's Marty Scorsese's best film. Unfortunately, audiences did not flock to see it, and it was pretty well ignored by the Academy. Still, I believe that *Silence* will stand alongside some of the best Ingmar Bergman, Fellini, and Pasolini films. I'm so glad we hung in, faced down all the naysayers, and made it, no matter what. That's what filmmaking should be about.

PART VI

WITH *THE IRISHMAN*, a new platform for audiences around the world to see a movie has taken hold. Although the film has the standard elements—script, cast, director, and producer—its distribution is experimental. Netflix is making *The Irishman* available through its streaming service to its subscribers, an audience of 125 million people worldwide, 56 million in America alone. Netflix, founded just twenty years ago to rent out DVDs they purchased from the major studios, now spends approximately eight billion dollars a year on movies, television shows, and documentaries. In order for them to keep their subscribers coming back (at ten to twelve dollars a month), they have to constantly supply them with new content (it seems funny that I'm describing films as content). Netflix's success has brought Amazon, Hulu, and even the television networks (CBS Now) into that same online, streaming marketplace. Some of the original films that Netflix or Amazon fund do get a limited theatrical release, at least in the United States. Why did Marty Scorsese, Bob De Niro, and I take Netflix over a Hollywood studio? Easy. The cost of financing. The marketing of a big budget film can run up to $100 million. That's OK for *Star Wars, Captain America, Black Panther*, or most of the Marvel or D.C. Comics films that are guaranteed worldwide audiences. *Avengers: Infinity War*, opening in May 2018, sold $1.6 billion worth of tickets after just four weeks. *The Irishman*, a character study, brilliantly played by Bob De Niro, would have a hard time competing in that comic book world. So along comes Netflix with their financial support, subscriber audience, and very little, if any, marketing cost. Netflix provides the opportunity to show *The Irishman* to over one hundred million movie fans.

I believe audiences will still go to the theaters to see movies, no doubt about that. I imagine that hundreds—no, thousands—of years ago, women, men, and children sat around a fire together to listen to someone tell a story. And we will still enjoy communal viewing in a theater as well as the streaming of a film on a screen at home, where you can see a show when you like it and as many times as you like it.

CHAPTER NINETEEN

Old Friends

THE IRISHMAN (2018)

A REUNION OF OLD friends and colleagues is a rare treat in the film-making process. If the old friends are Bob De Niro, Al Pacino, Joe Pesci, Marty Scorsese, and me, it's more than a real treat; it's an occasion for a celebration. *The Irishman* is just that.

In January 2013, all the actors, Marty Scorsese, and producers Emma Koskoff, Jane Rosenthal, and I came together at Bob De Niro's Tribeca office for a reading of *The Irishman* script. It was to be my eighth picture with De Niro, starting with *The Gang That Couldn't Shoot Straight* (1971), then *New York, New York* (1976), *Raging Bull* (1980), *True Confessions* (1981), *Goodfellas* (1990), *Guilty by Suspicion* (1991), and *Night and the City* (1992); my third film with Al Pacino since *Author! Author!* (1982) and *Revolution* (1985); my third with Joe Pesci since *Raging Bull* and *Goodfellas*; and my eighth collaboration with Scorsese since *New York, New York, Raging Bull, Goodfellas, Round Midnight* (1986, Marty as an actor), *Guilty by Suspicion* (also as an actor), *The Wolf of Wall Street* (2013), and *Silence* (2015). The script that was being read was written by Steve Zaillian (Academy Award winner for *Schindler's List* in 1993) based on the deathbed confession of Mafia hit man Frank Sheeran in Charles Brandt's book *I Heard You Paint Houses*. Brandt's book and Zaillian's screenplay devoted quite a bit of time to Sheeran's killing of Jimmy Hoffa, the famous (or infamous) head of the Teamsters Union who disappeared in July of 1975 (no body ever found). Pacino played the Hoffa role in the Tribeca reading, and Joe Pesci came out of retirement to play Russell Bufalino, the genial mob boss who had a hand in Hoffa's killing (and quite a few others). Bob De Niro was the

Irishman Frank Sheeran, who we first see as a soldier in Italy during World War II, killing German prisoners, then as a small-time crook, and then graduating to the FBI's famous list of Cosa Nostra criminals (one of the few non-Italians). Sheeran's good friend Jimmy Hoffa made him head of the Teamsters in Wilmington, Delaware, where his specialty was intimidation. Barry Primus, who goes back with me to *New York, New York* and *Guilty by Suspicion, Night and the City*, and *Life as a House*, joined the cast, as did Harvey Keitel as Angelo Bruno, one of the era's mobsters. Harvey, of course, goes back to *Who's That Knocking at My Door*, one of Marty's earliest films, and was opposite De Niro in *Mean Streets* and *Taxi Driver*. I never worked with Harvey, but we're longtime friends, and he starred in my son David's first directing effort, *Finding Graceland*, in 1999.

The title of the book *I Heard You Paint Houses* was based on Sheeran's recollection that when he first met Jimmy Hoffa, he was greeted by that remark. In gangster terms the paint referred to is the blood that splatters on a wall when a victim is shot in the head. Nice, coming from one of the most important leaders in the American labor movement.

After the Tribeca reading we all were enthusiastic and agreed to make the movie. It was, for Jane Rosenthal, the culmination of almost a decade of development. Jane and Bob De Niro read and optioned *I Heard You Paint Houses* in 2007 while they were researching another mob book, *The Winter of Frankie Machine*. They had Steve Zaillian adapt *I Heard You Paint Houses* and he delivered a very good draft in 2009. Jane never wavered in her passion for the movie in spite of studios low balling the budget and questioning its commerciality. A truly dedicated producer. However, several years elapsed while all of us went off to fulfill other commitments, Marty (and I) to *The Wolf of Wall Street* and *Silence*, Bob De Niro and Al Pacino to their films, and Joe Pesci to the golf course and his retirement (turned out he was so happy with his golf game, it wasn't easy to get him back to *The Irishman*. It took a lot of persuasion and ultimately his loyalty to Bob and Marty).

Marty, Emma, Jane, Bob, and I had a lengthy discussion and decided our principal actors would play all the ages of their characters. De Niro starts out playing Sheeran in his eighties and in his reminiscences plays a thirty-year-old, a forty-year-old, a fifty-year-old, and a

Martin Scorsese and Irwin Winkler
The Irishman

sixty-year-old. The same was true for Pesci, Pacino, and several other actors. That would take technology and money.

In August 2015, the technicians from George Lucas's ILM digital company met with our production people in New York. Marty Scorsese, Bob De Niro, Emma Koskoff, Jane Rosenthal, and I watched as Bob brilliantly redid a scene from *Goodfellas*. It was videotaped, and we ran it against a clip from the twenty-five-year-old original film. The ILM people told us that they would digitally "de-age" De Niro to look like he did all those years ago. Three months later, in November 2015, we saw the first results of the de-aging and knew that it could be done but that it would be slow and, yes, expensive.

In January 2016, I had lunch with Brad Grey, who told me Paramount wanted to distribute *The Irishman* but would not put up any of the financing. He also reminded me that Paramount owned the book and the Zaillian screenplay and we had to come to Paramount before we engaged other studios and/or financiers. I was not looking forward to the hunt for money, as raising the financing for *Silence* had been a roller coaster of now you have the money, now you don't.

After we finished shooting in Taipei on *Silence*, I met with Gaston Pavlovich, who had put up a third of the financing on that film, and told him about *The Irishman*. He was happy with his involvement on *Silence* and was eager to come in on *The Irishman*. We arranged for Paramount to give Pavlovich an option on the Zaillian script and the Brandt book with the understanding that, once he had the financing, he had to repay Paramount for all the costs they had incurred. At the Cannes Film Festival in May of 2016, Pavlovich sold the foreign rights to STX, a new American distribution company that had Chinese backing. STX quickly sold off individual territories. It was a lot easier for Marty Scorsese and me, as this time we didn't have to sit in a hotel room in Cannes and pitch to all the buyers. Things seemed to be in place until we got our de-aging estimate from ILM and Donald Trump got elected president of the United States. With Trump's rhetoric about our neighbors to the south, how we needed a wall (they would pay for it) to keep the Mexican drug dealers and rapists out of America, the peso dropped 25 percent, and Pavlovich couldn't cover the new budget. It looked pretty bad until Brad Grey, to my great surprise, said Paramount would finance the difference between the new budget and the money STX had committed. That lasted until I got back to my office from lunch with him.

Rick Yorn had wisely slipped *The Irishman* script to Ted Sarandos, chief content officer at Netflix, and he was very enthusiastic. Netflix, the streaming, online subscription service that had become a major force in the entertainment landscape, was excited about the script, Marty, and the cast (Oscar winners De Niro, Pesci, Pacino) and me. Sarandos quickly examined the budget and agreed to finance the film. Brad Grey, who had been very supportive of *The Wolf of Wall Street* (and made lots of money on it) and *Silence* (not so much), agreed to turn over the rights to Netflix. With Netflix aboard to fully finance *The Irishman*, it should have been easy. As usual, it wasn't. STX went back to the individual territories that they had sold the film to and told the buyers that *The Irishman* wouldn't be available to them, as the financing from

Irwin Winkler, Al Pacino, Robert De Niro
The Irishman

Mexico had fallen through. Several refused to accept the fact that *The Irishman* would not get made if they didn't give up the phantom rights they'd acquired. Several distributors threatened to go to their local magistrate and get an injunction against *The Irishman* and Netflix. Money finally won everyone over (it usually does).

Emma Koskoff, just as she had dedicated herself on *Silence*, went to work on the complicated physical production. There were 340 scenes, about twice the number of most films, and hundreds of locations to find. No accident, as Frank Sheeran practiced his craft all over the eastern seaboard, and we needed real locations (from the original thirty- to forty-year-old homes, bars, offices, restaurants, and factories) and would have to build the ones we couldn't find. With locations locked, sets built, and casting completed, we started shooting on September 18, 2017. Four years after the reading in Tribeca.

The shooting of *The Irishman* was a pleasure. Every day the actors seemed eager to start and reluctant to finish, even though these pros had been at it for four to five decades. *The Irishman* wrapped on March 5, 2018, and the postproduction process began—that is, in addition to the picture editing, sound editing, music, and normal visual effects, we would start getting to see the final "de-aging" of the actors.

As of this writing, we expect *The Irishman* to be in theaters and on Netflix in the fall of 2019.

I wonder if Bob De Niro, Joe Pesci, Al Pacino, Marty Scorsese, and I will ever get a chance to come together again on a project. I'm doubtful but hopeful.

EPILOGUE

Milo Ventimiglia, Tessa Thompson, Dolph Lundgren, Steven Caple Jr., Michael B. Jordan,
Irwin Winkler, Charles Winkler
Creed II reception, November 2018

THE PAST FIFTY YEARS of films and filmmaking that I've enjoyed (most times) doesn't end with the last sentences of this book. Not by any means.

Here are five films we're planning on making in the next year (or two).

I met with Steven Spielberg, and we decided to collaborate on *Sundown*. In the early 1990s, I'd read Henrik Ibsen's play *An Enemy of the People*. I believed that the story of two brothers representing the idealistic and the practical sides of human nature would make an interesting film set in the American West in the mid-nineteenth century. Post–Civil War America and its expansion has always been a source of great filmmaking, going back to silent films. I had worked with the writer David Eyre for several months, and when we were satisfied with the script, I thought I'd direct *Sundown*. Instead, I decided to direct

The Net. By the time I was free to direct *Sundown*, I had lost interest in doing so and found there was little interest from other directors. I had not thought about *Sundown* for the last couple of decades. That was, until I was asked by the Motion Picture Academy to host a dinner for the nominated producers for the Best Picture of 2017. During dinner I chatted with Kristie Macosko Krieger, who had produced *The Post* with Spielberg, and when she asked me if I had any scripts that Spielberg might be interested in, I scratched my head and recalled *Sundown*. In short order Kristie and Spielberg read and liked the script, and Charles Winkler, Spielberg, Krieger, and I met at Amblin Studios. Steven had now committed to direct the musical *West Side Story* and wasn't available to direct but wanted to produce *Sundown* with us through Amblin. Steven had a very good take on the script (weren't the plot and characters in *Jaws* similar?). We will go out to directors.

Stephen Sondheim and James Lapine's Pulitzer Prize–winning musical *Sunday in the Park with George* has been in my past and future since I saw it on Broadway in 1985 with Mandy Patinkin playing the post-Impressionist painter George Seurat. I was moved by Sondheim's brilliant score and Lapine's book dealing with the creation of art, especially one song, "Art Isn't Easy," something I've known all my life. I met with Sondheim and Lapine several times and thought they agreed for me to acquire the rights. I was surprised when, a few weeks later, Sondheim decided not to go forward. Thirty years went by, and James Lapine in an interview mentioned that he was sorry he and Sondheim hadn't made the deal for me to produce *Sunday* back in the 1980s. I called Lapine and told him I was as enthusiastic now as I was back in 1985. He has written a very fine adaptation of the play, and we are in discussions with Jake Gyllenhaal, who received great reviews for his performance in the 2017 Broadway revival, to star in the film version of *Sunday in the Park with George.*

Gershwin is another film I've been attempting to make for some thirty years. With scripts by John Guare and Paul Schrader, Marty Scorsese directing, Daniel Day-Lewis to play George Gershwin, and

Tom Hanks to play Ira—in spite of all those great talents, I could never convince the then-head of Warner Bros., Terry Semel, that anyone would be interested in the Gershwin music. The music of *Rhapsody in Blue, An American in Paris,* and *Porgy and Bess,* along with a great cast and fine script, couldn't convince Semel. I stayed with it all these years, and after seeing some very different musical films from the Irish writer and director (*Once, Sing Street*), I contacted John Carney, and he wrote a treatment for a Gershwin film that I like, Marty Scorsese likes, the Gershwin family likes, and two studios are eager to finance.

We finished the shooting of *Creed II* on June 12, 2018, in the New Mexico desert, and it is set for release Thanksgiving 2018. Quick, but the demand to see this chapter of the "Rocky" saga is very, very strong. The two-and-a-half-minute trailer that went online June 20 was seen by fifty million viewers (and, I assume, fans) in the first thirty-six hours. The dailies that I've seen, I believe, will please the fans of "Rocky" and "Creed." Last year in a conversation with our "Creed" star Michael B. Jordan, I offered him the opportunity to not only star in, but also to direct *Creed III.* Bob Chartoff and I offered the same opportunity to Sly Stallone to direct *Rocky II* after we finished shooting *Rocky.* I'm sure Michael B. will bring the contemporary audience to a new place.

On January 2011, Forrest Allen, eighteen, of Middleburg, Virginia, suffered a snowboarding accident that left him in a coma, unable to speak or walk. The Allen family engaged Susan Koch to document the journey, over four years, of Forrest's recovery with the guidance of Tom Sweitzer, a music therapist. The power of music to heal offered us an opportunity to make a mainstream movie of this incredible story. We will engage a writer to adapt Forrest Allen's story and have found that Tom Sweitzer's journey to becoming a music therapist is remarkable as well. *Music Got Me Here* quotes Plato:

> *Music gives a soul to the universe, wings to the mind,*
> *flight to the imagination, and life to everything.*

ACKNOWLEDGMENTS

OVER THE FIFTY-PLUS YEARS represented in the pages of this reminiscence, an enormous number of artists are portrayed. Actors, directors, producers, choreographers, novelists, screenwriters, playwrights, costume designers, wardrobe assistants, tailors, wardrobe shoppers, makeup artists, wig makers, hair stylists, composers, lyricists, musicians, cinematographers, camera operators, focus pullers, film loaders, sound mixers, sound editors, sound designers, casting directors, first and second and third assistant directors, film editors, production designers, set dressers, art directors, draftsmen, storyboard artists, unit still photographers, gaffers, grips, electricians, stand-ins, background extras, stunt persons, script supervisors, visual effect artists, location scouts, dialogue coaches, carpenters, painters, construction crews, runners, interns, negative cutters, color timers, digital engineers, print and lab technicians, title makers, first aid personnel, script clearance people, teachers for minors, researchers, production managers, production secretaries, motion control engineers, loop actors, teamsters, masseurs, trainers, studios executives, lawyers, agents, financiers, bankers, and of course, craft service folks that serve the snacks all day long.

Over the thousands and thousands of days working with these artists, I have grown to respect each individual craft, whether it's the makeup person who spent four hours every morning making Kevin Kline look like the seventy-year-old Cole Porter, or Sydney Guilaroff designing Liza Minnelli's hair for New York, New York, or the effects person preparing the blood for Sly Stallone to say "Cut me, Mick" in the fight between Rocky and Apollo Creed in Rocky, or Jane Fonda preparing for an exhausting dance marathon in *They Shoot Horses, Don't They?*, or the cinematographer Michael Ballhaus sitting next to me while color timing *Guilty by Suspicion*, or the location scouts finding several hundred period sets for *The Irishman*, or our costume designer shopping all over Los Angeles for the dress that Sandra Bullock needed for her running scenes in *The Net*.

I could go on and on. My forty-year relationship with Marty Scorsese and Bob De Niro is of particularly great significance. Through their enormous gifts of acting and directing, both men have had a profound influence on my filmmaking. The challenges of risk-taking, its rewards and disappointments, have been life lessons for me beyond the filmmaking process. The friendship of Marty and Bob has added to these chapters and my life.

In 1975 a young actor by the name of Sylvester Stallone walked into our offices and pitched an idea. Since then it's been quite a ride, and now, forty-three years later, we're still "flyin."

To my friend Ron Meyer, who literally pushed me into writing and then directing movies and changed my career for twenty happy years. Very few days go by when we don't share each other's ups (mostly) and downs (rarely).

For the past ten years I've enjoyed the producing partnership of two of my sons, Charles and David (Adam is a UCLA law professor). They have been intimately involved in all the Winkler Films productions and, most significantly, the later *Rocky* films. There would never have been a *Creed* without their creativity, persistence, and passion.

I could never have started and certainly could never have completed this book without the tireless commitment of my assistant Selina Gomeau. No amount of time or effort is too much for Ms. Gomeau; her eagle eye and cheerful patience spurred me on whenever my energy flagged or my mind wandered. She made *A Life in Movies: Stories from 50 Years in Hollywood* a reality, and for that I thank her profusely.

The persistent question "What does a producer do?" caused me, some years ago, to keep a diary of *just* what I did on a daily basis. I, on a whim, gave a copy to my friend, the legendary editor and publisher

Jason Epstein. To my surprise, Jason called a few days later and said that once he started to read the notes, he stayed up all night, as he couldn't put them down. Jason introduced me to the literary agent Michael Carlisle, who incredibly, enthusiastically (a lot more than I was), and quickly arranged for me to meet with Jamison Stoltz, executive editor at Abrams. Both gentlemen convinced me to turn my diary into a narrative, and to search my memory back to the early days of my career. Michael's counseling and Jamison's insightful, tireless, and confident editorial suggestions make this a much better work. For that I thank them both.

I wrote about my friendship with my partner of many years, Bob Chartoff, in a separate chapter of this book, but those mere words will never express my feelings with his passing.

From Margo and me to Charles, David, Adam, Sandra, Elizabeth, and Melissa; and especially to their children Maya, Sebastian, Dani, Eli, and Chloe:

> *Whatever you can do,*
> *or dream you can,*
> *begin it.*
> *For boldness has genius,*
> *power and magic*
> *in it.*
> —Goethe

FILMS I DIDN'T MAKE

It gives me no pleasure to make a list of what I *didn't* accomplish in spite of lots and lots of time, energy, resources, money, and commitment, but below is a list of attempts.

Even the films that don't get made have a story.

Here are two.

Lillian Hellman's *Uncle Willie*

Some films don't get made for obvious reasons. The script isn't good enough, the budget is too high, or the casting is unsuccessful, but I can't remember when an author told a star he wasn't cast right and that killed the project.

Bob Chartoff and I acquired a short story by Lillian Hellman, a successful Broadway playwright (*Toys in the Attic, The Children's Hour*) and Oscar-nominated screenwriter (*The Little Foxes*, 1942, *The North Star*, 1944). Hellman's *Uncle Willie* is a fact-based story of Hellman's gunrunning uncle set against the Latin American sugar wars in the early 1900s. Eric Roth (Oscar winner for *Forrest Gump*, 1995) wrote an excellent screenplay that Warren Beatty, at the top of his game, agreed to star in. With Warren attached, the exotic background, and the excellent script, we were certain it would be a very special film. We were delighted when Lillian Hellman came to Los Angeles, and we invited her to dinner with Beatty to join Margo and me. As we ordered our drinks, Lillian, who knew Warren quite well, remarked how much she admired Eric Roth's screenplay and asked who we were thinking of to play Uncle Willie. I very enthusiastically said, "Warren, isn't that great?" Lillian's answer was not only embarrassing, but it's the comment that killed the movie. She looked right at Warren and declared, "Oh, he'd make a terrible Willie." We never found a better Willie than Warren Beatty. He was perfect, but no matter how we tried, he wouldn't discuss it again.

The political thriller that never got made

While I was working on several scripts after the release of *The Net*, a studio head asked me to read a script he was very high on. It was an interesting thriller with a political background. I read the script, thought it was pretty good but needed lots of work, and I passed on it. The studio head wouldn't take no for an answer and asked if I would please meet with the writer and give him my thoughts. I agreed and had a pleasant session with the writer, who was very accommodating. When the next draft came in, I told the studio head I thought it was better, but I still wasn't willing to commit to direct the movie. He asked if I would meet with and give the writer my notes once again. I did, and, lo and behold, the next draft was very good, and I told the studio head I was now ready to direct the screenplay. He was delighted, telling me how happy he was that he hadn't let me walk away. He was right.

I went about casting the lead role and found my leading man, had lunch with him, and the studio head started negotiating his deal and mine as the studio prepared the budget.

All was moving along until the studio head was fired. The deal for the actor hadn't been firmed up, and a new studio head was to be announced shortly. The studio head who was fired called me and told me he was up for a job at another studio, and would I call the CEO at that studio, who he knew was a close friend of mine. I called my friend, but he said he didn't think the studio head was tough enough for the job. I reported my recent experience, that I had walked away from a thriller several times, and it was because of his insistence that I stayed with it. My friend then took another meeting with the studio head and hired him. After his hiring, the studio head took me to lunch and thanked me profusely for getting him his new job.

The newly installed studio head at the original studio read the thriller script, didn't want to do the film, and gave it to me in turnaround. I thought, well, this will be a cinch, called the studio head at his new job, and, would you believe it, he asked to read the script. I sent it to him, and, sure enough, it's on the list of films that never got made.

Some others

Lush Life
Explores the relationship between Billy Strayhorn and Duke Ellington,
based on *Lush Life: A Biography of Billy Strayhorn.*
Screenplay by Jay Cocks.

House of Mirth
Based on Edith Wharton's novel.
Screenplay by A. R. Gurney Jr.

Wolfboy
A teenager deals with the tragic and sudden death of his brother, based
on the novel *Wolf Boy* by Evan Kuhlman.
Screenplay by Chris Parker.

Porgy and Bess
The opera by George and Ira Gershwin and DuBose Heyward.
Trevor Nunn to direct a film version.

Vegas
A look behind the scenes of Las Vegas.
Screenplay by John Gregory Dunne and Joan Didion.

The Tempest
Contemporary adaptation of the Shakespeare play.
Treatment by Ray Bradbury.

Joe Louis
Portrayal of the life of boxer Joe Louis from his humble beginnings to
his rise to the top of the boxing world.
Screenplay by Robert Eisele.

Angel Eyes
A single mother will stop at nothing to protect herself and her daughter after an ill-advised one-night stand with a younger man leads to a fatal obsession.
Screenplay by Jay Cocks.

Pandora
An entertainer who uses the media for political purposes.
Screenplay by Carrie Fisher.

Richard III
A film version of the Shakespeare play in a contemporary political environment.

Paris Model
About a fashion model Marty Scorsese and I met on a location scout whose life was adrift with no real purpose.
Jay Presson Allen, John Guare, Nora Ephron, and Dennis Potter discussed to write the screenplay.

Brownsville Girl
A skillful loner with nothing to lose, a beautiful woman with everything to gain, a train full of money.
Based on the Sam Shepard/Bob Dylan song "Brownsville Girl." Screenplay by Jay Cocks.

Feel
A contemporary love story.
Screenplay by Israel Horovitz.

Paris Deserter
An American soldier deserts in Paris after his World War II traumas and is hunted by the military police.
Screenplay by David Rayfiel based on Victor Hugo's *Les Misérables*.

Infidels
F. Scott Fitzgerald in Hollywood.
Screenplay by Jay Cocks.

Kat and Mouse
Explores the complications of a modern-day family.
Screenplay by Naomi Foner.

Homage to Catalonia
George Orwell's personal account of his experiences during the Spanish Civil War.
Discussed adaptation with Harold Pinter, Derek Marlowe, David Cornwall, Trevor Griffin, Eric Roth. Screenplay by Walter Bernstein based on Orwell's book *Homage to Catalonia*.

Edie Sedgwick
The tragic story of Andy Warhol's New York muse.
George Plimpton to write screenplay. Irving "Swifty" Lazar to coproduce.

Empty Glass
A young coroner investigates the death of Marilyn Monroe.
Novel by J. J. Baker. Screenplay by J. J. Baker.

Mob Cop/Johnny Caruso
A man grows up in a mob family and joins the NYPD, which leads to compromised integrity and loyalty.
Screenplay by Nick Pileggi.

Sigma Protocol
While trying to avenge his brother's murder, a man unearths a lethal international conspiracy.
Screenplay by Julie Bush based on the Robert Ludlom novel.

Scarpa
True life story of Greg Scarpa, the notorious hit man for the Colombo crime family.
Screenplay by Steve Shagan with rewrites by Nick Pileggi.

People Not Places
A woman dying of cancer befriends a homeless man.
Screenplay by Ellen Furman.

Speed-the-Plow
Satirical look at two Hollywood studio executives and their secretary.
Screenplay by David Mamet based on his play.

Rules of Engagement
A modern take on Henrik Ibsen's *A Doll's House*.
Screenplay by Jeffrey Caine.

Ellida
An eccentric town beauty is seduced by a mysterious stranger.
Based on the play *Lady from the Sea* by Henrik Ibsen.

From Now On
A carpenter finds a newspaper page from the future, which shows him married to a wealthy, beautiful woman; he then struggles with the pre-ordained nature of his life.
Drafts by W. D. Richter, David Sheffield, and Barry Blaustein.

Spite House
True story of Bobby Garwood, the controversial Vietnam POW released after fourteen years in captivity.
Screenplay by Oliver Stone and rewritten by Paul Attanasio based on *Spite House: The Last Secret of the War in Vietnam* by Monika Jensen-Stevenson.

Dirt
Traces the history of NASCAR back to moonshine manufacturers who used their fast cars to outrun the law.
Screenplay by David Eyre.

Man on Third
Two brothers try to resolve their lifelong resentment, set against the Baltimore Orioles.
Screenplay by Mark Friedman based on his novel *Columbus Slaughters Braves.*

Special Interest
A woman Washington lobbyist.
Screenplay by Irwin Winkler and Rob Cowan.

A Perfect Divorce
An affable, upper-middle-class couple attempt to divorce each other amicably for the sake of their son.
Screenplay by Bruce Joel Rubin based on *A Perfect Divorce* by Avery Corman.

Nose for News
Screwball comedy, two newspaper reporters vying to solve a case.
Screenplay by W. D. Richter.

Chet Baker
The life of famed jazz musician Chet Baker.
Screenplay by Jay Cocks.

Compton
Inspired by the real-life events of Tim Lewis, a former professional baseball player, who returns to his hometown of Compton and begins coaching a Little League team while struggling with sobriety.
Screenplay by Irwin Winkler and Jose Ruisanchez.

Light Years
A contemporary love story based on James Salter's novel.

Out of Fashion
An out-of-touch fashion executive must move home to care for her autistic sister and learns the real secret to happiness.
Screenplay by Beth Henley.

Piano Man
A tragic love story set against the aftermath of a tsunami.
Screenplay by Mark Friedman.

Grounds for Dismissal
A teacher fights charges of sexual harassment when a brief affair with a colleague goes awry.
Screenplay by Theresa Rebeck.

Bloodlines
A woman on the run becomes entangled with a corrupt corporation.
Screenplay by Theresa Rebeck.

The Promise
A man gives up everything and puts tremendous strain on his wife and two daughters as he obsesses about finding the drive-by killer of his talented son.
Screenplay by Jack Olsen.

The Prosecutor
A New York prosecutor goes up against the mob and exposes a white-collar scandal.
Screenplay by Nick Pileggi.

Marines of Autumn
The battle of Chosin Reservoir and the U.S. Marines in Korea.
Screenplay by Ann Peacock based on James Brady's novel.

Day of the Rope
An FBI agent goes undercover in a right-wing white supremacist organization.
Screenplay by John Eskow.

Winds of Change
A doctor's life from World War II to Vietnam.
Screenplay by David Ayer.

Daniel Boone
Story of frontiersman Daniel Boone.
Screenplay by John Milius.

Busby Berkeley
One of the greatest choreographers of the Hollywood movie musical.
Discussed with directors Bob Fosse and Jerome Robbins.

Jack America
Jack Phelan, a self-made media mogul and celebrated owner of the Boston Red Sox, must analyze his mercurial life in order to solve the mystery of who tried to kill him.
Screenplay by Dick Beebe.

Sugar Mountain
A couple struggles to cope with their crumbling marriage when their daughter is the victim of a cyber crime at school.
Screenplay by Betsy Lerner.

Foreign Correspondent
NBC international reporter Richard Engel's capture (and escape) in war-torn Syria.
Story by Richard Engel.

Dreamland
An obsessed New Yorker builds Coney Island against all odds.
Screenplay by Kevin Baker.

The Politician
A short story by Jimmy Breslin.

PHOTO CREDITS